DIALECTICS AND SOCIAL THEORY
THE LOGIC OF CAPITAL

Ali Shamsavari

MERLIN BOOKS LTD.
Braunton Devon

British Library Cataloguing in Publication Data
Shamsavari, Ali
Dialectics and social theory: the logic of capital.
1. Marxism. Dialectical materialism
I. Title
335.4112

ISBN 0-86303-531-0

ISBN 0 86303 531-0
Printed in England by Antony Rowe Ltd., Chippenham, Wilts

47 Differentiating totality from generality
48 You cannot separate production from distribution

DIALECTICS AND SOCIAL THEORY

51 Double determination 52 The totality of production. 53 3 definitions of simple
66 S.3 relations of the totality. 75 The 2 notions of the commodity. 79 On specificity + relationship between form + content.
80 The need for concrete analysis of applying the wrong abstraction 82 The 2 problems of form analysis of classical PE 84 The 3 problems 88 If essence does not move beyond itself to the whole, then it regresses to a moment below the essence. 97 2 moments of a determination (i.e. Hegel's discussion of the soul) → it is an abstract moment plus a concrete actuality. → 98 2 points of this.
99 The contradiction of being implicit but not wanting to be 101 The whole must be defined in relation to the concrete
110 Distinguishing kantian analytic method from Hegel's dialectical synthetic method → use against CR. 112-113 criticising analytic method for subsuming external factors → use against CR
117 Hegel's characteristic of abstract generality. 120 There is a duality

not between concepts, but within both.

(128) Scientific analysis proceeds as a critle →
use against CR. (129) what unites the
beginning + the end is the very logic of the
movement. (132) The beginning must be
differentiated plus take the form universality
/ summarising the discussion of Hegel's notion
of the beginning / The 2 concepts of
universality. (133) The new level of simplicity
→ use this to criticise CR. → G.P. on this.
(134) The 'simple' notion of simplicity refers
to the Mer (relations) (CR). The complex notion of
simplicity subsumes the Mer. /summing up
Hegel's ideas about the beginning. (135) Good
quote on the difference between the 2 beginnings

(138) 3 points to criticise CR.

[space paper]

i) Suggest that it is linear - progressive

ii) It is simple abstract rather than simple, universal
immediate

iii) It est relations amongst objects not their
'subsumption' under a universality.

(139) Discussing method of enquiry + mode
of presentation. (165) Why money proves to
be self-moving value. (169) Within the CMP
circulation is both the basis of production and
one of its moments

For
FARZAD, SEENA AND SARA

PREFACE AND ACKNOWLEDGEMENT

The present work is a revised and enlarged version of an earlier work which appeared as a Kingston Polytechnic mimeo in 1983 under the title *Marx's Concepts in Capital in the Light of Hegel's Logic* (Shamsavari 1983). Over the years, as the work on this book was progressing, I have benefited immensely from the advice, assistance and encouragement of a number of friends and colleagues.

Professor Meghnad Desai has been of greatest help as he read the entire typescripts of both the 1983 work and the present one and made extensive comments and suggestions. Some of his very useful suggestions for the present book (including two wonderful graphs for the Hegel chapter) have not unfortunately been incorporated in the text as the typesetting was at an advanced stage when they arrived. I am particularly thankful to him for his superb Foreword to this book. I am also deeply grateful to Professor Bob Jessop and Dr Rajani Kanth for their very positive and encouraging comments on and reviews of this book.

My greatest thanks go to Paul Auerbach, my friend and colleague, who devoted a considerable amount of his valued time advising me on every aspect of the book, reading through several versions of the book as it was in the process of revision and correction and making extensive comments on substance as well as style and presentation. I am deeply grateful for all the hard work he has put into this project. Any errors or gaps of any sort that may have remained is entirely my responsibility.

September 1990   *Ali Shamsavari*

FOREWORD

The relevance of Hegel's writings for understanding Marx has been not so much a controversial area as (sometimes almost literally) a minefield. Opinions have existed on every side of the issue and sometimes as in the case of Georg Lukács terrible consequences have followed. The Hegel question lay dormant while the cobbler's son ruled in Muscovy. After that as the question was opened up, the answers to it refracted in many ways the state of the Left. Thirty-five years after the advent of the New Left we are no nearer agreement on the issue than before.

Paradoxically however now in 1990 after 'the end of history', some may argue that the search for any sort of answer is irrelevant. Stalin is dead as are Lenin and the Leninist political model. Who then is afraid of Karl Marx? With the glorious triumph of capitalism and the defeat of socialism, with democracy on their breath and VCRs in their homes, why should people, even intellectuals, worry about the Hegel/Marx question?

Anyone who will read Ali Shamsavari's profound (deep, scholarly, patiently instructive) book will no doubt be rewarded about the primary question of Hegel's relevance to any reading of Marx. In these few pages, I wish to bring out the reasons why this issue has festered for so long and how is it that its non-resolution has cost the socialist movement dearly.

I

It used to be a common conceit in the heydays of the 1960s to quote Lenin's dictum that you could not understand Marx's *Capital* if you had not read Hegel's *Logic*. Some of us went as far as to buy a copy of Hegel's *Logic* but few if any of us read it. One could as I know from my own case become an 'expert' in Marxian economics/political economy without reading Hegel even at one remove. This was not only due to the formidable difficulty of reading and understanding Hegel. It was also due to at least three factors: the status of economics in Marxism, Marx's own playfully and somewhat perversely misleading statements about Hegel and the deadening influence of the Third International on any creative and critical thinking about Marxism.

Gramsci is quoted sometimes as saying that the 1917 was a revolution against *Capital*. He meant the book, not the social relationship. From 1883 to 1913, Marx's economics had been subject of a lively debate on the Left as well on the Right. There are many names in the two forewords Engels wrote for the two volumes of *Capital* which show the early start of the debate. Then followed the Böhm Bawerk attack, the controversy with Bernstein, the debate on the Reproduction schemes that Rosa Luxemburg contributed along with Bukharin, Lenin, Tugan Baranowsky *et al.* The 'economic laws' of Marxism proved not easily tractable or even commonly agreeable upon.

The effect of this debate on Marxism was spread over two phases; in the first phase was an attempt to revise Marx's original model in a direction which would 'fit the facts' better, i.e. explain the so-called change in the business cycle, the failure of capitalism to collapse as was mistakenly thought was Marx's immediate prediction and to update and bring Marx in line with twentieth century reality. I will not comment on the epistemological poverty of this attitude; it should be obvious at least after reading this book if not before. I will however say that this attempt at revision which led to finance capitalism and later to monopoly capitalism proved to be theoretically shallow. For one thing it failed to replace Marx's theory by a better, or even an alternative, value theory. Monopoly capital was vulgar economics at its worst. As Marx characterized the original vulgar economics: 'It was therefore no longer a question, whether this theorem or that theorem was true, but whether it was useful to capital (substitute the *Party*) or harmful, expedient or inexpedient, politically dangerous or not. In place of disinterested inquirers, there were hired prizefighters; in place of genuine scientific research, the bad conscience and the evil intent of apologetic.' (Marx; *Capital*, vol 1, afterword to the second German edition [1873/1974], p.25)

Marx's original attempt at fashioning a critique of political economy using a labour theory of value was abandoned. The transformation of values into prices became an esoteric scholastic problem, irrelevant to the class struggle. Capitalism was going to collapse out of its own contradictions, without much further investigation because Lenin had said Marx had said it was so. This is not much of a caricature. In the halcyon 1960s and 1970s, one even heard it said that some propositions of Marxian economics may be true but were not in the interests of the proletariat. Truth was not objective, but class biased. We all had to become prizefighters.

Anyone perusing accounts of western Marxism written in recent years by Perry Anderson or Martin Jay will not discover any economist mentioned among the Gramscis, the Adornos and the Lukácses. High Marxism written in the post-war years, or even since 1930 ignored or evaded economic theoretic issues. Henryk Grossman is the last great figure in Marxian economics of the tradition that stretches back to 1883 but he was before 1930.

In place of Marx's theory we had a mishmash of some monopoly capitalism, some neo-classical theory of imperfect/monopolistic competition about 'excess profits', some Hobson/Keynes underconsumptionism and a lot of vulgar rhetoric relying on quotations. The result was demoralizing. In the space vacated by Marxists, economists moved in. They had a different epistemology, but they had habits of rigorous logical thinking. They did care whether this theorem or that was true; they examined Marx's propositions with care if not always sympathy. Once Sweezy had revived the long dead literature on value theory it was Winternitz and May and Seton, and later Samuelson and Morishima and Roemer who moved into systematizing Marx's theorems. Their approach was doggedly non-dialectical but at least sincerely logical. It was against this background that the controversy surrounding neo-Ricardian critique of Marx's propositions has to be seen. Rigorously non-dialectical as the others, the neo-Ricardians started from a position of partisanship favourable to Marx; they found logical, algebraic flaws in Marx's fundamental proposition that profits arise from surplus value and that surplus value is the only source of profit. (For a survey see Desai, M., The transformation problem, *Journal of Economic Surveys*, Vol.2, No.4, 1988, pp.295-333.)

As you read Ali Shamsavari's text, you will see some of the traps that we get into if we forget the dialectical context of Marx's economics. For the present I merely wish to emphasize that this débâcle of Marxian economics happened because Marxists had no philosophical foundations to their economics once it had become fashionable to neglect Hegel. Modern neo-classical economics whatever its other faults puts all its practitioners through a hard training in mathematics; you cannot be an economic theorist without grasping calculus, matrix algebra, some topology and differential equations. To be a Marxist economic theorist, a talent for invective was enough armed with quotations and a facility for using italicization! No wonder there has been no serious economic debate among the Marxists since the neo-Ricardian debate nearly a decade ago. Marxian economics is dormant if not dead; one can only hope that Ali Shamsavari's book will encourage many to acquire an expertise in Hegel to be able to do Marxian economics better.

II

But when it comes to understanding Marx's relation with Hegel, it has to be said that Marx himself is no help. He is playful and misleading in acknowledging his debt to Hegel. Ali Shamsavari is quite right in not taking Marx at his word but penetrating further into the many ways in which Marx is embedded in Hegel. To give my own favourite though perhaps trivial example. There is a famous quote from Marx much used by economists. 'Accumulate, accumulate; that is Moses and the prophets . . .' Now most people think this is *Marx's theory* of accumulation; i.e. that capitalists accumulate because that is their business as it were. If read in context it will become clear that Marx is here criticizing vulgar classical view about accumulation. The give-away is Moses and the Prophets. We do not read the Bible nowadays as Marx and indeed Hegel used to. Moses and the Prophets is an expression from the Gospel according to St Luke, and it stands for *outdated, obsolete* doctrine. Hegel uses it in his *Philosophy of Right* almost as a throwaway line as does Marx. If we do not know the Bible, Hegel or Marx, it is easy to think that Moses and the Prophets means authority.

But aside from the many ways in which Ali Shamsavari makes clear the context of many of Marx's statements especially the deep, hidden meaning in their Hegelian roots, we have to know that Marx's relationship with Hegel is itself a problem. Hegel died before Marx had even left high school. Marx did not begin as a student of philosophy, but wished to follow in his father's footsteps as a lawyer. It was only while recovering after a severe illness that he discovered Hegel and from then on to his father's dismay was converted to philosophy. By the time he came to Hegel however two things had happened. In official circles, Hegel's domination in academic philosophy was being challenged; the Prussian Minister for Education was being persuaded to purge the Hegelians from positions of academic influence. The young Hegelians on the other hand were using his philosophy as a weapon to attack the established order, beginning significantly with an attack on Christianity. Strauss's *Life of Jesus* was the first salvo in this battle. Bruno Bauer who was to be Marx's mentor albeit for a short time was working on his tome on Christianity while struggling for tenure at Bonn. In this climate Marx was both a critic of Hegel but denied university appointment since he was a young Hegelian after all. He had to submit his thesis in Jena since Berlin and Bonn had been purged of Hegelian influences.

Another seminal influence on Marx's critical attitude to Hegel was of course Feuerbach. Feuerbach's anthropological inversion of Hegel was the intermediate step towards Marx's materialist critique. But that and all Marx was trained as a philosopher and his *method*, not his methodology, was that of immanent criticism. This meant absorbing completely the doctrine one was challenging and subverting it *from within*. Thus Marx had to be a good Hegelian before he could transcend Hegel. He used the same method with classical political economy, especially with Ricardo. Hence the frequent confusion especially in material not carefully prepared for publication by Marx (i.e. most of his collected works) where it is hard to draw the line between when he is being Hegelian [Ricardian] and when he is criticizing Hegel [Ricardo].

Between 1842 when he wrote his *Critique of Hegel's Philosophy of Right* and 1850 when he and Engels had abandoned The German Ideology to the gnawing criticism of the mice Marx was engaged in coming to terms with Hegel but especially the young and increasingly not so young Hegelians as well as others like Stirner who were climbing on the anti-Hegelian bandwagon. Throughout this debate, Marx's attitude to Hegel is one of critical respect; while he knows Hegel has his problems, he has nothing but contempt for the young (anti-) Hegelians as *The Holy Family* shows us.

This episode in Marx's creative life between the *Economic and Philosophical Manuscripts* and the 'economic' works — *A Contribution to the Critique of Political Economy* onwards, between say 1844 and 1851 or almost 1857, is unexplored especially by those of us who concentrate on Marx's economics. But much of Marx's hide-and-seek with Hegel — his playful reference to how he adopted Hegelian expressions just to annoy those who neglected Hegel as a dead dog, his almost unconscious adoption of many of Hegel's favourite quotations (e.g. Hic Rhodus, hic saltus, Moses and the Prophets, etc), his very careful use of phrases such as *it appears* (some of which are assiduously detected by Ali Shamsavari to get at the real intent) — comes from this long engagement with Hegel. Hegel's philosophy was to Marx what calculus and linear algebra is to a modern day economist — the tools of trade, the basic language. In trying to understand Marx without any acquaintance with this language we (and I include myself among these) have been in the position that economists were between 1871 and 1935 when they tried to understand Walras's General Equilibrium without knowing the mathematics. Nothing but untold reams of confusing arguments resulted from this.

The analogy is not perfect of course as no analogy is. To understand Hegel in this day and age is much harder work than picking up calculus. The relevance of Hegel to Marx is also nuanced as Ali Shamsavari demonstrates. But it will be increasingly hard to be able to pretend that we can 'do Marx' without a smattering of Hegel.

III

Luckily, or unluckily perhaps, we have plenty of time to grasp Hegel. It may have been possible in the 1960s or even 1970s, as we chanted

"We shall fight, we shall win
London, Paris, Rome, Berlin"

to say that overthrowing capitalism was a more urgent task than understanding the origins of profit in surplus value (a misreading of the eleventh thesis on Feuerbach). But now at the end of history, we have plenty of time. The one sect that claimed apostolic succession from Marx and which excoriated revisionism although it had been one of the first revisers, Leninism has shot its bolt. It had the first chance to prove its worth and after seventy-odd years in all its variants — Stalinism, Maoism, Trotskyism — it stands discredited. Neither the revolution nor the critique of the revolution from within Leninism could have foreseen the extent of rejection of the Leninist model. The Soviet workers are not going forward to the Trotskyist solution nor staying with the Stalinist one; the flight to capitalism is complete, the lingering delusions of the third way notwithstanding. In China where the break came ten years earlier, the débâcle is even more complete with the excesses of the Khmer Rouge in Cambodia a gruesome footnote on applied Maoism.

The worst enemies of Marxism failed to predict the speed of the ignominious collapse of the Leninist state; their critique was mild compared to what is now coming out of Eastern Europe and USSR. At the very least, one thing is certain. In the narrow economic sphere, the sphere in which socialism was going to do better than the irrational capitalist system, in delivering the material goods and services, socialism failed abysmally. One can recite the litany of excuses, but at the end of the day one has to ask was it the fault of our theory that we failed to foresee the demise of (real existing) socialism? Much worse was it not a blatant fault of the theory that we failed to foresee the continuing dynamism — contradictions and all — of capitalism? Seventy and more years after it had been labelled to be in terminal decline — the highest phase — capitalism is alive and kicking. Its coverage is even more global than was thought possible but a decade ago. There are variants *within* capitalism — Swedish, Japanese, German, American — but none outside.

How do Marxists come to terms with this fundamental reversal to their expectations? One can of course deny that anything serious has happened and watch the tickertape carefully for the next collapse of the stock markets. One can go on mouthing platitudes about the profound and continuing crisis of capitalism (seventy years on and still running, better than *The Mousetrap*). Or as I would prefer and I am sure Ali Shamsavari would agree we could go back to our studies and reunderstand Marx's theory of history to grasp the significance of what has happened. There is no hurry; no Stalinist orthodoxy stands ready to chop off our heads, no Party to expel or purge us. We have our books and we need to go back to our schools.

Towards the end of this book Ali Shamsavari takes up some of these larger issues — issues of transition from feudalism to capitalism, from capitalism to socialism and you will see that much new light is thrown by rereading Marx through old Hegel. I would say that the generation of Kautsky, Luxemburg, Bukharin, Hilferding and Lenin were in too much of a hurry to revise Marx. They were hasty in thinking that capitalism had matured or reached its highest phase. It had but covered a small part of Europe and North America; imperialism as Hobson appreciated was as much feudal/aristocratic in its nature as finance capitalistic. In the polities of capitalist countries the aristocracy rather than the bourgeoisie ruled as Arno Mayer has recently shown in his *Persistence of the Old Regime*.

It was not till after the Second World War that capitalism came into its own, defeating fascism on the one hand and conceding the demand for mass democracy without which it could not have defeated fascism. The forty-five years of more or less continuous economic growth — accompanied necessarily by cycles and occasional but short-lived crises, accompanied by the spread of mass democracy in the near periphery (Iberia, Southern Europe) and then in the farther periphery, the waves of technological revolutions in electronics, communication, transport, the growing mobility of labour and capital till we have arrived at a global division of labour — have brought us to a stage when it is fatuous to think that somehow the forces of production are being fettered by the relations of production and that a transition is imminent. A transition was not imminent in 1914 nor is it now.

This is not to say that there are no contradictions, or that the capitalist system is trouble free. Dialectics tells us that every time a system looks triumphant is the moment to seek its Achilles' heel, which is often its strongest point. The global financial network and the international division of labour have made capitalism vulnerable to attack from almost anywhere (as I write this the Iraqi invasion of Kuwait is affecting all the stock markets and may cause a global recession at the very least, when a month ago the boom seemed everlasting). Growth has brought fragility to financial markets as the US Savings and Loan sector shows. The global market in finance is useful for laundering the money of the global drug trade. The ecological threat is no longer local, but is as internationally mobile as is capital; as the pollution of the Rhine, the Union Carbide disaster in Bhopal, or Chernobyl showed. In these days of just-in-time inventories, a slowdown in Ford at Dagenham can cause layoffs in Germany the next day. As the system finds new solutions so new problems arise. That is the dialectical nature of the world.

There is much then to understand yet about the dynamics of capitalism before we can plan for socialism. History luckily does not end. The owl of Minerva may fly only at dusk, but then every dusk is followed by a new dawn. The intervening night is the time for preparation. It will be hard work, but books like the present one will be of great help in that task.

September 1990   *Meghnad Desai*

CONTENTS

ABBREVIATIONS

The works by Hegel, Marx and Engels cited most frequently in this book are listed below together with the abbreviation used for each throughout the text. For fuller details of each work consult the Bibliography.

EL.	Hegel, G. W. F., 1873, *Logic*, tr. by W. Wallace
LHP.	Hegel, G. W. F., 1892, *Lectures on the History of Philosophy*, in 3 volumes, tr. by E. S. Haldane & F. H. Simon, rep. 1974
Ph.R.	Hegel, G. W. F., 1952, *Philosophy of Right*, tr. by T. M. Knox
PM.	Hegel, G. W. F., 1967, *The Phenomenology of Mind*, tr. by L. B. Baillie
LL.	Hegel, G. W. F., 1969, *Science of Logic*, tr. by A. V. Miller
Ph.N.	Hegel, G. W. F., 1970(a), *Philosophy of Nature*, in 3 vols. tr. by M. J. Petry
Ph.M.	Hegel, G. W. F., 1971, *Philosophy of Mind*, tr. by W. Wallace and A. V. Miller
TSV. I.	Marx, K., 1963, *Theories of Surplus-Value*, Part I
TSV.II.	Marx, K., 1968, *Theories of Surplus-Value*, Part II
TSV.III.	Marx, K., 1971, *Theories of Surplus-Value*, Part III
CR.	Marx, K., 1970, *A Contribution to the Critique of Political Economy*
G.	Marx, K., 1973, *Grundrisse*
C.I.	Marx, K., 1976(a), *Capital*, Vol. 1
C.II.	Marx, K., 1978(a), *Capital*, Vol. 2
C.III.	Marx, K., 1981, *Capital*, Vol. 3
SW.	Marx, K. & Engels, F., 1969, *Selected Works*, in 3 vols.
SC.	Marx, K. & Engels, F., 1975, *Selected Correspondence*, 3rd Edn.
LC.	Marx, K. & Engels, F., 1983, *Letters on Capital*

INTRODUCTION

The present work narrowly conceived is a study of Marx's methodology in his economic works (*Capital* in particular) and its relation to Hegel's philosophy and logic. In a broader sense it is a defence of the relevance and place of the dialectical approach in social theorizing against the hegemonic claims of the analytical approach (i.e. what Hegel calls 'analytic cognition' and Marx the 'analytical method') which characterizes the basic methodology of the mainstream social sciences today.

In the past two decades or so a number of Marxist intellectuals have attempted to distance Marxist thought from Hegel, explicitly or implicitly. For this group, the task of extricating Marx from all Hegelian connections has been an essential part of the legitimation of Marxist thought in a twentieth century context. Hegel, the 'mystical', the 'idealist' philosopher has been considered a major obstacle in establishing the scientific credentials of Marx in modern analytical philosophy and in the social sciences.

This modern anti-Hegelian movement is by no means limited to a group of like-minded Marxists or interpreters of Marx. Its network includes prominent Marxist philosophers such as Louis Althusser and Lucio Colletti and their followers, neo-Ricardian Marxist economists such as Ian Steedman, and analytical philosophers such as G. A. Cohen.[1] The work of the latter has in fact led to a new trend in Marxist scholarship, appropriately labelled 'analytical Marxism', which is represented by the works of Jon Elster and John Roemer.[2] One consequence of this attempt to distance Marx from Hegel has been an explicit or implicit denial of the relevance of dialectics and a tendency to adopt an analytical methodology.[3]

My purpose is not to deny the analytical aspects in Marx's work. In fact, it was Marx himself who left his interpreters in doubt about his intellectual debt to Hegel.[4] Furthermore, what I have elsewhere called Marx's 'shame-faced' Hegelianism can also be traced to motivations and concerns similar to those behind the modern anti-Hegel trend.[5] It is not my intention to degrade the value and the legitimate role of the analytical approach in any scientific research programme. I firmly believe that the standards of clarity set by Steedman and Cohen, for instance, must be followed rigorously in the social sciences. However, the anti-Hegel trend, by dismissing dialectics not only obviates a significant aspect of Marx's thought but also deprives itself of a most powerful method particularly

1

suited to social research and scholarship.

Although clarity is much to be admired in any scientific project, it is no substitute for truth. A true idea, even if it is wrapped in obscurity, is superior to a falsehood stated with perfect clarity. In order to highlight the problems of a purely analytical approach to Marx which attempts to bypass Hegel, I will discuss one particular example which deserves special attention, a modern interpretation of Marx's theory of history (i.e. historical materialism) in an analytical fashion: Cohen's 'defence' of historical materialism. I have singled out Cohen at this stage for the following reasons:

a) Despite the fact that Cohen's work has been extensively criticized since its appearance in 1979 it continues to be very influential, especially in the Anglo-Saxon world.

b) Cohen's work represents a conscious attempt at an analytical method and presentation, and for this reason is particularly suitable as a focal point in revealing the pitfalls of the analytical approach.

Cohen's Defence of Marx

Cohen's approach to Marx's theory of history is an archetypal case of the application of the analytical method. Cohen himself characterizes his interpretation as 'technological determinism'. As this interpretation is not unique to Cohen but spans a long history going back to certain formulations by Marx and Engels and finding classic expression in works such as Plekhanov's *The Development of the Monist Theory of History* and Bukharin's *Historical Materialism: A System of Sociology*,[6] I shall not deal with the validity of this interpretation at this juncture. Cohen has been criticized from various points of view, such as the discrepancy between his interpretation and Marx's works on historical development.[7] While I sympathize with this line of criticism, my main concern here is rather with the methodology that produces this interpretation.

The foundation of Cohen's interpretation consists of a strict analytical separation between the material and the social aspects of production, leading to a fixed opposition between the two.

To validate the separation between the material and the social aspects of a mode of production Cohen uses an analogy that is highly revealing:

> If we consider a statue from the point of view of its matter we abstract from its form, and we describe it under that abstraction by stating what it is made of. Yet what it is made of does now have the form of the statue. It has both material

2

and formal characteristics. So it is with men and productive forces. They have material and social characteristics, but *no social characteristics may be deduced from their material characteristics*, any more than the statue's shape may be deduced from its matter. (Cohen 1979, pp.91-2)

This conception of the form/content relation used by Cohen derives from the spatial-geometric metaphor Plato had in mind while formulating his philosophy of forms: these forms are independent of the material realization of their idea, as a geometric figure is indifferent to any material content.[8] And since human beings in their productive as well as their artistic activity give forms to objects, the form-giving process is external to the material object. The relationship between the worker or artist and the material can be described in Hegel's words as 'external teleology'. But there are other relationships in nature and society that cannot be so described. Here we may turn to 'internal teleology', which was upheld by both Aristotle and Hegel[9] and which was inspired by their study of organic life, in which the spatial-geometric concept runs into serious difficulty: the form and purpose, far from being external and indifferent to the 'material content', emanate from it. Thus Hegel formulates the form/content relation in the following way:

i) Form and content pass into each other, i.e. form is transformed into content and content into form.

ii) The content includes the highest form, i.e. content is empty without the highest form achieved in the development of the form/content relation.

The following quotation from Hegel's *Logic* will clarify these points further:

When the form . . . is not reflected into self it is equivalent to the negative of the phenomenon, to the non-independent and changeable: and that sort of form is the indifferent or External Form.

The essential point to keep in view about the opposition of Form and Content is that the content is not formless, but has the form in its own self, quite as much as the form is external to it. There is a double sort of form. At one time it is reflected into itself. That form is identical with the content. At another time it is not reflected into itself. That is the external existence, which does not at all affect the content. We are here in presence . . . of the absolute relation or proportion between content and form: according to which the one lapses into the other . . . . (EL. pp.208-9)

Form and content are a pair of characteristics frequently employed by the reflective understanding, especially in the way of looking on the content as the essential and independent, the form on the contrary as the unessential and dependent. Against this it is to be noted that both are in fact equally essential; ... the two (content and form) are distinguished by this circumstance, that matter, though implicitly not without form, still in being one thing or another manifests a disregard of form, whereas the content, as such, is what it is only because *the matured form is included in it*. Still the form comes before us sometimes as an existence indifferent to and external to content .... In a book, for instance, it certainly has no bearing upon the content, whether it be bound in paper or in leather. That however does not in the least imply that apart from such an indifferent and external form, the content of the book is itself formless. There are undoubtedly books enough which even in reference to their content may well be styled formless: but want of form in this case is the same as bad form, and means the absence of the right form, not the absence of all form. So far is this right form from being unaffected by the content that it is rather the content itself. A work of art that wants the right form is for that very reason no right or true work of art .... Real works of art are those where content and form are throughout identical. (EL. p.209, Additions, emphasis added)

Let us now explore the implications of Hegel's analysis for Cohen's methodology. Suppose, following Cohen's approach we were to examine the production relations of capitalism at a relatively advanced stage, for instance, after the completion of the industrial revolution. These production relations we will take to be its social form and the productive forces its content. If we now apply Hegel's formulations above, this content (the productive forces) includes the 'mature' form, i.e. mature capitalism as a social form. Is this reasonable? If we examine Marx's account of the development of productive forces under capitalism since the sixteenth century up to the period of the industrial revolution in *Capital I* (Chapters 13, 14 & 15 comprising over two hundred pages), we may conclude that in the earlier stages of capitalism capitalist enterprises simply took over the productive forces available to them from older forms of production, e.g. the hand-loom, without developing the technology of production. Even at the stage of manufacture, which required extensive division of labour, the technology remained basically unchanged. With the advent of large-scale machine-based production made possible by the industrial revolution, however, capitalism begins transforming the forces of production 'in its own image'. Thus large-scale industry, the core of capitalist productive forces (the content of capitalism) increasingly exhibits the characteristics of the mature social form that now belong to this content. Thus Hegel's formulation fits well with Marx's perception of capitalist development.

Cohen's formulation of the content/form relationship as applied to

4

capitalism on the contrary is, if anything, really only a special case or, in Hegelian terms, a 'particular'. That is to say, far from being a truly general theory of the forces and relations of production it is a 'regional' theory applicable only to the early stages of a mode of production when the new social form stands in external relation to the stock of productive forces handed down by older modes of production. Only in this special historical phase can the 'purity' of Cohen's categories be preserved.

To avoid misunderstanding, let me say that I am not suggesting that the forces of production, technology, science or in general the creations of the human mind and of human labour are somehow 'locked-into' a given social form from which they cannot or should not be freed. To make such an assertion would be to commit an error opposite to that of Cohen. The forces of production have (at least partially) a life of their own, but one can say that these forces will be in external relation to new social forms as long as they are not transformed, modified or adapted by these forms. I believe that the problems of 'dualistic' development in developing countries as well as the search for market or market-type mechanisms in centrally-planned economies arise from the external nature of the forms of technology borrowed: these technologies have a degree of maturity emerging from the social relations of advanced capitalism that stands in sharp contrast with the existing social relations of production in developing and centrally-planned economies. In one case (central planning) the social form has failed to transform these forces of production in its own image and has maintained an external relation to them. In the other case (underdevelopment) the existing social form has not matured enough to absorb these forces of production as its own.

When we abstract from a social form of production, what is left is not simply the material substance of the relationship between human beings and nature in general. The forces of production do not express the relations of people to nature in general, but are specific to the abstracted social form. It is only when we abstract from these specific forces that we arrive at the material relationship between people and nature in general, a relationship of no particular interest from the point of view of social analysis. The man-nature relationship is almost always mediated by the social relations of production and the forces of production, which are inseparably connected to each other.

Thus we are dealing not with two levels, i.e. the productive forces and the relations of production, but three:

i) The general material relations of society with nature.

5

ii) The specific forms taken by these relations in human societies (the productive forces).

iii) The social relations within which these productive forces function (the productive relations).

What ideally fits Cohen's analogy is level (i), which like the piece of marble does not reveal the social form taken by these relations. This however, does not apply to level (ii), which must be included along with (iii) in that social form. Cohen's error is to identify (ii) with (i). It is this identification that, for instance, prevents him from appreciating Marx's criticism of J. S. Mill's characterization of the 'laws of production' as eternal and the 'laws of distribution' as transient and dependent on social arrangements (Cohen, 1979, pp.108-11).

At one point where Cohen quotes Marx in support of his thesis, the quotation has the opposite effect:

> So if we look through the social form we discern something conceptually separate from it: the *human* — here opposed to *social* — interaction with nature which is material production. Having 'nothing to do with social form' it is "the productive activity of human beings in general, by which they promote their interchange with nature, divested not only of every social form and well-defined character, but even in its bare natural existence, independent of society, removed from all societies . . . an expression and confirmation of life which the still non-social man in general has in common with the one who is in any way social." [quoted from *Capital III*, by Cohen] (Cohen 1979, p.99)

In this quotation Marx identifies the content of different modes of social being not with productive forces, but with the productive relation of individual human beings with nature. But this concept is so general (expressing features that are shared by both the social and the non-social man, in Marx's words) as to be practically empty and useless. If Cohen had also identified the invariant material aspects of society with the necessity for the existence of labour, or indeed with those pre-conditions without which neither society nor production would exist (e.g. the force of gravity) then this procedure would be unobjectionable, but useless. Cohen identifies these material aspects with productive forces — elements of the social existence that have already been 'formed' by social relations.

For Cohen the changes made by society to nature (which encompass the existing stock of productive forces) become a permanent feature of the material content of the society, 'part of the landscape'. But some of these changes to nature under capitalism (or indeed in the centrally planned economies) are threatening to destroy the very natural basis of society. Thus some productive forces may become unproductive if not destructive. Cohen may dispel these problems by declaring that such cases do not fit his definition of productive force and should be crossed out in his 'list' or 'catalogue' of productive forces. But such a procedure would avoid the essential task of defining these productive forces in a meaningful way.

To abstract from the social form hoping, through this process of abstraction, to find the material relations of society with nature is like abstracting from a biological form in order to find the material relation of that form with nature. But it is precisely the biological form that structures those material relations in a specific way. If we abstract from that form we have also abstracted from the material content.

There are two kinds of abstractions involved here:

a) If we abstract from the social form of a specific mode of production what is left is *not* the material relations with nature but the productive forces specific to that social form.
b) If we abstract from social form in general then we are left with the general material relations of human beings with nature. But then these relations are so general that they can hardly be distinguished from those between any other species and their external nature.

Thus in neither of the above abstractions do we end up with productive forces in general.

The methodological foundation of Cohen's project is thus quite weak. This weakness arises from the search for pure categories in social analysis where, if present, they are irrelevant. The separation between the material and social aspects of society is based on a particular interpretation of the form/content relation which is realized only in particular, specific circumstances whether in thought or in reality (e.g. Cohen's own examples of how the structure of a bridge is separate from its constituent parts and the formal structure of an argument is distinct from the statements that make up the argument [Cohen 1979, pp.33-6]). Thus, far from leading to a general theory, these pure categories apply only in particular circumstances.

In order to substantiate more specifically the general critique of Cohen's methodology attempted above I will now focus on Cohen's treatment of productive forces.

Cohen defines the forces of production in the following way:

> To qualify as a productive force, a facility must be capable of use by a producing agent in such a way that production occurs (partly) as a result of its use, and it is someone's purpose that the facility so contribute to production. (Cohen 1979, p.32)

This definition involves three distinct concepts:

i) A *producing agent*
ii) The *productivity* of the facility
iii) The *purpose* of production.

But all of these concepts (which remain presumed and undefined in Cohen's text prior to the definition of a productive force) are inextricably linked to social relations of production. Unless we consider elementary situations in which either production directly serves the biological needs of the individual producer (the classical isolated hunter or fisherman), or the productive activity itself is a source of utility for the individual (hunting for pleasure), there is no way in which the concepts of 'producing agent', 'productivity', 'purpose of production' or indeed production itself can be determined independently of not only the ensemble of social relations of production but also superstructural elements. There are, in addition, serious conceptual difficulties with Cohen's definition when we come to consider his basic list of productive forces:

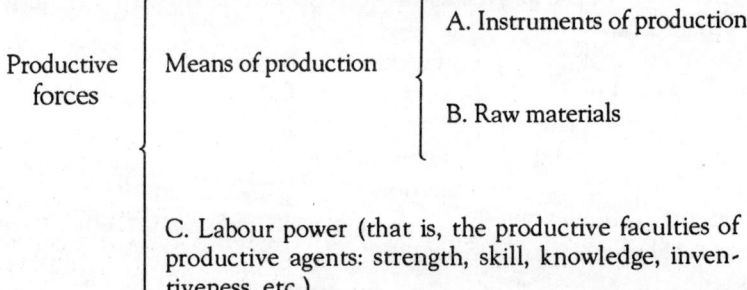

(Cohen 1979, p.32)

(Cohen expands this list in the course of his discussion to include many more items, but this extended list need not concern us here.) The first problem with this basic list is that it is not really a proper list of productive forces. Rather it roughly corresponds with the elements of the labour process as defined by Marx in *Capital I*:

> The simple elements of the labour process are (1) purposeful activity, that is work itself, (2) the object on which that work is performed, and (3) the instrument of that work. (C.I. pp.284-5)

Therefore unless we are prepared to identify the stock of the productive forces of society with the elements of labour process, Cohen's basic list is not acceptable. In particular the inclusion of raw materials in this list is inappropriate, as a raw material, although necessary for most productive activities is not a productive force, as we shall see below. But this item is especially damaging to Cohen's case for other reasons that will become apparent in the following discussion of the elements of Cohen's basic list.

1. Raw Materials

Cohen begins by rejecting Marx's definition of raw material. Marx defines a raw material as a special class of the subject of labour that has already been processed by prior labour. According to Cohen, Marx's criterion is neither necessary nor sufficient for an object of labour to qualify as raw material. Although Cohen himself does not give us an alternative definition for raw material, one can surmise from context that for him a raw material is an object that is physically transformed in the act of production, a concept that is based on the literal meaning of the term 'raw' (uncooked, unprepared, untransformed) and thus roughly corresponds to the commercial use of the term raw material.

For instance, Cohen says that a tree in the 'virgin' forest (not a raw material according to Marx) is a raw material when it is made into a totem pole. Iron ore, which is not a raw material in mining (according to both Marx and Cohen) 'is a raw material in the sense that there is *some* labour process in which it functions as such, but is not a raw material in mining . . .' (Cohen 1979, p.38).

> If iron ore is not raw material in mining, it is also not raw material for the labour of the truck driver who takes it to the mill, even though it is 'filtered' by the miner before it is transported. Nor is timber raw material for the lumberjack when the forest is not virgin but the product of planting. (Cohen 1979, p.39)

From these examples it is obvious that for Cohen a raw material is an

9

object that is physically transformed in the labour process. Cohen's treatment of Marx's categories is objectionable in that instead of trying to understand these categories, he substitutes his own definitions and then criticizes Marx's categories because they do not match his own definitions. Thus if we look at both of the examples used by Cohen in the above quotations, it is not true, as Cohen claims, that for Marx iron ore is not a raw material in processes other than mining. As Marx says:

> If... the object of labour has, so to speak, been filtered through previous labour, we call it raw material. For example, ore already extracted and ready for washing. (C.I. p.284)

Similarly timber for lumberjacking is a raw material if the forest is not virgin but the product of prior planting. As Marx says, all industries except extractive industries use raw materials, including agriculture — except when 'it starts by breaking up virgin soil' (C.I. p.287).

Marx's criterion is not identical to Cohen's. For Marx, it is not the *physical* transformation in a labour process that determines an object of labour as a raw material, but essentially the *social* transformation, i.e. the fact that a raw material is not an object of labour furnished by nature (an untransformed object, 'raw' in the ordinary sense of the word but not in Marx's sense) but the product of a previous labour process. Physical transformation (in the narrow sense implied by Cohen) is neither necessary nor sufficient for an object to be a raw material. It is not sufficient because the tree in the virgin forest transformed into a totem pole is not a raw material in Marx's sense (unless the tree has already been cut down), as it is not the product of previous labour. Neither is it a necessary condition because iron ore transported by the trucker is a raw material for his labour although it is not physically transformed in this process.

Cohen's misreading of Marx's definition of raw material is very typical of his treatment of Marx's categories in general. Cohen wants to define productive forces in complete isolation from the relations of production. Having (wrongly) identified raw material as a force of production he finds Marx's definition disturbing for his method because this definition has reference not to an object in general that can be physically transformed into another object but to a product of previous labour, implying the existence of a social connection. Thus Marx uses a *social* as opposed to a *physical* criterion — one that enables him, for instance, to distinguish between purely extractive industries and non-extractive ones. Non-renewable resources constitute the object of labour in extractive industries (non-raw material) while renewable resources

10

(raw materials) form the object for other industries including agriculture.

2. The Instruments of Production

If we look at instruments of production beyond relatively simple tools, they are not only products of other processes of production (like raw materials) and thus socially determined but also, as in the case of machinery, they are interrelated parts of a productive complex whose operation requires the existence of a skilled work force, the availability of the requisite infrastructure, e.g. power supplies, roads, etc. and also superstructural elements such as laws and regulations and a general cultural environment that supports the production methods used. Thus the use of every major productive facility in modern industrialized societies depends not only upon the existence of a skilled labour force but also on supporting services and an infrastructure of both a technical and a managerial nature that are closely bound up with the social relations of production. It even demands the presence of such super-structural elements as an appropriate legal system and the support of government policies and activities.

In recent years two significant phenomena have forced Western culture to recognize the importance of these infrastructural and super-structural elements for the operation of modern industry. One is Japanese management methods and in particular the just-in-time (JIT) production management techniques.[10] A second phenomenon concerns the problems associated with technology transfer from developed to less developed countries.

The JIT production methods in Japan clearly show that productivity and efficiency cannot simply be understood in terms of the production technology and activities inside an enterprise, but to a large extent involve the social-institutional arrangements between enterprises and in general the 'business culture' of a country. For this reason, Japanese factories in Western countries could not simply hire local labour and put them to work without prior training and continuing efforts at acculturation.

When we consider technology transfer not between two industrialized countries (Japan and United Kingdom, for instance), but from a developed country to a less developed one, the analytical separation of the techniques and instruments of production from the social conditions of production runs into further difficulties. The transfer of modern technologies to developing countries has raised serious problems con-

11

cerning the appropriateness of many of these technologies and has led to a considerable literature on intermediate or appropriate technology. Some of these problems have involved the effects of modern technology on income distribution, the difficulties of manning, servicing and maintaining modern equipment, the diffusion of technical know-how in the local economy, the use of local resources and even the suitability of the products of modern technology to the needs of poor countries. These problems have made it evident that technology is generated in very specific social-institutional settings and its use in other settings requires considerable adaptation of the technology itself. Thus the forces of production cannot be separated from other features of an economy.[11]

One particular example that has received considerable attention concerns the difficulties encountered in the course of the application of the high-yielding varieties of seeds (HYV), or modern varieties (MV) also known as the 'Green Revolution' technology in Asia and Latin America.[12] It has been shown by many studies that this technology was not neutral with respect to ownership patterns (the relations of production) as richer farmers had a better chance of using this technology due to the necessity of purchasing complementary inputs such as fertilizers. Although a more recent study[13] questions the non-neutrality of this technology in the Asian context, it categorically confirms the non-neutrality of the use of another 'material force of production' new to less developed countries, i.e. tractors: rich farmers have considerable advantage in their use. Based on my personal observations in the north-west of Iran in mid-1970s, where the oil boom had led to the virtual depopulation of rural areas and, thus, made mechanization of farming, in view of high rural wages, economically sensible, even rich farmers were averse to the adoption of tractors. This decision was due mainly to the lack of complementary services and infrastructure, such as repairing, maintaining and servicing facilities in the rural areas. In a developed country a tractor may seem to be a powerful productive force whose use in farming is relatively unproblematic: all you need is a driver and fuel. In a less developed country any potential tractor driver, i.e. a person with the requisite skills is most probably an individual who would rather work and live in an urban area: mechanics who would be able to repair tractors are scarce and are found mostly in cities. Fuelling stations could be a hundred miles away from where the tractors are used and the roads may be unsuitable for towing a broken-down tractor to the nearest city for repairs. Thus a programme for the mechanization of agriculture, if not accompanied by major changes in the infrastructure of the economy as

12

well as shifts in government policy away from 'urban bias', can easily turn a rural area into a graveyard for tractors. It is evident, then, that superstructural elements are not easily separable from the instruments of production.

3. Labour-Power

Labour-power, according to Cohen, is a 'productive force' although the worker is not. For Marx the distinction between the worker and his/her labour-power is not just analytical, but to a large extent an historical product, which though not initiated by capitalism has been developed immensely under capitalist conditions of production. It is only under capitalism that labour-power becomes fully commodified and commodification itself is part of a social process. Thus labour-power is a productive force that cannot be considered in isolation from the social relations of production and cannot be conceived as an invariant productive force under all conditions of society. If we adopt a narrow definition of labour-power as 'brawn' power then its effectiveness as a productive force is limited to the most primitive conditions of production or to particular branches of the economy in which mere physical exertion of labour is essential. Interpreted in a broader sense to include 'brain' power as well, the character of labour-power varies in different forms of society. (According to Marx the worker invariably exhibits both of these aspects in the labour process: it is only under certain conditions of production that one aspect is strengthened at the expense of the other.) The significance of the education of the labour force and investment in human 'capital' has attracted a good deal of attention in recent years. When one looks at this education one can also treat it analytically and regard it simply as a productive asset which becomes part of the labour-power of the worker, but the education of workers is also intimately linked to the superstructure: labour-power does not function as an 'autonomous' productive force.

Thus none of the 'basic' productive forces discussed above lend themselves to pure definitions that set them apart from relations of production and/or the social superstructure. Although one may find some justification in Marx for such analytical definitions, the latter were preliminary notions, working hypotheses for both Marx and Engels in their early attempts to formulate a new theory of history. Furthermore, these definitions were not conceived with the analytical purity that Cohen attempts to impart to them. Cohen's work as a defence or a

13

critique of Marx remains largely irrelevant, if not outright false.

The Objectives and the Plan of the Present Work

As opposed to the anti-Hegelian trends mentioned above, it is the central contention of this book that the dialectical method as developed by Hegel constitutes a central influence on Marx's economic and historical studies, and that, furthermore, this method in itself is valid and essential for social theorizing.

The primary aims and objectives pursued in this book are:

1. (i) To identify a core of ideas about methodology based on Marx's explicit and implicit statements on this issue and his critical comments on classical political economy; (ii) to trace these ideas to Hegel's philosophy in general and his *Logic* in particular. (Part I)

2. To demonstrate, based on a detailed study of certain key concepts in *Capital* that a consistent and coherent structure can be identified. (Part II)

3. (i) To develop a critique of Marx's theorizing in certain key areas, such as value theory, based on the analyses in Parts I & II; (ii) to demonstrate how the analysis of the present work throws light on many controversies surrounding Marx's theory of history (historical materialism), the transition from feudalism to capitalism, economic development in the 'third world', the role of markets under socialism, etc. (Part III)

My object is not to search for the 'true' Marx, nor would I claim to offer an impartial and totally objective view. Marx has been and will continue to be subject to diverse and often contradictory interpretations. All this said, however, it would be wrong to give up the search for some form of objectivity in interpreting Marx. The elements of the objectivity I have tried to achieve in this book can be described in the following way:

(i) Marx's project, i.e. as evident from his explicit statements about the 'critique' of political economy.
(ii) Marx's explicit methodological statements (as, for instance, contained in the *1857 Introduction*).
(iii) The structure of Marx's concepts in *Capital*.

If it can be demonstrated that Hegelian philosophy sheds considerable light on the above elements, then we have an objective standard by which to judge Marx's work.

14

Marx was no doubt influenced by other intellectual traditions, e.g. classical political economy, utopian socialism and even the Greek classics. These influences cannot be claimed to form a coherent body of knowledge even though they were synthesized in Marx's thought: there remains, for instance, a definite conflict between the Hegelian and the Ricardian influences. To hope to reconstruct a completely coherent Marx who had synthesized all these traditions to produce a thoroughly harmonious and coherent doctrine is futile, unrealistic, unnecessary and at best an intellectual pastime. A dynamic approach, on the contrary, would attempt to produce a coherent standard by which to judge Marx in his successes as well as his failings. The 'true' Marx is a dead Marx. On the other hand the living Marx is riddled with contradictions. But this circumstance, far from being a hindrance is an advantage, a source of strength rather than weakness. Thus I offer no apologies for treating Marx's thought as living, developing and capable of further development. If one can show that a coherent body of thought exists in Marx, it can help to illuminate not only the central problems Marx was concerned with in his time but also key problems in the contemporary world — the struggle for economic development, the transition from capitalism to socialism, the reform and transformation of existing socialism, the struggle for human rights and protection of the environment, current economic crises, etc. The legitimacy of this procedure would then be justified even if it stood in conflict with other specific and outlying aspects of Marx's thought.

Marx's Project in Capital *and its Relation to Hegel's* Logic

Marx's first public announcement of his debt to Hegel's dialectics in *Capital* appeared in the postface to the second German edition of the first volume of that work. In this postface he goes over some of the reviews that appeared in various countries following the publication of the first edition of *Capital I* in 1867.

One particular review of the first volume of *Capital* by the Russian economist I. I. Kaufman especially interested Marx. Kaufman, in his review, declared that Marx in his method of presentation was 'the most idealist of philosophers, and indeed in the German, i.e. the bad sense of the word'. But as far as the factual material of his work is concerned Marx, according to Kaufman, 'is infinitely more realistic than all his predecessors in the business of economic criticism . . . He can in no sense be called an idealist'. Marx finds no better way of answering Kaufman's criticisms than to quote him at length. After reproducing a long quotation from Kaufman's review, Marx says:

> Here the reviewer pictures what he takes to be my own actual method, in a striking and, as far as concerns my own application of it, generous way. But what else is he depicting but the dialectical method? (C.I. p.102)

After referring to his method as dialectical Marx goes on to confront the dichotomy Kaufman alleged to exist between Marx's 'idealist' form of presentation and his 'realist' treatment of factual material. But, as we will see, instead of directly meeting his critic's charge of an 'idealist' form of presentation, he attempts to steer clear of the latter by making a distinction between the method of inquiry and the method of presentation:

> Of course the method of presentation must differ in form from that of inquiry. The latter has to appropriate the material in detail, to analyse its different forms of development and to track down their inner connection. Only after this work has been done the real movement can be appropriately presented. If this is done successfully, if the life of the subject-matter is now reflected back in the ideas, then it appears as if we have before us an *a priori* construction. (C.I. p.102)

A superficial reading of the above quotation may suggest that in fact Marx concedes the point of his critic by intimating that the method of presentation, by creating the appearance of an '*a priori* construction', appears as 'idealistic'. It may seem that Marx is defending himself from the charge of idealism by making the above distinction between the two methods. From the context of Marx's dialogue with his Russian critic it would seem that Marx is trying to say that his dialectical method should be sought at the level of his method of inquiry rather than presentation where the Hegelian ('idealist') influence is more manifest. But would not this reduce the method of presentation and, therefore, the Hegelian influence to mere 'formalism' or, at worst, a 'formality'?

These doubts become stronger when Marx follows the above comments by declaring that his 'dialectical method is in its foundations, not only different from the Hegelian, but exactly opposite to it' (C.I. p.102). Why? Because Hegel was an 'idealist' while Marx is a 'materialist'! These are strong words, implying a radical disjunction between Marx's dialectical method and the Hegelian one. But if Marx's method is in such direct opposition to Hegel's dialectics, is there any common ground left between the two besides the obvious terminological connection represented by the word 'dialectics'?

Marx continues his commentary, still strengthening doubts about

16

his relation to Hegel in the following way:

> I criticized the mystificatory side of the Hegelian dialectic nearly thirty years ago, at a time when it was still in fashion. But just when I was working on the first volume of *Capital*, the ill-humoured, arrogant and mediocre epigones who now talk largely in educated German circles began to take pleasure in treating Hegel in the same way as the good Moses Mendelssohn treated Spinoza in Lessing's time, namely as a 'dead dog'. I therefore openly avowed myself the pupil of that mighty thinker, and even, here and there in the chapter on the theory of value, coquetted with the mode of expression peculiar to him. (C.I. pp.102-3)

In the above passage Marx is clearly protective with respect to Hegel to the point of 'coquetting' with his particular mode of expression and even declaring himself 'the pupil of that mighty thinker'.

What can we conclude from these comments but that Marx used Hegel's terminology, his peculiar mode of expression, 'here and there in the chapter on the theory of value', simply to show his respect to 'the mighty thinker'? Is Marx's relation to Hegel simply a terminological and at best a formal one? This is, indeed, how Althusser, for example, interprets Marx.[14]

But the question is — why should Marx protect Hegel by 'coquetting' with his terminology and by declaring himself Hegel's pupil if Marx's method owes nothing to Hegel's *Logic*?

The answer to this question is very clear to Marx, in spite of all the doubts raised by his earlier comments. There is for Marx a 'rational kernel' in Hegel, which although encased in a 'mystical shell' forms the common ground between Marx and Hegel.

> The mystification which the dialectic suffers in Hegel's hands by no means prevents him from being the first to present its general forms of motion in a comprehensive and conscious manner. With him it is standing on its head. It must be inverted, in order to discover the rational kernel within the mystical shell. (C.I. p.103)[15]

Marx continues the above passage by giving a broad description of the 'rational kernel' of Hegel's dialectics, describing it as 'in its very essence critical and revolutionary'. His description, however, is so general and so brief that it has little value for understanding what Marx considers to be rational in Hegel's *Logic*. This, however, is not our main concern here.

Surely what Marx attributes to Hegel above cannot be reduced to a mere formal method of presentation, even less to a terminological borrowing (a 'coquetting'). This point is supported by comments that

Marx makes in his private correspondence, especially when he was writing the manuscripts known as the *Grundrisse* during 1857-9.

In a letter dated 14th January 1858 Marx communicates the following to Engels:

> ... I am discovering some nice arguments. For instance, I have overthrown the whole doctrine of profit as it has existed up to now. The fact that by mere accident I again glanced through Hegel's *Logik* ... has been of great service to me as regards the *method* of dealing with the material. If there should ever be time for such work again, I should very much like to make accessible to the ordinary human intelligence — in two or three printer's sheets — what is *rational* in the method which Hegel discovered but at the same time enveloped in mysticism ... (SC. p.93)

Marx is admitting here that Hegel's *Logic* rendered him 'great service' in his critique of the classical theory of profit. Marx's criticism of Ricardo's doctrine led to the formulation of the former's theory of surplus-value, which is one of the central tenets of Marx's theory in *Capital*: if Hegel's *Logic* helped Marx in 'overthrowing' the classical doctrine and in the formulation of his new theory this again could not have been a mere 'formal' or 'verbal' influence. In fact Marx himself refers to the 'rational' aspect of Hegel's method and considers it worth his while to popularize this method if he ever should find time for such work.

While Marx was engaged in preparing the above-mentioned manuscripts (the *Grundrisse*), another well-known figure in the German socialist movement, Ferdinand Lassalle, was planning to present political economy in a Hegelian fashion. Marx evaluates Lassalle's attempt in a letter to Engels, dated 1st February 1858 (just two weeks following the above-mentioned letter), in the following way.

> I can see from this one note that the fellow [Lassalle] is proposing to present political economy in the Hegelian manner in his second great opus. He will learn to his cost that to develop a science by criticism to the point where it can be dialectically presented is an altogether different thing from applying an abstract ready-made system of logic to vague notions of a system of this kind. (SC. p.95)

Marx is clearly distinguishing between a formalistic application of dialectics to political economy ('applying an abstract ready-made system of logic ...') and a critical application (developing 'a science by criticism to the point where it can be dialectically presented ...'). Although Marx meant this as a criticism of Lassalle's project, it illuminates at the same time the nature of Marx's own project, which was in fact nothing more

18

or less than critique of political economy 'to the point where it [could] be dialectically presented'. This point is stated very clearly and explicitly in a letter to Lassalle himself three weeks after the above letter to Engels:

> The first work in question is *critique of the economic categories*, or, if you like, the system of bourgeois economy critically presented. It is a presentation of the system and simultaneously, through this presentation, a criticism of it. (SC. p.96)

Here Marx makes it abundantly clear that his project is to criticize classical political economy ('economic categories', 'the system of bourgeois economy') and that this criticism cannot be separated from the presentation of classical political economy, i.e. it is a 'critical presentation'.

What emerges from Marx's comments above is that

a. Marx describes his method of treatment as a 'critique'. Critique, for him, cannot be construed as anything but the critical method developed by German critical philosophy from Kant to Hegel, culminating in Hegel's dialectical logic.
b. The method of treatment (critique, dialectical method) cannot be separated from the method of presentation. Thus if the method of treatment itself is not critical, dialectical then the method of presentation can only be dialectical in a 'forced' way, i.e. in Marx's own words, such a presentation will involve the application of 'an abstract, ready-made system of logic' (precisely what, in Marx's view, Lassalle was attempting).
c. It is clear that even in the apologetical statement in *Capital* quoted above what Marx means by 'presentation' is not formalism or style, but the very *comprehension of the phenomena resulting from the inquiry*.

Thus, based on Marx's own public pronouncements and private communications, one may conclude that Marx's *Capital* owes substantially more to Hegel's *Logic* than a mere form of presentation. The next question is the substance of this methodological debt. As we saw above Marx wrote very little on this subject. We do have the *1857 Introduction*, a text rich in methodological insights,[16] and the chapter on value in *Capital I*, where Marx attempts an explicit dialectical presentation.[17] But, ultimately, it is Marx's actual work in *Capital* and all his other related texts that should serve and historically have

19

served as the primary source material for the reconstruction of Marx's method.

Notes to Introduction

1. Althusser (1969), Althusser and Balibar (1970); Colletti (1973), Steedman (1977); Cohen (1979). Althusser is discussed in Chapters One and Two. Colletti is referred to in Notes to Chapter Two. A review of Cohen is given below in the Introduction.
2. Elster (1985), Roemer (1981); Roemer has edited a collection of articles under the title *Analytical Marxism* (Roemer 1986) that contains several contributions that largely adopt the analytical methodology.
3. Significant exceptions to this tendency, apart from the Frankfurt School which has always been influenced by at least a residue of Hegelian thought, are to be found in Eastern Europe and Japan. Banaji (1980) refers to some East European sources. Japanese contributions include Uno (1980), Sekine (1980, 1981, 1984) and Itoh (1980); see also Sekine (1975) as well as his assessment of Uno contained in Uno (1980); Albritton (1986) is a comprehensive survey of the Japanese contribution to Marxist theory.
4. For a discussion of the ambiguities and hesitations in Marx's own evaluation of the Hegelian 'debt' see the final section of the Introduction below.
5. See Shamsavari (1986).
6. Plekhanov (1956); Bukharin (1969).
7. For instance see Miller (1984) where the author attempts to show that the few quotations from Marx forming the foundation of Cohen's interpretation stand in sharp contrast to Marx's historical analysis, e.g. the development of capitalism (Miller 1984, Chap.5).
8. One may question Cohen's methodology even at the level of the analogy he is using. Cohen's whole argument rests upon identifying matter (or content) with the marble and the form with the statue (minus its material). But the matter or content of an artistic form may well be thought of not as the physical material it is made of, but the ideas, feelings, etc. expressed by that form, which are not readily separable from what Cohen considers as form (in opposition to matter). The same content (form for Cohen) can be expressed equally well using a different material, e.g. metal or wood (although different materials inevitably convey different artistic feelings). Here the material substance would be the form of the artistic content. Thus what Cohen considers as the indifference of content can be turned into an indifference of form.
9. Aristotle, in opposition to Plato, had advanced the conception of the form/content relation to a higher level with his concept of 'final cause'. Hegel later proceeded in a similar way in his opposition to Kant (who had already abandoned his earlier formulation in his third *Critique*) with the concept of 'internal teleology'. For a discussion of Aristotle's differences with Plato see Allan (1952), Chaps. 2 & 3. Hegel addresses the question of teleology in both versions of his *Logic* (LL. pp.735-54; EL. pp.296-303) and other works, e.g. *The Phenomenology of Mind* (PM. pp.284-327). Kant's third *Critique* is the *Critique of Judgement* (Kant, 1952) which followed his previous Critiques, i.e. *Critique of Pure Reason* (Kant, 1929) and *Critique of Practical Reason* (Kant, 1956). For Hegel's evaluation of the contribution of Kant's third *Critique* see Chapter Four, Section III, below.
10. On Japanese manufacturing techniques see Schonberger (1982), Monnden (1981a, 1981b, 1981c) and Dilworth (1989), Chap. 9.
11. For a major study of the questions of technological dependence, appropriate technology and technology transfer see Stewart (1978). See also Clark (1985), Chap. 8 and Fransman (1986). Schumacher (1973) remains a classic on appropriate technology.
12. For a radical approach to the Green Revolution see Cleaver (1972), Fatami (1972), Frankel (1971) and Griffin (1974).

13. Yujiro Hayami, 'An assessment of the green revolution', in Eicher & Staatz (1984).

14. See, for instance, Althusser's Preface to *Capital* Volume One (1969) which appeared in English in Althusser (1971).

15. The idea that Marx appropriated the 'rational kernel' of Hegelian system was originally suggested by Engels in his 1859 review of Marx's *Critique* (Marx, 1970). Engels's views on this question are discussed in detail in Chapter One below. For a critique of the 'extraction' metaphor see Althusser (1969), Chap. 3. Of course Althusser's otherwise interesting analysis is intended to purify Marx's method of all Hegelian traces.

16. For a detailed study of *1857 Introduction* see Chapter Two below.

17. See Chapters Eleven & Twelve below.

PART I

MARX'S METHOD AND HEGEL'S LOGIC

CHAPTER ONE

THE COMPLEXITY OF 'SIMPLE' CONCEPTS IN MARX'S CAPITAL

Marx uses the term 'simple' to characterize a number of concepts in *Capital*. Some prominent examples are Simple Commodity Production, Simple Circulation of Commodities, Simple Reproduction and Simple Co-operation (or the 'Simple Shape of Co-operation', as Marx puts it). The theoretical status of these concepts has found a variety of diverse interpretations, beginning with Engels's primarily historicist view. As different views on this question imply different interpretations of Marx's methodology in *Capital* I will review three major views of Marx's 'simple' concepts (hereafter S-concepts) as an introduction to the subsequent discussions in this book.

I will start with Engels's view of Marx's method, which has become known in the literature as an 'historicist' interpretation. I will then deal with two other rival interpretations, the structuralist and the rationalist, that have evolved largely in response to the historicist position. I shall conclude the chapter by a brief discussion of the reasons why none of these positions are adequate to the essence of Marx's method in spite of the fact that each provide valuable insights into the intricate conceptual structure of Marx's *Capital*.

Before proceeding to a detailed review of these three approaches I will offer an elementary characterization of them:

i) The historicist approach conceives of 'simple' as an historically 'first' relation. In other words, S-concepts refer to historically prior relationships. The major presumption here is that history develops from simple to complex forms.
ii) The structuralist approach views 'simple' as a simple relation, not necessarily historically first but structurally subordinate to a

25

'complex' whole.

iii) The rationalist argument does not interpret S-concepts as representing a reality, i.e. a simple relation that is historically prior or subordinate to a real complex whole. In this approach 'simple' refers to an abstract idea, or an abstract model representing a mental abstraction from a complex reality, which is then used to explain the latter.

I. The Historicist Interpretation

A. Engels: The First Simple Beginning

Shortly after the publication of Marx's A *Contribution to the Critique of Political Economy* (1859), Engels published a review of the work[1] in which he offered his own interpretation of Marx's method in political economy. The salient feature of Engels's reading in that review is that he attempts to relate Marx's method to his own interpretation of Hegel's philosophy. Before outlining Engels's views let us see why the direct linking of Marx's method to Hegel's *Logic* came to Engels so naturally.

Engels who as a young Hegelian in his youthful days was very well versed in Hegelian philosophy[2] developed a special interest in methodological questions not only in relation to Marx's work in political economy but also, somewhat independently, in connection with developments in the natural sciences. Thus we find Engels trying to show the relevance of Hegel's philosophy to developments in biology and physics precisely in the same period in which Marx was struggling with Hegel's *Logic* in his critical presentation of political economy. In a letter dated 14th July 1858, in which Engels asks Marx for a copy of Hegel's *Philosophy of Nature*, he makes the following comments:

> This much is certain: if he [Hegel] had a philosophy of nature to write *today* the facts would come flying to him from every side . . . . The microscope has led to even more important results in chemistry. The main thing which has revolutionised the whole of physiology . . . is the discovery of the cell . . . . Everything is a cell. The cell is Hegel's "being-in-itself" and during its development it undergoes exactly the Hegelian process, resulting finally in the "idea", i.e., the particular complete organism.
>
> Another result which would have pleased old Hegel is the correlation of forces in physics, or the law that under given conditions . . . mechanical energy is transformed . . . into heat, heat into light, light into chemical affinity, chemical affinity . . . into electricity, electricity into magnetism . . . .
>
> So much is certain: comparative physiology gives one a withering contempt for the idealistic exaltation of man over the other animals. At every step

26

one is forced to recognise the most complete uniformity of structure with the rest of the mammals, and in its main features this uniformity extends to all vertebrates and even — in a less distinct way — to insects, . . . , etc. The Hegelian business of the qualitative leap in the quantitative series is also very fine here. (SC. pp.101-2)

It was this keen interest in the methodology of science and its relation to Hegelian dialectics that eventually led Engels to produce his famous methodological texts such as *Anti-Dühring, Feuerbach: The End of Classical German Philosophy* and *The Dialectics of Nature.*[3] Given this background, with Marx's letters to him expressing the former's renewed interest in Hegel's *Logic* and explaining the fine points of his work on political economy,[4] Engels was bound to take Marx's methodological perspectives seriously. It was in this spirit that Engels attempted a bold interpretation of Marx's method, the first of its kind. Let us now examine this interpretation. What impressed Engels most of all about Marx's work on political economy was that it represented 'a systematic integration of the whole complex of economic science', 'an interconnected development of the laws of bourgeois production and bourgeois exchange' (SW.1, p.511). Engels immediately related this aspect of Marx's work to Hegel:

Since Hegel's death hardly any attempt has been made to develop a science in its own inner interconnection. The official Hegelian school had appropriated from the dialectic of the master only the manipulation of the simplest tricks, which it applied to anything and everything, often even with ludicrous clumsiness. (SW. 1, p.511)

Here, Engels is reacting negatively to the 'official Hegelianism' that came in vogue in Germany after Hegel's death. At the same time he is implying that Marx succeeds in salvaging what is best in Hegel out of the wreckage of the Hegelian system caused by his official followers. What is best in Hegel, according to Engels, is described in the following way:

What distinguished Hegel's mode of thought from that of all other philosophers was the tremendous sense of the historical upon which it was based. Abstract and idealist though it was in form, yet the development of his thoughts always proceeded parallel with the development of world history and the latter is really meant to be only the test of the former. If, thereby, the real relation was inverted and stood on its head, nevertheless, the real content entered everywhere into the philosophy; all the more so since Hegel — in contrast to his disciples — did not parade ignorance, but was one of the finest intellects of all time. He was the first who attempted to show a development, an inner coherence, in history . . . (SW. 1, p.512)

27

Engels is paying tribute to Hegel on two counts:

1. Hegel's 'sense of the historical', his attempt to show that history unfolds with an inner logic and coherence.
2. The parallelism between Hegel's thoughts and the course of history. Engels clarifies the last point by stating the following:

'This epoch-making conception of history was the direct theoretical premise for the new materialist outlook, and this alone provided a connecting point for the logical method, too.' (SW. 1, p.513)

He then goes on to express, in words reminiscent of Marx's own characterization of his relation to Hegelian logic in the Postface to the second German edition of the first volume of *Capital*,[5] Marx's relation to Hegel in the following way:

> Marx was, and is, the only one who could undertake the work of extracting from the Hegelian logic the kernel which comprises Hegel's real discoveries in this sphere, and reconstructing the dialectical method, divested of its idealistic trappings, in the simple shape in which it becomes the only true form of development of thought. The working out of the method which forms the foundation of Marx's criticism of political economy we consider a result of hardly less importance than the basic materialist outlook itself. (SW. 1, p.513)

It is clear from the above quotation that for Engels the 'rational' kernel of Hegelian logic forms the backbone of Marx's critique of political economy and that Marx's method in this critique ranks equal in importance to the materialist standpoint.

Having established the Hegelian foundation of Marx's method, Engels proceeds to give his interpretation of this foundation in the following way:

> The criticism of economics, even according to the method acquired, could still be exercised in two ways: historically or logically. Since in history, as in its literary reflection, development as a whole also proceeds from the most simple to the more complex relations, the historical development of the literature of political economy provided a natural guiding thread with which criticism could link up, and the economic categories as a whole would thereby appear in the same sequence as in the logical development. This form apparently has the advantage of greater clearness, since indeed it is the actual development that is followed, but as a matter of fact it would thereby at most become more popular. History often proceeds by leaps and zigzags and it would thus have to be followed up everywhere, whereby not only would much material of minor importance have to be incorporated, but there would be much

interruption of the chain of thought; furthermore, the history of economics could not be written without that of bourgeois society and this would make the task endless, since all preliminary work is lacking. The logical method of treatment was, therefore, the only appropriate one. But this, as a matter of fact, is nothing else but the historical method, only divested of its historical form and disturbing fortuities. The chain of thought must begin with the same thing with which this history begins, and its further course will be nothing else but the reflection of the historical course in abstract and theoretically consistent form; a corrected reflection but corrected according to laws furnished by the real course of history itself, in that each factor can be considered at the point of development of its full maturity, of its classic form. (SW. 1, pp.513-14)

Let us now examine Engels's argument in the above quotation. His argument can be analysed into the following constituent elements:

a) In history, as well as in thought (for Engels, the literary reflection of history), 'development proceeds from the most simple to the more complex relations'. Thus the movement of real (history) is parallel to the movement of thought.
b) However, 'history often proceeds by leaps and zigzags'. The implication is that the course of history does not run as smoothly as the movement of thought.
c) The logical method is the 'only appropriate one', since this 'is nothing else but the historical method, only divested of its historical form and disturbing fortuities'.

From the above points it may be concluded that the logical method is an 'ideal' reflection of the historical movement and thus the truly historical method. In this conclusion, however, the only function assigned to thought is that of smoothing, averaging and idealizing the real movement of history.

The main methodological thrust of Engels's argument leads to the conclusion that 'the chain of thought must begin with the same thing with which this history begins, and its further course will be nothing else but the reflection of the historical course in abstract and theoretically consistent form'. But the activity of thought cannot be limited in this way. Engels almost contradicts his whole argument by adding that the reflection of history in thought is a 'corrected' one: 'corrected according to laws furnished by the real course of history itself, in that each factor can be considered at the point of development of its full maturity, of its classic form'.

This last point puts Engel's entire 'historicist' chain of argument

29

in doubt. If each factor can be considered from the vantage point of its full maturity there is no reason why the chain of thought should begin with the same thing with which history begins.

Leaving this point aside for the moment let us examine the exact nature of Engels's account of the dialectical method.

> In this method we proceed from the first and simplest relation that historically and in fact confronts us; here, therefore, from the first economic relation to be found. We analyse this relation. Being a relation of itself implies that it has two sides, related to each other. Each of these sides if considered by itself, which brings us to the way in which they behave to each other, their interaction. Contradictions will result which demand a solution. But as we are not considering here an abstract process of thought taking place solely in our heads, but a real process which actually took place at some particular time or is still taking place, these contradictions too, will have developed in practice and will probably have found their solution. We shall trace the nature of this solution, and shall discover that it has been brought about by the establishment of a new relation whose two opposite sides we shall now have to develop, and so on. (SW. 1, p.514)

Engels's characterization of the departure point of the method above involves three facets:

1. The beginning is with a 'simple', in fact, simplest relation.
2. This 'simple' is historically first.
3. This 'simple' is also a relation confronting us in the contemporaneous reality: 'the first economic relation to be found'.

The fact that Engels identifies the logical and the historical 'first' is squarely based on a particular 'historicist' reading of Hegel, which may be supported by quotations such as the following from Hegel:

> The thinking or figurate conception which has before it only a specific, determinate being must be referred back to the previously-mentioned beginning of the science made by Parmenides who purified and elevated his own figurate conception, and so, too, that of posterity, to *pure thought*, to being as such and thereby created the element of science. What is the first in the *science* had of necessity to show itself *historically* as the first. (LL. p.88)

What is not very clear in Engels's commentary is the how and why of the simplicity of the beginning and the contemporaneous reality of the simple relation. What Engels has in mind is obviously Marx's analysis of the 'commodity' which, while being the unit of wealth under capitalism, is at the same time a relation that is a lot older than capitalism.

30

Engels's standpoint can be best understood if we turn to Marx's concept of 'simple commodity production' and Engels's interpretation of it thirty-five years after the publication of Engels's review of Marx's *A Contribution to the Critique of Political Economy*.

B. What is so simple about 'Simple Commodity Production'? (Marx and Engels)

It was the publication of volume three of *Capital* by Engels in 1894 that gave the latter an opportunity to put his historicist position to a real test.

In the third volume of *Capital* Marx presents his theory of production prices. These prices deviate systematically from the labour-values of the first volume of *Capital*. These deviations are explained by Marx on the basis of: 1) The necessity for a general rate of profit due to competition among capitals invested in different departments of production and 2) the different organic composition of capital existing between these branches of production.

The disjunction between the two systems created a semblance of contradiction between the labour theory of value of volume 1 and the production price theory of volume 3. While for Marx's opponents this meant an unresolvable contradiction,[6] Marx's followers attempted to reconcile the two systems. One such attempt came from Engels himself. In his Supplement to the third volume,[7] while reviewing various responses that had followed the publication of the third volume, Engels presents his own explanation of the relationship between the theory of the first volume and that of the third.

Here is Engels's own summary of his lengthy explanation:

> To sum up, Marx's law of value applies universally, as much as any economic laws do apply, for the entire period of simple commodity production, i.e. up to the time at which this undergoes a modification by the onset of the capitalist form of production. Up till then prices gravitate to the values determined by Marx's law and oscillate around these values, so that the more completely simple commodity production develops, the more do average prices coincide with values for longer periods when not interrupted by external violent disturbances, and with the insignificant variations we mentioned earlier. Thus the Marxian law of value has a universal validity for an era lasting from the beginning of the exchange that transforms products into commodities down to the fifteenth century of our epoch. (C. III. p.1037)

Engels thus relegates the functioning of the law of labour-values to pre-capitalist forms of the production of commodities ('simple commodity production') while he assigns the task of the regulation of price ratios under capitalist production to the system of production prices. This is Engels's historicist method of reconciling the contradiction between the two systems of volume 1 and volume 3.

Engels, who had formulated his own interpretation of the Hegelian dialectics in a historicist manner some thirty-five years earlier in relation to Marx's work, could now rely on Marx's authority and offer his interpretation with greater confidence. We do in fact find in Marx passages in which he is advancing an interpretation very similar to Engels's:

> The exchange of commodities at their values, or at approximately these values, thus corresponds to a much lower stage of development than the exchange at prices of production, for which a definite degree of capitalist development is needed . . . . Apart from the way in which the law of value governs prices and their movements, it is also quite appropriate to view the values of commodities not only as theoretically prior to the prices of production, but also as historically prior to them. (C. III. p.277)

Engels's interpretation is by no means the only one to be found among individuals sympathetic to Marx. As we will see below Conrad Schmidt and Werner Sombart advanced a completely different interpretation of Marx's method.

II. *Responses to Historicism*

A. *The Impact of the* 1857 Introduction

The challenge to the historicist position, although present at the time when Engels published his supplement to volume 3, gained considerable strength after the publication of a 'general introduction' to Marx's critique of political economy, a text found by Kautsky among Marx's unpublished works in 1903.[8] This work, variously known as the 'Introduction to the Grundrisse' or the '1857 Introduction', although referred to in Marx's Preface to *A Contribution to the Critique of Political Economy* (1859)[9] apparently had remained unknown to Engels. In this work Marx explores methodological questions in relation to both Hegel's *Logic* and classical political economy — questions of the same nature as the ones Engels deals with in his 1859 review of Marx's work.

Although published in 1903, this text remained unknown to a great majority of thinkers and theoreticians of the Second International or perhaps was ignored by them because of their 'mechanistic-evolutionist' conception of historical materialism.[10] There were isolated cases in which

Marxist analysts found this text of great value for understanding Marx's method, as testified by the work of the Russian economist I. I. Rubin in 1920s (see below). But it was only in the 1950s and 1960s that this work gained the status of a fundamental source material for the study of Marx's methodology.

In what follows I will briefly discuss those points in Marx's *1857 Introduction* that have been of particular importance for the main twentieth century challenges to the historicist position, leaving a fuller discussion of the text for the next chapter.

In the *1857 Introduction* we find Marx criticizing Hegel for identifying the thought-process with the process of real history. According to him

> ... Hegel fell into the illusion of conceiving the real as the product of thought concentrating itself, probing its own depths, and unfolding itself out of itself, by itself, whereas the method of rising from the abstract to concrete is only the way in which thought appropriates the concrete, reproduces it as the concrete in the mind. But this is by no means the process by which the concrete itself comes into being. (G. p.101)

In the above passage, Marx, while criticizing Hegel for his 'idealism', i.e. for his conception of real movement as thought-process, is making the point that the method of advancing from the abstract to the concrete (i.e. the way the process of real history unfolds for Hegel) 'is only the way in which thought appropriates the concrete . . .' Thus this method is the way thought-process produces concrete concepts and therefore cannot be identified with the process of real history.

Marx's comment above contradicts certain historicist arguments used by Engels (and in other places by Marx himself) and as such it has served a number of interpreters in their critique of the historicist conception of Marx's methodology. Note that the word 'simple' that characterized both the beginning in thought and the historical 'first' in the historicist version now appears to be a characteristic of thought only.

This is one dimension of Marx's discourse. However there is another facet of his thought that is mentioned in a passage immediately following the previous one. As if to make his point clearer he uses an example:

> For example, the simplest economic category, say, e.g. exchange value, presupposes population, moreover a population producing in specific relations; as well as a certain kind of family, or commune, or state, etc. It can never exist other than as an abstract, one-sided relation within an already given, concrete, living whole. (G. p.101)

33

Recall that Marx had established simple as a thought-construct in the previous passage. In this latter passage he seems to be bringing back some reality into 'simple'. Here simple is designated as an abstract, one-sided relation subsumed under a concrete, living whole. This latter dimension of Marx's view is also intended as a critique of historicism and has been used by commentators as such.

The reason I have distinguished between two dimensions in the conceptualization of 'simple' above is that each of the two main trends of the anti-historicist school that I referred to earlier stand squarely on one of these two elements. Let us now look at these two trends more closely.

B. *The Structuralist Position*

What I call the structuralist position in relation to the question of method originated primarily in the works of Louis Althusser.[11]

Based on certain passages in *1857 Introduction*, such as the ones we quoted in the previous section, and the following one Althusser arrives at a particular interpretation of the role of 'simple' concepts in Marx.

> It would therefore be unfeasible and wrong to let the economic categories follow one another in the same sequence as that in which they were historically decisive. Their sequence is determined, rather, by their relation to one another in modern bourgeois society, which is precisely the opposite of that which seems to be their natural order or which corresponds to historical development. The point is not the historic position of the economic relations in the succession of different forms of society. Even less is it their sequence 'in the idea' (Proudhon) ... Rather, their order within modern bourgeois society. (G. p.108)

Marx in the above passage turns the historicist thesis upside down by declaring that the sequence of economic categories is determined by their order in the modern capitalist economy and not by their historical order of appearance. He even goes so far as to declare that the former 'is precisely the opposite' of the latter. Althusser is not prepared to go as far. He thinks that any disjunction between the structural and the historical order is a sufficient condition for overthrowing the historicist position.

Let us now look at Althusser's version of the 'simple' concept and its relation to the whole.

Althusser refers to Mao's 'simple process' which contains 'only a single pair of opposites'. He also refers to Lenin's characterization of dialectics as 'the splitting of a single whole and the knowledge of its contradictory parts'. But he takes issue with these notions and finally

34

declares that "this 'simple process with two opposites' in which the whole is split into two contradictory parts is precisely the very womb of Hegelian contradiction". (Althusser 1969, pp.194-5).

After having dismissed Mao's and Lenin's notions of 'simple' processes, Althusser, on the grounds that they are derived from Hegel (whose dialectics, according to Althusser, is the direct opposite of Marx's dialectics), goes on to give his own view of the place and the function of the 'simple category' in Marx's method:

> Marx does not only show that every 'simple category' presupposes the existence of the structured whole of society, but also, what is almost certainly more important, he demonstrates that far from being original, in determinate conditions, simplicity is merely the product of the complex process. This is simplicity's sole claim to existence . . . . (Althusser 1969, p.196)

Althusser's argument can be summarized in the following way:

1) The 'simple category' presupposes a complex whole and, therefore, it is not 'original'.
2) 'Simplicity' is a product of the complex whole.

The conclusion seems to be that the simple category is fully subordinate to the complex whole.

What can be the implication of this characterization of the 'simple category' for Marx's method? Althusser himself does not elaborate further on this point but we can infer his view from attempts at a structuralist approach to Marx's method by people influenced by Althusser. What I call the structuralist position is best summarized in the following passage from Fine and Harris (1979):

> In the *Grundrisse* he [Marx] describes it [his method] as starting from the complexity of the superficial world and constructing the most simple, highly abstract concepts. From these, with their interrelations and their internal contradictions, increasingly complex concepts are developed until the complexity of the world of appearance is reproduced in thought or on the page. The important point is that this process is neither purely idealist, existing in thought independent of reality, nor arbitrary. Instead the concepts produced and their logical order are in accordance with material reality. (Fine and Harris 1979, pp.6-7)

In short:

1. Science starts from the complex reality and constructs 'the

most simple', highly abstract concepts.
2. Through the interrelations and contradictions of these concepts more complex concepts are produced.
3. The complex concepts in (2) are developed to the point where the real complex is reproduced in thought.
4. The succession of the phases 1-3 is neither idealistic nor arbitrary because the logical order of concepts is in accordance with material reality. The conclusion is that the 'thought process parallels those of reality'. (Fine and Harris 1979, p.8)

What we have here is an identification of the 'real' with 'thought' — an identification which was the main feature of the historicist position. The only difference is that in the latter the thought process parallels the real historical movement, while in the former it moves with layers of a contemporaneous reality. Any good Althusserian would suspect an identity of the 'problematic' between the historicist and the structural representation of Marx's method. The only change that occurs between these two alternative positions is that while in the historicist version the logical 'simple' is identified with an historically first or primitive relation, in the structuralist thesis the 'simple category' corresponds to a simple relation coexisting with and subsumed under a more complex whole. In other words, in both the historicist and the structuralist interpretations, the movement from simple to concrete, which is supposed to be a thought-process, is the mirror image of the historical movement or evolution in one case and a reflection of the complex structure of the whole in the other.

In both interpretations, 'simple' is identified as a simple reality, although it is at the same time retained as a concept, a concept of a simple reality. Thus a unity of the real and thought emerges in the form of something that is simple both conceptually and in reality.

I believe that this tendency to conflate thought and reality is ultimately to be explained by the reflection (copy) theory of knowledge which is an integral part of 'official' Marxism. The identification of 'simple' with an historically primary reality or a contemporaneously subordinate relation yields a simple relation in which thought corresponds to reality in an unambiguous way.

C. The Rationalist Position

What I call the 'rationalist' position is another major response to the historicist position, but its origins are much older than the structuralist response. In this approach 'simple' is conceived basically as a logical, theoretical concept or a thought-construct, which while functioning as a means of grasping reality, is irreducible to any given fact, whether past or present.

The origins of this position go back to the controversies surrounding the status of the labour theory of value in Marx's *Capital* which began with the posthumous publication of the third volume of *Capital* in 1894. We have already referred to these controversies in the previous section, mentioning Sombart and Schmidt in particular. The views of these two thinkers represented an alternative to Engels's historicist interpretation of Marx's method. This is why Engels devoted part of his Supplement to a discussion and rebuttal of their views. This is how Engels summarizes their ideas:

> He [Sombart] discusses the significance of value in Marx's system and arrives at the following result. Value is not present at the phenomenal level, in the exchange relationship of capitalistically produced commodities; it does not dwell in the consciousness of the agents of capitalist production; it is not an empirical fact but an ideal or logical one . . .
> Schmidt, too, has his formal reservations about the law of value. He calls it a scientific *hypothesis* put forward to explain the actual exchange process, which proves the necessary theoretical point of departure, illuminating and indispensable even for the phenomena of prices under competition, which appear completely to contradict it . . . . Schmidt declares that the law of value in the capitalist form of production is a fiction, though a theoretically necessary one. (C. III. p.1031-2)

Thus, in the works of these two thinkers discussed by Engels, we have the beginnings of the rationalist approach. Both of them conceive of Marx's labour theory of value not in terms of an historically first simple exchange economy nor of a simpler structure embedded in the contemporary capitalist system, but essentially as a logical, theoretical construct necessary for the conceptualization of the workings of the capitalist economy.

These ideas, however, remained in the background for a long time, overshadowed by the authority of Engels's interpretation of the method of *Capital*.

It was only the publication of Marx's *1857 Introduction*, with its strong anti-historicist themes, that led to the emergence of the rationalist approach as a serious challenge to historicist position. One of the most systematic attempts to unseat the latter came from I. I. Rubin in 1928.

Basing his argument on Marx's *1857 Introduction* Rubin makes the following comments on the historicist position:

> Marx emphasizes that the method of moving from abstract to concrete concepts is only a method by which thought grasps the concrete, and not the way the concrete phenomenon actually happened. This means that the transition from labour-value or simple commodity economy to production price or the capitalist economy is a method for grasping the concrete, i.e. the capitalist economy. This is a theoretical abstraction and not a picture of the historical transition from simple commodity economy to capitalist economy. (Rubin 1972, p.255)

Rubin thus rejects the historicist position by concluding that what is projected as the movement of history from simple to complex (with the logical order following it) is really an image of the movement of thought beginning with simple concepts and arriving at more concrete concepts.

Fifty years after Rubin wrote the above lines we find two modern economists arguing on the same lines independently, apparently unaware of Rubin's work:

> ... What Marx was looking for in the labour theory of value was not the abstract description of a pre-capitalist period from which he could derive developed capitalism genetically, but rather the theoretical tools which would allow him to get to the bottom of capitalist economic relations .... The idea of abstract labour belongs, thus, to the very essence of the concept of value. (Morishima and Catephores 1978, p.188)

In the 'rationalist' interpretation Marx's simple, abstract concepts such as simple labour-value and simple commodity production are interpreted primarily as thought-constructs, concepts that are not identifiable with a concrete reality, whether a primal stage of history or a contemporaneous real relation.

The rationalist conception comes closest to the essence of Marx's method compared with other positions discussed above. However, it suffers shortcomings, at least in the form presented by Rubin and also by Morishima and Catephores, leading it to degenerate into either the structuralist position or into the empiricist model-theory in social sciences. Let me quote these authors again, starting with Rubin:

> The labour theory of value and the theory of production price differ from each other, not as different theories which function in different historical periods, but as an abstract theory and a concrete fact, as two degrees of abstraction of the same theory of the capitalist economy. The labour theory of value only presupposes production relations among commodity producers. The theory of

production price presupposes in addition, production relations between capitalists and workers, on the one hand, and among various groups of industrial capitalists on the other. (Rubin 1972, p.257)

Although still strongly rationalist in his approach, Rubin wavers on the question of whether the system of production-prices refers to a 'concrete fact' or represents a theory. Then he slightly corrects himself on this issue by referring to the labour theory of value and the theory of production prices as representing 'two degrees of abstraction'. He then seems to suggest that these two different theories are pertinent to two different sets of relations in the capitalist system: one set being simpler and involving relations between commodity producers and the other being a complication of the first, representing a further development of the relations of production. But this closely approaches the structuralist position by proposing two 'regional' theories relevant to two different hierarchically articulated regions in the economy.

Morishima and Catephores are led on to a similar track:

Marx viewed the concepts of value and abstract labour as acquiring some sort of reality only in advanced capitalism. If he constructed an abstract system of simple commodity production to illustrate the workings of value without disturbance, if he started his analysis in Capital with the concept of value, this he did, not because he considered the pre-capitalist economy as the locus of the concept of value . . . but because he wanted to make a logical simulation, in order to identify the effects of the capitalist ownership of means of production upon exploitation, the concentration of ownership and the production prices of commodities. The model of simple commodity production was constructed for this purpose . . . (Morishima and Catephores 1978, pp.189-90)

In this conception the theoretical status of 'simple' concepts in Marx is reduced to the function of 'logical simulation' or model-building. Thus 'simple commodity production' is a model in which certain essential characteristics of the capitalist mode of production, such as the ownership of the means of production, is assumed away so that the impact of these characteristics on, say, price ratios, can be studied when they are brought back into the picture (model).

This conception is by no means confined to the rationalist school: here several very different positions on Marx's method find a common ground.[12]

As an example, Ronald Meek who maintained fundamentally an historicist position as developed by Engels in relation to the transformation problem[13] found some common ground with the rationalist school. This common ground was nothing but the recognition by Meek of Marx as a model-builder in 'a long and respectable tradition', dating back to the classical political economy. Thus: 'Marx's postulation of an abstract pre-capitalist society based on what he called "simple" commodity production was not essentially different in aim from Adam Smith's postulation of an "early and rude" society inhabited by deer and beaver hunters'. (Meek 1973, p.303)

Exactly the same tendency to view Marx's procedure as model-building — i.e. as a process in which 'complex' reality is simplified into a preliminary model in which 'complicating' factors are first ignored but then brought into the model as so many factors that improve the 'predictive' power of the model — can be seen in the structuralist position of Fine and Harris referred to above. In their interpretations too, the 'simple' functions as a simplified model of reality, which has to go through a process of complication in order to achieve 'concreteness' or 'reality'. Let me conclude this section by clarifying what I consider to be the common ground of all three interpretations of Marx's method, which were considered above.

III. A *Critique*

All these positions ultimately end up with postulating a simple structure which, having been discovered, should serve as a stepping-stone, a departure point or a beginning for scientific inquiry. In one case this simple structure is an historically first condition, in the other a simple contemporaneous relation subsumed under a more complex whole, and in the third case, it is a simple concept, a logical construct or simple model. After identifying this simple beginning, the journey of inquiry traverses the path from this simple beginning to the concrete or complex end-result. Again in one case this journey is a movement in time, in the other case it is an ascendence from the ground floor to the top of an existing structure and in the third case it is a progress in thought from a simple model to a more complex (therefore, more realistic) model. In all three cases the end-result is a concrete, whether thought or real, which must correspond to reality.

The common problematic shared by these approaches is a rigid and fixed opposition maintained between the 'simple' and the 'complex': complexity can in no way be regarded as exhibiting a simplicity in its own right, nor can simplicity be viewed as representing a complexity. Ultimately an 'analytical' approach underlies these conceptions.

Thus in the historicist approach 'simple' refers to an historically first relation which is in opposition to a more developed complex whole. In the structuralist approach 'simple' represents a simple relation of a complex whole and finds its sole justification and determination in relation to the latter, to which it is completely subordinate. In the rationalist approach (especially in the modern version represented by Morishima-Catephores) simple refers to a simple thought, concept or model.

In spite of this fixed opposition there seems to exist a relationship between the two aspects. Here again we find a common ground. In all the three schools we have considered, the process of knowing reality, knowing it in as complete a manner as possible, invariably involves a passage from 'simple' to 'complex'.

What is the basis for the opposition between the simple versus the complex? Is this a 'simple reproduction' of the fundamental opposition between thinking and being, between thought and reality — an opposition characterizing such diverse philosophies as those of Descartes, Spinoza and Kant? Let us briefly pursue this idea.

If we start from the premise that in all three conceptions there is a direct correlation between the couples (simple, complex) and (thought, reality), it may be contended that while this correlation can be regarded as a fair description of the old rationalist school of Schmidt-Sombart, it can in no way characterize the historicist and the structuralist schools. One may say, for instance, that both of these schools, while maintaining that reality is complex, admit of simple real relations. There is no doubt that these coincidences between simple concepts and realities exist (implying a correspondence between thinking and being so fundamental to the theory of knowledge of 'official Marxism'). What is more, there are one-to-one correspondences between real existences and their theoretical reflections. Simple concepts correspond to simple realities and complex concepts to complex realities. Thus thinking reflects being in both the historical sequence (historicism) and the structural order (structuralism). In short, thinking simply reflects being.

If we now raise the question as to the criterion that distinguishes simple from complex, it will become clear that in fact no such criterion is provided by any of the schools. We end up with identifying complexity with reality (which intuitively makes sense: reality is complex because it represents a multiplicity of events, factors, dimensions, etc.) and simplicity with thought. Ultimately, thinking has to submit to the complexity of reality and somehow 'reproduce' it in thought (complex thought?). Thus thinking as complex merely reflects the complexity of reality; it has no autonomy, i.e. it cannot be complex in its own right. Thought is complex only when it reflects a complex reality.

Thinking is denied an autonomous complexity. In these approaches only a reproduction of complex reality can qualify as a complex thought. The upshot is that complexity cannot characterize thinking as opposed to being and therefore thinking must be 'simple'. The simplicity of thought rises to complexity only when it strives to contemplate 'complex reality'. The reality of simple relations may seem to negate this polarization of simple and complex as reflections of thought and reality. This contradiction, however, is only apparent: in both the historicist and the structuralist conceptions simple relations are not really 'real', i.e. they suffer from a 'diminished sense' of reality, the simple relation in one case having faded away with the coming of the complex whole and in the other subsisting as a subordinate relation.

In the modern rationalist approach we find a culmination of this classical dichotomy between thinking and being. In this conception simple does not refer to a prehistoric existence nor does it represent a subordinate 'layer' of the existing reality. Following the old rationalist school of Schmidt-Sombart and the rationalist aspect of Rubin, it simply identifies simplicity with thought. Thus 'simple' is not a feature of reality but a simple thought-construct or a model — a tool for understanding reality. However the modern rationalist school does not rest content with simple models; it tends to build ever more complex models. Why? The only logical answer is that since knowing is about reality, models that help us in understanding reality should correspond to reality. They should be complex. The result? Reality is complex!

Thus the movement from simple to complex in all three schools is an attempt to 'approximate' reality, to 'reproduce' reality in thought. It is a process of thought: the simple asymptotically approaches reality. This movement, however, is the form in which the fixed opposition between simple and complex is reproduced rather than resolved.

What unites all these three approaches is an 'essentialism' based on the essence-appearance or content-form opposition and ultimately 'empiricism'. In the 'essentialist' problematic, the function of knowing is to start from reality (phenomena, appearances, forms, etc.) and search for its essence. The essence thus found then illuminates the phenomena from which it was derived, i.e. results in the knowledge of reality. This conception is very popular among Marxists, perhaps because Marx spoke approvingly of the analytical method, the scientifically correct method of political economy[14] and also he occasionally made comments such as 'all science would be superfluous if the outward appearance and essence of things directly coincided'.

Marx did not find the method of political economy adequate. In a number of occasions he spoke of the 'genetic' or dialectical method that should complement the analytical approach of political economy.[15] This is why a number of interpreters have suggested that in Marx's method there is a 'reverse' journey from the discovered essence back to phenomena or forms of appearance, a kind of synthetic method. This synthesizing process can be detected in all three positions discussed above. In different shapes we have the identical process of complication from simple to complex. But this is only a more sophisticated form of essentialism which reproduces the fixed opposition of essence/appearance or content/form dichotomies. What we have is still what Hegel calls 'analytic cognition', Marx the 'analytical method' and Althusser 'the empiricist' problematic. This approach explains the persistence of tendencies to move in a parallel fashion with the ordering of real objects, to conflate simple concepts with simple realities, to simulate the real in models, etc., in all the positions examined above. As we shall see later in the present work Hegel's *Logic* attempts to overcome the fixed oppositions of essence and appearance. And it was this logic that Marx was trying to follow. The fallacy of essentialism consists in that in moving from essence to appearance, essence remains untouched and therefore appearance retains its separation from, and fixed opposition to, essence.

The various interpretations of Marx's method as outlined in the preceding sections, I believe, do not by themselves succeed in capturing the depth and breadth of Marx's logic in *Capital*. Each of these approaches illuminate some but not all aspects of this logic and, therefore, they remain abstract and one-sided.

In the next chapter we will show, among other things, that Marx's views about S-concepts exhibit a complexity that goes beyond the one-sided characterizations offered by the three schools discussed so far.

I started this chapter with a discussion of Engels's review of Marx's book of 1859. I wish to end the chapter by a quotation from Marx's letter to Engels after the publication of that work and before Engels's review of that, in which Marx hints at the possibility of such a review:

> In case you do write something, you should not forget 1) that Proudhonism has been extracted by its roots, 2) that in its simplest form — in the form of *commodity* — the *specific* social (and in one way *absolute*) character of bourgeois production has been analyzed. (LC. pp. 68-9)

43

1. This review was published in two parts in *Das Volk*, a German weekly published in London, No. 14, August 6, 1859 and No. 16, August 20, 1859. The translation used here is taken from Marx and Engels, *Selected Works* in 3 Vols. (1969), Progress Publishers, Moscow. A slightly modified translation is to be found in Marx, K., (1970) *A Contribution to the Critique of Political Economy*, Progress Publishers, Moscow.

2. For Engels's intellectual interests in his youth see McLellan (1977), Chap. 1 and Carver (1981), Chaps. 1-3.

3. *Anti-Dühring* was published in 1877-8 and *Feuerbach* . . . in 1888. *The Dialectics of Nature* believed to have been written in the mid-1870s, was first published after his death. (See McLellan, 1979, p.56)

4. On Marx's renewed interest in Hegel's *Logic* see the Introduction.

5. This work is discussed in detail in the Introduction above. In that text, for instance, Marx talks about his 'extraction' of the 'rational kernel' of Hegelian philosophy. This is exactly how Engels characterizes Marx's relation to Hegel in his review of Marx's earlier work in 1859.

6. E.g. Böhm-Bawerk, E. von, 1898, *Karl Marx and the Close of his System*, in Sweezy (1949).

7. Engels, F., *Supplement and Addendum to Volume 3 of Capital* (C. III. pp. 1027-47).

8. The German original was first published in the magazine *Die Neue Zeit* in 1903. It is part of the manuscripts written by Marx in 1857-9, which was first published under the title *Grundrisse der Kritik der Politischen Ökonomie (Rohentwurf)*, Moscow, 1939. It was reprinted in Berlin in 1953. The first English translation appeared under the title *Grundrisse* in 1973 (this is the translation used throughout this book, unless otherwise indicated). The first English translation of *1857 Introduction* appeared under the title "Introduction to the Critique of Political Economy" in Marx, K., *A Contribution to the Critique of Political Economy*, Kerr, Chicago, 1904.

9. Marx's reference is given in Note 4 to Chapter Two below.

10. For a brief discussion of the Marxism of the Second International and the Hegelian response to it see Callinicos (1976) Chap. 1.

11. Althusser is also discussed in Chapter Two. For a general introduction to Althusser see Callinicos (1976). Benton (1984) attempts a detailed survey of Althusser's theories and their influence as well as post-Althusserians and their critics. Structuralism as an intellectual movement can be traced to the seminal work of Ferdinand de Saussure (Saussure, 1974) on Linguistics. It has been applied in numerous fields as diverse as anthropology (e.g. the work of Lévi Strauss) and literary criticism (for a review of the range of these applications see Sturrock [1986] and for a critique of structuralism as applied to criticism and linguistics from the viewpoint of the 'deconstructionists' such as Jacques Derrida see Norris [1982]). The application of Structuralist principles to Marx's method is relatively recent; it predates Althusser and is not limited to him. Maurice Godelier's 'System, Structure and Contradiction in *Capital*' published in 1966 (English translation in Milliband and Saville [1967]) and *Rationality and Irrationality in Economics*, (published in 1966, English translation: Godelier [1972]), part II, represent an attempt to interpret Marx's method in structuralist terms.

12. Sweezy (1942), pp.11, 19, 23, Desai (1974), Chap. XI and Rosdolsky (1977), p.565 represent varying degrees of a rationalist position.

13. Meek's position was challenged by Morishima and Catephores in the mid-1970s in their debates on the historical transformation problem, resulting in the formulation of the ideas presented above (see Morishima & Catephores [1975 & 1976] and Meek [1976]). For a more detailed discussion of these debates see Shamsavari (1987).

14. See Chapters Two and Three below.

15. See Chapter Three below.

CHAPTER TWO

MARX'S METHOD I: INTIMATIONS FROM THE 1857 INTRODUCTION

I begin this study of Marx's method with a review of Marx's *1857 Introduction* for three reasons. First, this work is one of the few texts in which Marx gives us his own reflections on scientific methodology and the theory of knowledge and thus is an invaluable guide for understanding the method of *Capital*.[1] Secondly, this text, having been long recognized as a major methodological work, has served as the departure point for a number of interpreters of Marx's method and in this capacity it has led to many useful insights into Marx's method as well as many misinterpretations.[2] Finally, this work, as we will show in Chapter Four, was directly influenced by Hegelian philosophy[3] and, therefore, is of specific value for the purposes of this study.

However, in order to avoid misinterpretation, it is important to bear in mind that this text was part of Marx's preparatory notebooks on economics which eventually led to the writing of his *Capital*. Thus we are dealing with a text in which Marx merely explores questions of logic and methodology for himself, without stating results — a work not intended for publication, as is evident from its subsequent suppression in Marx's first major published work on economics, *A Contribution to the Critique of Political Economy*.[4] For this reason, the text under consideration must be handled with utmost care.

The *1857 Introduction* is divided into four sections. The first two sections deal with certain fundamental economic concepts such as production and distribution as well as the interrelations between production, distribution, exchange and consumption. The third section is on the methodology of the classical political economy. In what follows I shall first discuss sections 1 and 2 and in the second part of this chapter I will concentrate on section 3. Section 4, which is a short collection of elliptical notes, will not be discussed below.[5]

I. FROM RATIONAL ABSTRACTION TO THE CONCRETE WHOLE (A CRITIQUE OF GENERIC CONCEPTS)

Marx begins his text by a general critique of naturalism — an ideology shared by both the eighteenth century French *philosophes* and the British classical economists. Marx mentions 'the individual and isolated hunter and fisherman' of Smith and Ricardo and the 'natural state' of Rousseau's *Contrat Social*. In both of these cases a 'natural', free individual is presupposed. But this natural, free individual is presumed to belong to some pre-capitalist past. Marx, however, points out that this free individual, projected back in history, is a product of *civil society*, rather than its prehistory. Thus the free individual or the isolated hunter is a product of modern bourgeois society and not an historical predecessor. Neither is this individual, as some believed, 'merely a reaction against over-sophistication and a return to a misunderstood natural life' (G. p.83). Marx says that, in fact, if we go back in history the individual person is not really free, as he/she is part of a community. Thus the basis of naturalist philosophy is not some pre-modern free savage but the 'free' individual of civil society:

> In this society of free competition, the individual appears detached from the natural bonds, etc. which in earlier historical periods make him an accessory of a definite and limited human conglomerate. (G. p.83)

Thus naturalism seems to involve an abstraction based on the contemporaneous historical experience and a projection of this abstraction back to earlier history and, perhaps, also to future societies. Marx thinks that this kind of generalization is wrong since it abstracts from the very specific features that determine the individual in each particular society. One may claim, however, that although this generalization is wrong, naturalism has 'unconsciously' managed to determine the nature of the individual in a specific society, i.e. civil society. Can we deduce, therefore, that the generalization implicit in naturalist ideology is in reality not a 'generality' but a 'particular'? Let us now follow Marx more closely:

> *Production in general* is an abstraction, but a rational abstraction in so far as it really brings out and fixes the common element and thus saves us repetition. Still, this *general* category, this common element sifted out by comparison, is itself segmented many times over and splits into many determinations. Some determinations belong to all epochs, others only to a few. Some determinations will be shared by the most modern epoch and the most ancient. No production will be thinkable without them; however, even though the most developed languages have laws and characteristics in common with the least developed, nevertheless, just those things which determine their development, i.e. the elements which are not general and common, must be separated out from the determinations valid for production as such, so that in their unity . . . their essential difference is not forgotten. The whole profundity of those economists who demonstrate the eternity and harmoniousness of the existing social relations lies in this forgetting. (G. p.85)

46

As an example of this 'empty' generalization (generic concept), Marx refers to the manner in which economists identify capital, a social relationship of production with the instruments of production: 'No production is possible without an instrument of production, even if this instrument is only the hand . . . . Capital is, among other things, also an instrument of production, ... Therefore capital is a general, eternal relation of labour; that is, if I leave out just the specific quality which alone makes "instrument of production" . . . into capital' (G. pp.85-6).

Can we conclude from this that the general category, e.g. 'production in general', which specifies the most essential elements true for all times and places, or 'instrument of production', which exists in all historical epochs of production in one form or another, is really not general at all but a 'particular'? Let us be more specific. Marx mentions 'the hand' as a possible instrument of production. Now it is obvious that in all forms of production, human hands (as in manual labour, for instance) play a role. This general assertion is so broad and self-evident that it is almost empty. However, one may assert that human hands played a much more important role in production prior to the introduction of machinery (and even more so before tools were made). Thus one can very well say that in certain *particular* historical forms of economy human labour unaided by tools etc. plays a dominant role. Therefore a generalization that reduces the concept of instrument of labour to such a low level as to include human hands is either empty or else a 'particular', i.e. it is a characteristic of a particular period of production. This interpretation is supported by Marx in the paragraph immediately following the above discussion:

> If there is no production in general, then there is also no general production. Production is always a *particular* branch of production — e.g. agriculture, cattle-raising, manufactures, etc. — or it is a *totality*. (G. p.86)

Thus production is either a *particularity* (a particular branch of production) or a *totality*. Now this is the first time when 'totality' is mentioned in Marx's text. It is clear that Marx is introducing this concept as a category that unites generality and particularity. Thus an economic system is a totality and not a generality. The generality itself is negated and reduced to a particularity and, at the same time, the concept of totality replaces that of generality as a 'true' and no longer empty generality. A totality, unlike the empty generality, cannot be reduced to a particular; rather, particular moments are subsumed under the totality. Marx ends the paragraph under discussion by these words: 'Production in general. Particular branches of production. Totality of production.'

Marx then goes on to elaborate this theme further:

It is the fashion to preface a work of economics with a general part — and precisely this part figures under the title production (see for example J. S. Mill) — treating of the *general preconditions* of all production. (G. p.86)

But none of all this is the economists' real concern in this general part. The aim is, rather, to present production — see, e.g. Mill — as distinct from distribution, etc. as encased in eternal natural laws independent of history, at which opportunity *bourgeois* relations are then quietly smuggled in as inviolable natural laws on which society in abstract is based. (G. p.87)

Marx continues this discussion by pointing out that 'quite apart from this crude tearing apart of production and distribution and of their real relationship' one can also generalize about distribution. 'For example, the slave, the serf and wage labourer all receive a quantity of food which makes it possible for them to exist as slaves, as serfs, as wage labourers' (G. p.87). Marx is thus criticizing a conception of the economy in which production always obeys general laws common to all forms of production but where distribution is specific ('production in general plus a specific distribution of income'). His point is that one cannot separate production from distribution and, furthermore, if the laws of production form a generality, so can the laws of distribution.

Marx concludes his section on production in the following way:

There are characteristics which all stages of production have in common, and which are established as general ones by the mind; but the so-called *general preconditions* are nothing more than these abstract moments with which no real historical stage of production can be grasped. (G. p.88)

Once again Marx confirms our earlier conclusion that generalities based on the common element are either empty ('with which no real historical stage of production can be grasped') or are 'abstract moments'. The discussion in Section II of the present chapter will show that these abstract moments are particular relations subsumed under a totality.

In the second section of this text Marx discusses the 'general relation of production to distribution, exchange, consumption'. Right from the beginning Marx starts questioning the very logic of this division of the economy between distinct spheres, which was popular in his time and has continued to be so to date.[6]

The obvious, trite notion: in production the members of society appropriate (create, shape) the products of nature in accord with human needs; distribution determines the proportion in which the individual shares in the product;

48

exchange delivers the particular product into which the individual desires to convert the portion which distribution has assigned to him; and finally, in consumption the products become objects of gratification, of individual appropriation. (G. pp.88-9)

He continues by stating that these segments of the economy form a 'regular syllogism': production is the generality, distribution and exchange the particularity and consumption the singularity in which the whole is combined. Marx grants that this scheme is indeed coherent but states that it is shallow (G. p.89).

Marx is judging the above conception of the economy (as consisting of three or four interlocking segments) in the same way as he treats the idea of 'production in general' in the first section. In other words, we can say that this conception of the economy is at worst a tautology and at best a particularity.

In this conception, the economic 'whole' is split up into distinct phases; furthermore, these distinct stages form a linear chain leading from production to consumption, each phase naturally leading to the next one. It turns out that this conception is only applicable to certain particular forms of economy, e.g. 'Robinson Crusoe' types of self-sufficient communities, i.e. what Marx identifies as a 'single subject'. Marx demonstrates the error of generalizing this conception to all economies by referring to Say,[7] for instance, for whom 'when one looks at an entire people, its production is its consumption' (G. p.94).

The problem with this conception is that while it attempts to produce a coherent picture of the economy consisting of phases and moments, this coherence suffers from two closely related shortcomings:

i) The division between moments does not follow any logic, i.e. it is arbitrary. In reality it is a unitary process divided up into phases in the same way as one may divide an assembly line into arbitrary stages. The distinction between phases merely 'exists' but is not essential. An essential division would involve autonomy and independent activity for each moment.

ii) It presumes a strict one-way causation running from production to consumption (or vice versa).

In the remainder of this section we will attempt to discover if Marx is able to offer an alternative view that avoids these pitfalls.

Closely following the above discussion on the relationship between production and consumption Marx states:

49

> With a single subject, production and consumption appear as moments of a single act.... In society, however, the producer's relation to the product, once the latter is finished, is an external one, and its return to the subject depends on his relations to other individuals. He does not come into possession of it directly. Nor is its immediate appropriation his purpose when he produces in society. *Distribution* steps between the producers and the products ... (G. p.94)

Marx now turns to distribution:

> In the shallowest conception, distribution appears as the distribution of products, and hence as further removed from and quasi-independent of production. But before distribution can be the distribution of products, it is: (1) the distribution of instruments of production, and (2), which is a further specification of the same relation, the distribution of the members of society among different kinds of production. (G. p.96)

Marx is attempting to overcome the separation between production and distribution by grounding distribution firmly in the conditions of production. But, more significantly, distribution is placed at the very root of production itself:

> Ricardo, whose concern was to grasp the specific social structure of modern production, and who is the economist of production *par excellence*, declares for precisely that reason that *not* production but distribution is the proper study of modern economics. This again shows the ineptitude of those economists who portray production as an eternal truth while banishing history to the realm of distribution. (G. pp.96-7)

Thus distribution is not only not separate from production but is a determinant factor of the nature of production itself. Based on Marx's earlier discussion of production it is obvious that distribution like production is either a totality or a part of totality. J. S. Mill considers distribution to be specific to every particular society while conceiving production as having laws that are common to all societies. Marx's criticism is that Mill's specific distribution is based on a more fundamental distribution that goes into the heart of production. It is obvious that Marx is 'enlarging' and deepening the concept of production to *include* distribution: 'The question of the relationship between this production-determining distribution, and production, belongs evidently within production itself' (G. p.97). This clearly confirms that the second concept of distribution is subsumed under production itself and, thus, as a result the concept of production itself has been widened and deepened to include distribution. Marx explains the nature of the relationship between production and distribution in the following way. He says that if it is claimed that 'since production must begin with a certain distribution of the instruments of production' this means that distribution has precedence over production. Marx opposes this argument by declaring that 'production does indeed have its determinants and preconditions, which form its moments'. Thus production considered not as an empty generality or a particular but as a totality has its moments, e.g. distribution. But how does distribution (or any 'determinants' and 'pre-conditions') that may historically precede a given system of production become a moment of it?

> At the very beginning these may appear as spontaneous, natural. But by the process of production itself they are transformed from natural into historic determinants, and if they appear to one epoch as natural presuppositions of production, they were their historic product for another. Within production itself they are constantly being changed. The application of machinery, for example, changed the distribution of instruments of production as well as of products. Modern large-scale landed property is itself a product of modern commerce and of modern industry, as well as the application of the latter to agriculture. (G. p.97)

Thus the process of the production itself determines whether or not a 'natural' pre-condition of production becomes an 'historic', specific moment of the totality. Marx conceives the relationship between production as a totality and its moments in the following way. He says that distribution, exchange, consumption, etc. 'all form the members of a totality, distinctions within a unity':

> Production predominates not only over itself, in the antithetical definition of production, but over the other moments as well. The process always returns to production to begin anew. That exchange and consumption cannot be predominant is self-evident. Likewise, distribution as distribution of products; while as distribution of the agents of production it is itself a moment of production. A definite production thus determines a definite consumption, distribution and exchange as well as *definite relations between these different moments*. Admittedly, however, *in its one-sided form*, production itself is determined by the other moments. (G. p.99)

In this remarkable passage every concept finds a *double determination*. Distribution is explicitly defined in two ways, i.e. as distribution of products *and* of means of production among agents: it is in the latter sense that distribution is a 'moment' of production. Clearly this is a distinction between production-determined and production-determining distribution. Furthermore, production itself leads a double existence, i.e. production in its 'antithetical definition' or its 'one-sided form', i.e. material production (the labour process) and as the totality, which is the predominant factor. So far it is clear that production in the latter sense is defined as the totality which determines its own constituent parts as well as the relations among them. What about exchange and consumption? Marx admits that these in fact determine production in its one-sided form. But can we find a determining role for these moments, similar to distribution — an autonomy in relation to the totality? Marx is silent on this question. These asymmetries in Marx's treatment can be represented as in Diagram 1. However if these asymmetries are removed then we have a more consistent, coherent and symmetric system as shown in Diagram 2.

DIAGRAM 1

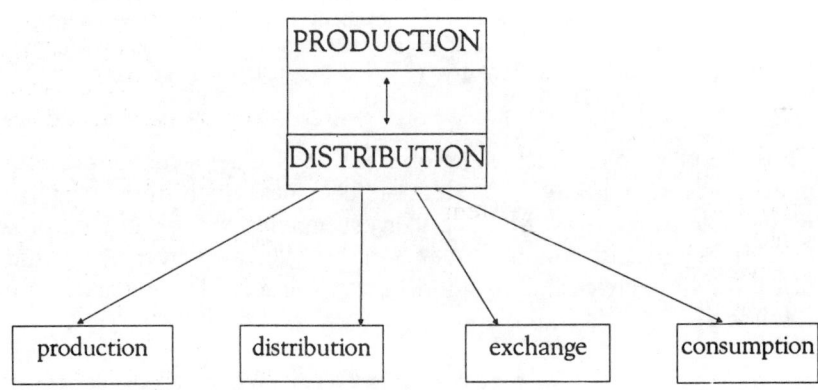

DIAGRAM 2

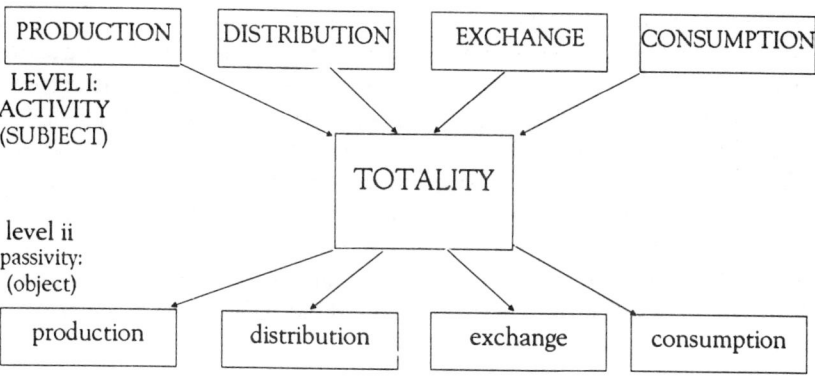

The system presented in Diagram 2 shows what I call Marx's Duality Model (or D-model for short). In this model all the elements of the economy appear at two different levels. At Level (I) these elements are active and determine the totality. At level (ii) they are passive and are determined by the totality.

My interpretation can be justified on the following grounds. If production is defined as a system that includes production in the narrow sense, with the distribution, exchange and consumption of products as passive elements, then the totality is abstract (empty) or it is a particular. On the other hand if every element is allowed the possibility of some degree of autonomy or independent activity, then the totality is no longer abstract but concrete. For example, based on Marx's earlier reference to how changes in the application of machinery changed the distribution of both instruments and the products, one can say that production in the narrow sense, as in this example, and exchange and consumption as well are each capable of changing the distribution of the instruments of production and thereby influencing production as a totality. This is the only way to escape a one-sided interpretation based on a fixed opposition between 'parts' and the 'whole' which leads to the determination by wholes on the one hand and determination by parts on the other.

Our conclusions in this section may be summarized in the following way: Marx's text explicitly criticizes three closely related concepts:

a) Production in general,

b) The general pre-conditions of production,
c) The economic system as a linear-teleological structure consisting of production, distribution, exchange and consumption.

Marx shows that these concepts are 'abstract', i.e. empty: (a) there is no production in general or general production; rather there are either specific branches of production or else production must be conceived of as a totality; (b) none of the general pre-conditions helps one to determine a specific social form of production; these so-called pre-conditions are historically transformed and function as moments of the present economic order, e.g. the primacy of agriculture; finally (c) by examining the concept of distribution Marx problematizes the traditional distinctions between production, distribution, etc. and attempts to show that it is not only true that distribution cannot be conceived in isolation from production but that it is in a sense identical with production; he makes similar comments about other moments of the economic structure.

Marx's text has a number of difficulties that I have attempted to resolve above:

i) Marx explicitly states that generic concepts are deficient in that they do not determine the differential and specific nature of a reality (e.g. the concept of production in general does not determine the specific nature of the capitalist mode of production). While they are useful, for instance, for taxonomical purposes, their precise place and function is not made explicit by Marx. These concepts (if they are not to be empty) must refer to particularities. Thus their specific generality reduces them to their opposites. These may refer to historically past forms of production or specific moments of an advanced economic structure.

ii) Marx clearly calls for a transcendence of the generic concepts, a rise from these to more universal concepts (totalities). But there is no clear indication in his text as to how more concrete (though not less general) concepts that escape the weaknesses of the generic concept can be formed. I have attempted a preliminary solution in the form of Marx's D-model. In this model each aspect or moment — moments derived from the analytical distinction that generates generic concepts of the economic system — functions at two levels, in two modes, a passive and an active mode. In the passive mode each element is what the generic concept represents in reality, i.e. a particular moment subordinate to a concrete totality. In the active mode these moments rise above their

54

purely 'prehistoric' or 'regional' insignificance and overcome their particularity, achieving universality through their activity and influence on other moments.

Our conclusions raise an important methodological question concerning the relationship between the general and the particular. In the analytical (as opposed to the dialectical) conception there is a fixed opposition between particularity and generality. This opposition takes many forms. For instance, science may be characterized as dealing with general concepts as opposed to particular ones; or the beginning of a science may be characterized as a concrete object as opposed to an abstract one.

Our discussions so far have demonstrated that Marx's text precisely problematizes this fixed opposition.[8] Thus one form of generality is turned into its opposite and is characterized as a particular, while particular moments of the social whole are elevated to the position of universality. From this it is clear that Marx is trying to overcome this abstract opposition by positing a higher degree of generality that not only does not stand in opposition to particularities but can only exist in active relation with them. This, indeed, is Marx's view of scientific concepts and is confirmed in the third section of the *1857 Introduction* to which we now turn.

II. THE QUESTION OF THE BEGINNING

A textual reading of section 3 of the *1857 Introduction* which is entitled *The Method of Political Economy* has led to a number of misinterpretations of Marx's methodology. A salient example of this reading is the virtual identification and confusion of Marx's method with the method of classical political economy. This conception is supported by Marx's analysis, which seems to imply that scientific method begins with 'simple', abstract concepts and ends up with a 'thought-concrete'. Such an interpretation would characterize the method of classical political economy as 'the scientifically correct method' (as Marx calls it) and thus raise questions about the specific scientific status of Marx's own project.

The problem with the above line of interpretation is that while Marx's text begins with such a view, the concept of the 'simple' beginning is subjected to an intensive criticism in the course of its development. This critique yields three distinct concepts of the 'simple', as we will show below. Thus the whole idea of 'the scientifically correct method' of political economy, which figures prominently at the beginning of Marx's discourse, is put in doubt by the ensuing exploration and critique in the course of this text.

Marx begins with a discussion of the history of political economy. The path historically followed by political economists at the inception of political economy, Marx says, is characterized by the fact that they always began their inquiry 'with the real and the concrete'. This beginning, however, represents 'a chaotic conception of the whole' which by further analysis and determination must yield simpler concepts, 'thinner abstractions' until 'the simplest determinations' are arrived at. From this point 'the journey would have to be retraced until' we arrived at the concrete — a concrete, however, 'not as the chaotic conception of a whole, but as a rich totality of many determinations and relations' (G. p.100).

The first path, i.e., the path from the living concrete to the 'simplest determinations' ('determinant, abstract, general relations such as division of labour, money, value, etc.'), is the one followed by economists in the seventeenth century. The second path, i.e., the path that begins with simple relations and leads up 'to the level of the state, exchange between nations and the world market', viz. concrete wholes, is the one followed by the classical school of political economy. The latter represents 'obviously the scientifically correct method'. Along this path, we arrive at a 'concrete', by way 'of the working up of observation and conception into concepts'. This concrete is to be distinguished from the real concrete; it is a 'concrete in the mind', or a 'concrete in thought', i.e., 'a reproduction of the concrete by way of thought' (G. pp.100-101).

> Along the first path the full conception was evaporated to yield an abstract determination; along the second, the abstract determination led towards a reproduction of the concrete by way of thought. (G. p.101)

Marx's characterization of the method of classical political economy as 'obviously the scientifically correct method' raises a problem: what is it that distinguishes Marx's own method from the method of political economy, in other words in what does the specificity of Marx's method consist? If the method of political economy is the scientifically correct method, then, from the 'scienticist' perspective taken by some interpreters, Marx's method should directly coincide with the method of political economy. This thesis is explicitly or implicitly accepted by many followers of Marx. Admitting this identity of method between Marx and political economy would now pose a new question, replacing the previous problem: in what does the novelty of Marx consist, compared to political economy? Those who adhere to the thesis of the identity of method and

56

who, at the same time believe that Marx has made tremendous advances over classical political economy, have had to invent new concepts by which to analyse the specific difference between the project of political economy and that of Marx. Prominent among this group are those who believe that what distinguishes Marx from the political economists is a difference in the 'content' or the 'object' of their theoretical pursuits. For these interpreters, Marx's 'theoretical revolution' occurs not at the level of method, but at the level of object or content. According to them there is a continuity of method (scientific methodology) from the political economists to Marx. The discontinuity occurs at the point where Marx breaks away from the discourse of political economy and starts exploring an entirely new domain (presumably armed with the same methodology).[9]

The problem with the above line of interpretation is that it takes Marx's characterization of the method of political economy at its 'face value' and fails to interpret it. Marx, on a great number of occasions, discussed and clarified his agreements and disagreements with the classical political economists. It is only on the basis of the totality of his explicit judgements on the classical political economy (for instance, in his *Theories of Surplus-value*) and his implicit critique of it in *Capital* that the distance between Marx and political economists should be conceptualized. Since we shall deal with this issue at length in the next chapter, we will now limit ourselves to the following comments.

Marx's characterization of the method of political economy as the scientifically correct method is purely relative and *formal*. In contrast to the procedure of the economists of the seventeenth century, who started with 'concrete totalities', the method of the classical political economy is theoretical and 'analytical' in that it begins with concepts and proceeds to comprehend, to grasp the concrete totality in thought through these concepts. The path of the scientific method leads from simple, abstract concepts to concrete conceptions. Thus, Marx believes that the path of scientific inquiry must begin with simple determinations. But how are we to interpret the nature of these 'simple' concepts? The discussion below shall demonstrate that the concept 'simple' must itself be scrutinized and criticized, i.e. it must be 'interpreted'.

Marx first establishes that simple abstract categories form the beginning of 'the scientifically correct method' via a detour in which he criticizes Hegel's confusion of the movement of thought from the abstract to the concrete with the movement of real history (a point with which we shall not concern ourselves at this point). He then comes back to the question of the nature of 'simple' concepts and determinations:

57

Hegel, for example, correctly begins the *Philosophy of Right* with possession, this being the subject's simplest juridical relation. (G. p.102)

Here, once again (this time in the case of Hegel) the validity of the method of rising from abstract and simple categories to 'concrete in thought' is emphasized (note the use of the word 'correctly'). However, with the ensuing sentence, the nature of this 'simple' starting point is subjected to an intensive questioning and critique.

But there is no possession preceding the family or master-servant relations, which are far more concrete relations. However, it would be correct to say that there are families or clan groups which still merely *possess*, but have no *property*. The simple category therefore, appears in relation to property as a relation of simple families or clan groups. In the higher society it appears as the simpler relation of a developed organization. But the concrete substratum of which possession is a relation is always presupposed. One can imagine an individual savage as possessing something. But in that case possession is not a juridical relation. It is incorrect that possession develops historically into family. Possession, rather, always presupposes this 'more concrete juridical category'. (G. p.102)

A careful examination of this intricate and dense passage would reveal that for Marx the concept 'simple' is by no means unequivocal; rather, Marx is trying to develop the concept of the simple category in several directions and is presenting to us various shades of meaning with which the concept 'simple' is impregnated.

We shall now attempt to disinter the different interpretations of 'simple' in Marx's commentary.

We distinguish three aspects, sides or meanings of the concept of simple, which are listed below.

S.1: *Simple as an elementary, historically prior or primal relation ("a relation of simple families")*
S.2: Simple as an elementary relation coexisting but subsumed under a complex and developed whole ("the simpler relation of a developed organization")
S.3: Simple as a relation that presupposes a more concrete (complex, many-sided) development, e.g. a juridical relation ("But the concrete substratum of which possession is a relation is always presupposed"; "Possession . . . always presupposes this 'more concrete juridical category'") [10]

The bracketing or the subsumption of three different concepts (S.1, S.2 and S.3) above under a single category ('simple'), as attempted by Marx in the above-quoted passage is truly remarkable and defies our conventional and ordinary way of understanding. And this is why the entire history of interpretations of Marx's *Capital* (beginning with Marx's own and Engels's commentaries on the status of simple concepts in *Capital*) shows that the task of distinguishing between these various conceptions of the 'simple' and (given such a distinction has been made) holding fast to it is not easy and can run into serious difficulties, as we have seen in Chapter One. The reasons for these failures are many and cannot be fully explored here. At this point, we will limit ourselves to the following comments.

Part of the difficulty of comprehending differences in the various meanings of 'simple' in Marx's work is a result of the way in which Marx himself handles the issue not only in the *1857 Introduction*, but also in *Capital*. Marx's non-systematic treatment in the former text can be understood due to its exploratory nature. It is more difficult, however, to comprehend the lack of clarity and precision on this issue in *Capital* itself. We will show in the following chapters how in his theoretical practice, i.e. in *Capital*, Marx uses different concepts of 'simple' without making explicit the differentiations between them and/or showing the grounds for the communality of these different shades of meaning (justifying, thereby, the use of a common word, i.e. simple, to designate them).

The main reasons for these confusions (which begin with Marx himself and then spread throughout the entire history of Marx-interpretation) run much deeper: there are serious semantic and conceptual difficulties in making, for example, a proper distinction between something which is 'simple' because of its elemental nature and something which is 'simple' by virtue of its purity and universality. Words such as 'simple', 'mere' and 'pure' are often used synonymously in common parlance. Furthermore, words like 'elemental' and 'primitive' may be used synonymously: what is first and basic in thought and analysis (a spatial meaning) may be interpreted as something historically or chronologically first (a temporal meaning).

In the ordinary way of thinking it is easy to conceive S.1 or S.2 as simple, since these concepts designate a *single* relation among many, whether conceived as a historically 'lone' forerunner or a presently 'forlorn' residue or 'survival'. A system consisting of many relations articulated with each other in a complex way cannot be comprehended as 'simple'. How can a category based on the highest development and presupposing the richest possible determinations (S.3) be characterized as 'simple'?

The communality of and the interrelations between these three determinations of 'simple', i.e. their unity, will become apparent in Chapter Four as well as Parts II and III of this work, after we have analysed a number of key concepts in *Capital* and demonstrated the presence of a more or less constant structure, based on Hegel's *Logic*, in all of these concepts. In this chapter we shall limit ourselves to a detailed discussion of the three concepts of 'simple' in Marx's text, in which we distinguish these concepts from each other as clearly as possible.

S.1 Simple as an Historical Prius

Marx, after criticizing Hegel for 'conceiving the real as the product of thought concentrating itself, probing its own depths, unfolding itself out of itself, by itself', i.e. for identifying the movement of thought with the movement of real history, and stating that 'the method of rising from the abstract to concrete is only the way in which thought appropriates the concrete, reproduces it as the concrete in the mind' and that this is by no means the process by which the concrete itself comes into being, goes on to raise the question of whether or not 'simpler categories also have an independent historical or natural existence predating the more concrete ones' (G. p.102).

Here, Marx uses the example of the simple category 'possession' which serves as the point of departure in Hegel's *Philosophy of Right*. After disposing of the argument that this category can be made to express a simple relation historically preceding family, property, etc., he goes on to say:

> There would still always remain this much, however, namely that the simple categories are the expressions of relations within which the less developed concrete may have already realized itself before having posited the more many-sided connection or relation which is mentally expressed in the more concrete category; while the more developed concrete preserves the same category as a subordinate relation. Money may exist, and did exist historically before capital existed, before banks existed, before wage labour existed, etc. Thus in this respect it may be said that the simpler category can express the dominant relations of a less developed whole, or else those subordinate relations of a more developed whole which already had a historic existence before this whole developed in the direction expressed by a more concrete category. To that extent the path of abstract thought, rising from simple to combined, would correspond to the real historical process. (G.p.102)

The above passage may be interpreted as an admission by Marx to the possibility of an exclusive identification of simple categories with historically prior relations. And, indeed, Marx having given this conception the highest chances of revealing itself, is conceding that, in a sense, the thesis according to which simpler categories express dominant relations of less developed wholes, or the subordinate relations of more developed ones (i.e. those with a historically prior existence before developing in the direction expressed by the more concrete category) possesses a certain validity.

However, immediately after this passage, Marx begins questioning the universal validity of this thesis, having already given it as much credit as possible:

> It may be said on the other hand that there are very developed but nevertheless historically less mature forms of society, in which the highest form of economy, e.g. co-operation, a developed division of labour, etc. are found, even though there is no kind of money, e.g. Peru. (G. p.102)

Money was mentioned by Marx in the previous quotation as an example of simple categories expressing the dominant relations of less mature conditions of production, although in the case of money it can be said that it achieves its highest potential in more developed societies (e.g. in capitalist economies). But now we are told that this correlation between the development of the economy and the development of the money-form is by no means universal: the Incas of Peru had achieved a high degree of economic development without using money. This observation undermines any attempt to construct a correspondence between 'the path of abstract thought, rising from simple to combined' and 'the real historical process', i.e. the path of scientific advance and the path of historical development. More specifically, the whole idea of the identification of the beginning in science with the historically prior relations is put into serious doubt.

Marx on a number of other occasions refutes the universal truth of this identification of the beginning in science with historically prior relations. For example, after discussing another simple category, i.e. labour, he states:

> One could say that this indifference towards particular kinds of labour, which is a historic product in the United States, appears, e.g. among Russians as a spontaneous inclination. But there is a devil of difference between barbarians who are fit by nature to be used for anything, and civilized people who apply themselves to everything. And then in practice the Russian indifference to the specific character of labour corresponds to being embedded by tradition within a very specific kind of labour, from which only external influences can jar them loose. (G. p.105)

The point of the above passage is that the simple category 'labour' which is based on an indifference to specific kinds of labour and which forms the point of departure for political economy, presupposes the most developed conditions of production: it thus cannot be reduced to some historically less developed form, as in a less developed society where a similar indifference to specific types of labour may be observed.

Another example is provided by the question of the role of ground-rent or landed property under capitalism:

> For example, nothing seems more natural than to begin with ground rent, with landed property, since this is bound up with earth, the source of all production and of all being, and with the first form of production of all more or less settled societies — agriculture. But nothing would be more erroneous. (G. p.106)

This example, in a way slightly different from the examples cited above, shows that the correlation between the order or sequence of concepts in science and the historical sequence of forms corresponding to them lacks a solid foundation.

The scientific beginning cannot be identified with the historical beginning. It seems natural to start with ground-rent, which is an expression of those relations of production that have historical primacy. But this is wrong:

> In all forms of society there is one specific kind of production which predominates over the rest, whose relations thus assign rank and influence on the others. It is a general illumination which bathes all the other colours and modifies their particularity. It is a particular ether which determines the specific gravity of every being which has materialized within it. (G. pp.106-107)
>
> It would therefore be unfeasible and wrong to let the economic categories follow one another in the same sequence as that in which they were historically decisive. Their sequence is determined, rather, by their relation to one another in modern bourgeois society which is precisely the opposite of that which seems to be their natural order or which corresponds to historical development. The point is not the historic relations in the succession of different forms of society. Even less is it their sequence 'in the idea' (Proudhon) . . . Rather, their order within modern bourgeois society. (G. pp.107-8)

Thus the primacy of concepts is not determined by their historical primacy but by their primacy in modern bourgeois society, in which the historical order and sequence is reversed.[11]

These examples show that while Marx concedes in a limited way the interpretation of 'simple' as a concept expressing an historically prior

62

relation, he questions the validity of this conception by citing counter-examples. He is fully aware of the difficulties of generalizing this thesis.

Our discussion of S.1 so far has made one point clear: the simple beginning in science cannot be identified with S.1, i.e. the concept of a simple relation historically preceding a more complex whole. We now consider S.2 to see if it qualifies as a proper scientific beginning.

S.2 Simple as a Relation Subordinate to a Complex Whole

This concept represents simple relations subsumed under larger and more complex wholes.

In one respect S.1 and S.2, besides their simplicity, are of the same nature: both concepts designate single, isolated relations. In case of S.1 the reference is to an isolated relation in the past in relation to a higher development in the future. In case of S.2 the relation is a single, isolated moment of an existing whole. Thus the only difference appears to be that S.1 is a temporal concept, while S.2 is a spatial one. Furthermore in a passage cited above Marx, at one point, identifies these two concepts:

'. . . The simple categories are the expressions of relations within which the less developed concrete may have already realized itself [S.1] . . . , while the more developed concrete preserves the same category as a subordinate relation [S.2].' This comment by Marx suggests another interpretation of S.2 (besides the one given in the beginning of this section, namely, S.2 as a concept of simpler relations subordinate to larger wholes), i.e. S.2 as a concept of an historically prior relation. This interpretation, which virtually merges S.2 into S.1, raises a serious question:

There are many examples in Marx's works of simple, historically prior relations that are preserved in higher stages of development. And we may claim that more developed and complex social structures are able to salvage relations from their past and to make them serve the purposes of the new structure to a fuller extent than in less developed structures. But surely these preserved relations have entirely different modes of functioning in the new setting compared to their historically original forms. Thus an S.2 may be related to some S.1 as its original form but this does not mean that the two can be identified. Marx himself is aware of the distinction when he refers to 'divergent positions which the same category can occupy in different social stages . . .' (G. p.108)

This leads us to a sharper characterization of S.2: S.2 denotes relations (whether original or carried over from the past) which function as subordinate relations in a complex whole and whose mode of functioning is determined by the totality of which they form mere moments (in case they are carried over from the past, their function is determined by the existing whole and not by their historical origin). It can also be added that unlike S.1, S.2 presupposes a higher development since it denotes partial, subordinate relations of more developed wholes. There are numerous examples of S.2 in *Capital*, such as simple circulation as a subordinate moment of capitalist production and merchant's capital as a special form of capital subsumed under industrial capital.

The question before us now is whether or not S.2 can serve as the beginning in science. Marx's answer is clear and unequivocal.

> Ground rent cannot be understood without capital. But capital can certainly be understood without ground rent. Capital is the all embracing economic power of bourgeois society. It must form the starting-point as well as the finishing point, and must be dealt with before landed property. (G. p.107)

This comment not only rejects the idea that S.2 can serve as the beginning point in science, but also unmistakably points to S.3 as such a beginning.

S.3 Simple as the Most Developed Whole

S.2 presupposes a higher development and a concrete whole — it is a concept of a simple relation subsumed under a developed whole. S.3 also presupposes higher development, but it designates not an aspect of this higher development but this development in its entirety. Let us first see what Marx says about this interpretation of the concept 'simple'. His comments can be rephrased as follows.

Possession, as 'the subject's simplest juridical relation', which 'correctly' forms the beginning in Hegel's *Philosophy of Right*, can in no way be reduced to either a simple relation of possession among communities in which 'property' has not developed or to the 'simple' fact of 'possessing something' by an individual savage (S.1). Rather, far more concrete developments, such as family and master-slave relations, are needed for the concept of possession to become a juridical relation of the subject. Thus the concept of possession, unless it is identified with the mundane and ordinary meaning of the word 'possession', can in no way express possession as a legal relation and therefore, on the basis of this conception, we cannot say, for instance, that the family develops on the basis of possession. The most we can claim is that possession appears in a higher social organization as a subordinate relationship (S.2). But this relationship already presupposes a higher development: as we have seen S.2 does not qualify as the starting-point in science.

In Hegel the concept of possession as the simplest juridical relation of the subject must be based on the richest and fullest development of juridical relations in society.

Marx makes the same point when he discusses the category 'labour':

> Labour seems quite a simple category. The conception of labour in this general form — as labour as such — is also immeasurably old. Nevertheless, when it is economically conceived in this simplicity, 'labour' is as modern a category as are the relations which create this simple category. (G. p.103)

Once again (exactly like in the case of 'possession') we are confronted with a simple category which presupposes far more concrete relations: it 'is as modern . . . as are the relations which create this simple category' and, thus, it cannot be reduced to a prehistoric simple fact of 'labouring' (or to labour as the eternal condition of production): it is not an abstraction of the 'simplest and most ancient relation' (S.1). Nor can it be reduced to a particular variety of labour subordinate to the totality of the system of division of labour in society (S.2).

> Now it might seem that all that had been achieved thereby [conceiving labour in general as the wealth-producing activity, regardless of its specific forms] was to discover the abstract expression for the simplest and most ancient relation in which human beings — in whatever form of society — play the role of producers. This is correct in one respect. Not in another. Indifference towards any specific kind of labour presupposes a very developed totality of real kinds of labour, of which no single one is any longer predominant.
>
> The simplest abstraction, then, which modern economics places at the head of its discussions, and which expresses an immeasurably ancient relation valid in all forms of society, nevertheless achieves practical truth as an abstraction only as a category of the most modern society. (G. p.104)

Thus in the simple category 'labour' although an expression is found that is 'valid for all forms of society', we find a product enriched by the wealth of highest development. Furthermore, this category possesses 'full validity' only for the most highly developed conditions of production:

> This example of labour shows strikingly how even the most abstract categories, despite their validity — precisely because of their abstractness — for all epochs

are nevertheless, in the specific character of their abstraction, themselves likewise a product of historic relations, and possess their full validity only for and within these conditions. (G. p.105)

Clearly, for Marx S.3 represents neither a simple prehistoric or historically first relation (or, as a matter of fact, a fundamental relation valid for all times and places) nor a simple, partial relation subsumed under a larger whole (regardless of whether or not this relation has a prior historic origin). S.3 is the concrete whole itself, but presented in a particularly simple form: it is the whole world reflected in a drop of water.

We saw above that neither S.1 nor S.2 qualified as the points of departure in science. Let us see now whether S.3 can serve this role.

I believe that Marx's answer to this question is contained in the following extraordinary passage:

Bourgeois society is the most developed and the most complex historic organization of production. The categories which express its relations, the comprehension of its structure, thereby also allows insights into the structure and relations of production of all the vanished social formations out of whose ruins and elements it built itself up, whose partly still unconquered remnants are carried along within it, whose mere nuances have developed specific significances within it, etc. Human anatomy contains the key to the anatomy of the ape. The intimations of higher development among the subordinate animal species, however, can be understood only after the higher development is already known. (G. p.105)

This passage, whose implications cannot be fully explored here, suggests that science begins at the apex of development and then descends down the heights, but only to embrace the entire growth — root, stalk, branch and fruit.

Based on the above observations I conclude that S.3 is the starting point for Marx. However, in the light of our discussions so far one question naturally suggests itself: Marx, in the beginning, charted out the movement of thought from simple, abstract categories to the 'concrete in thought', a path presumably followed by classical political economy. He even chided Hegel for reading into this movement an historic development from simple relations to concrete and complex organizations. The conclusion he reaches, however, suggests that the beginning, although still simple, presupposes the wealth of the entire development (S.3). And, thus, in a sense, his 'concrete-in-thought' is indistinguishable from S.3, i.e. the end and the beginning merge with each other. Section III below will take up the question of the beginning in *Capital* and show that a number of approaches to these questions are

66

inadequate due to a lack of recognition of S.3-type concepts in Marx.

That for Marx the point of departure and the end-product are, in a sense, identical cannot be doubted. For example, in one of the previously quoted passages, he says that capital 'must form the starting-point as well as the finishing point . . . .'

We cannot at this point deal with this paradox of circularity. However, there is one aspect of this riddle to be discussed here by way of conclusion.

We have shown that the concept of 'simple' is not a self-evident one: it must be interpreted and that this is in fact what Marx does in his discussion on the method of political economy in the 1857 *Introduction*. We have also concluded that among the three main interpretations of 'simple' to be found in Marx's text, namely S.1, S.2 and S.3, only S.3 qualifies as the proper beginning for science. S.3, however, is based on the end result, on the 'concrete in thought', which should presumably develop out of simple beginnings. If these simple beginnings are identified with S.3, we have a circular movement. That is precisely Marx's view of the method. Classical political economy starts from 'simple' categories but the latter are not of the same type as S.3. Marx's text constitutes a critique of the nature of the concepts with which political economists begin their discourse.

The economists of the seventeenth century began with real, concrete totalities and ended up with abstract and simple categories. Classical political economists, in contrast, began with these simple concepts and by a 'reverse' movement arrived at 'thought concretes'. Marx's procedure cannot be assimilated with either of these movements.

Marx criticizes Hegel's 'confusion' of the movement of thought from simple to concrete with the real historic evolution from elemental to complex relations, the conclusion being that the movement from simple to complex is a characteristic of thinking, which can in no way be projected back to the course of real history. But Marx's own explorations in the 1857 *Introduction* show that even the movement of thought cannot be captured by this 'simple' scheme. These explorations show that thought passes through a much more complicated path than this. Indeed Marx's earlier criticism of Hegel may be reversed now: history may develop from the simple to the complex, but human thinking might not follow such a path. Thus the path of the 'scientifically correct' method of political economy may indeed correspond to the path of real history but it might not represent the true movement of thought.

We have seen how Marx's analysis in effect problematizes the fixed opposition between generality and particularity and then how the rigid opposition between simplicity and complexity, the abstract and the concrete, and the beginning and the end product of scientific activity are similarly problematized. Here I wish to compare the duality model presented above with the three-fold determination of simple concepts in the S-model. Diagram 3 is a representation of this relationship.

Let us recall that in the D-model the elements of the totality appear in two opposing functions, i.e. as active elements (subjects) and as passive elements (objects). We identified the latter with the 'common element' represented by a one-sided abstraction, i.e. the historical 'constant' which is a particular (if not empty) and not a true universal. The former were identified with activity, subjectivity and autonomy approaching an identity with the totality itself. Now turning to the S-model we can see that S.3 represents the concrete totality and thus level I of the D-model. It is also clear that from relations represented by S.1 there is a double transformation. On the one hand the historically prior relationship is elevated to the status of a determining moment of the whole (S.3) and on the other hand it is reproduced as a subordinate and passive element (S.2).

DIAGRAM 3

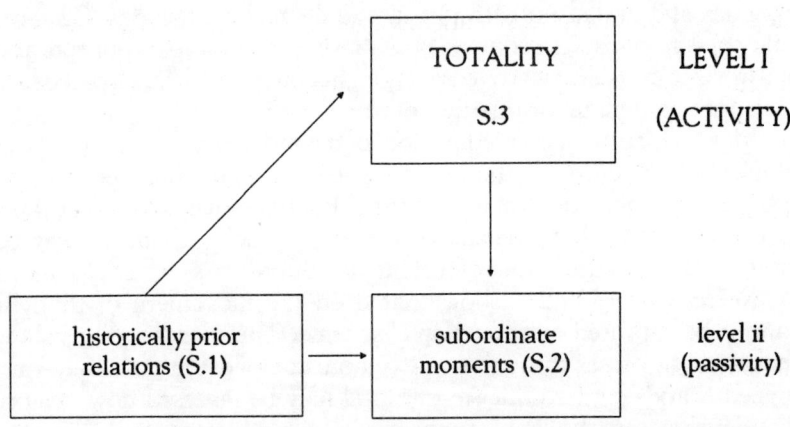

The two models developed in this chapter, i.e. the D-model and the S-model, will dominate our exposition in Part II of this work, where their validity will be tested by their application to Marx's concepts in *Capital*.

The three approaches to Marx's method reviewed in Chapter One, i.e. the historicist, the structuralist and the rationalist, all fail to confront the complexity of simple concepts in Marx and produce a one-sided interpretation. Diagram 4 illustrates the relationship between these approaches and the three sides of the simple concepts developed above.

DIAGRAM 4

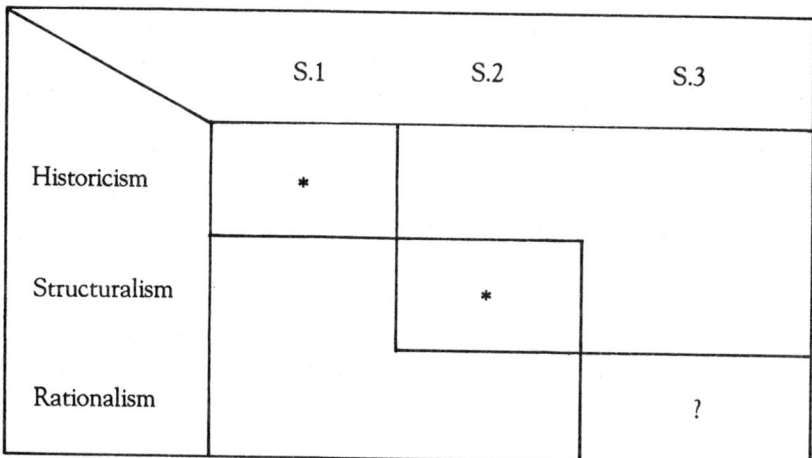

The reason for the question mark in front of the category of 'rationalism' in Diagram 4 is that while in the older version of the rationalist approach of Schmidt and Sombart we have an intimation of S.3, the fuller conception of S.3 as presented in this chapter is not achieved, especially in the modern variant of rationalism represented by Morishima and Catephores. In the next section we discuss two concrete examples of Marxist theorizing which also present a one-sided interpretation of Marx's method.

III TWO APPLICATIONS

A. De Brunhoff on Marx's Theory of Money

In what follows we will discuss some aspects of Suzanne De Brunhoff's approach to Marx's theory of money, an attempt to formulate social theory on the basis of generic concepts.

De Brunhoff begins her search for a 'general' theory of money by stating that

> The Marxist theory of money interests us primarily because of its integration
> with the theory of the capitalist form of production. Since money is part of the
> machinery of capitalism, its role is determined by its functions within the entire
> pattern of capitalist economic relations. (De Brunhoff 1976, p.19)

Thus a Marxist theory of money is important because it is part of the Marxist theory of capitalism. In reality money is also 'part of the machinery of capitalism', playing a role 'determined by its functions' under capitalism. Clearly, we should expect De Brunhoff to develop a theory of money adequate to the capitalist mode of production. While stressing the importance of money in the capitalist economy to the point of stating that the analysis of money as an 'integral part' of the capitalist mode of production 'can offer an explanation of the fundamental relationship of adjustment and maladjustment between the "real" and the "monetary" in terms of the financing of accumulation and its cyclical metamorphoses', she ends up by rejecting the primacy of a theory of money specific to capitalism:

> But it is not enough to formulate a *theory of the specific form of money*, i.e. of
> those monetary phenomena which persist or recur in contradistinction to other
> economic phenomena. (De Brunhoff 1976, p.19)

De Brunhoff favours a general theory of money applicable to all monetary economies — a theory which subsumes the specifically capitalist theory:

> Hence a theory of money applicable to the capitalist system must be subsumed
> under a theory of money in general, valid for every monetary economy; in other
> words, a general theory of money. (De Brunhoff 1976, p.19)

The author does not clarify what she means by a 'monetary economy'. If this means an economy in which money object exists then almost all historical forms of economy would be characterized as monetary. On the other hand, if it refers to an economy in which economic relations and transactions exhibit a high degree of monetization then only the capitalist economy would qualify as a monetary economy. If the latter interpretation is favoured, then it is not clear what a general theory of money applicable to *all monetary economies* means. De Brunhoff's object is to produce a generic concept of money that would be the common denominator of the most diverse conditions of production in which money is used. She tries to justify her procedure by claiming that it is based on Marx's view of method (De Brunhoff 1976, pp.20-5). According to her interpretation of this method one should construct general concepts, e.g.

commodity, money, applicable to all forms of production in which commodities and money exist. Then one should proceed to construct more complex and more specific concepts and models into which the general concepts and categories are integrated.

De Brunhoff regards the following three 'traditional' functions of money as the elements of a general theory of money. Money is a) a measure of value; b) a medium of circulation and c) an instrument of hoarding (De Brunhoff 1976, pp.25-45). These are indeed some of the important functions of money under capitalism. But numerous historical and anthropological studies have demonstrated the following points:

i) A 'general purpose money' that plays all these functions is relatively new in history.

ii) The further we go back in history the greater are the chances that we encounter 'limited purpose' money or monies, i.e. there is no single object that has all the modern functions of money or that different objects play different 'money-like' roles.

iii) The origins of money can be traced to a much earlier period than the beginnings of commodity production and exchange; in other words money pre-exists commodity exchange and markets. Money in those earlier stages served as means of compensation and exchanging gifts.[12]

Against this historical background one may legitimately claim that a general theory of money should not be restricted to commodity producing economies only, as De Brunhoff attempts to do. But more significantly these historical points indicate the absurdity of an attempt to apply the analytical method to an evolutionary object such as money. This method hopes to achieve a *complete* definition of money in abstraction from its *most developed* conditions of existence. But this procedure involves a contradiction: on the one hand we want to define money as completely as possible; on the other hand some of the functions of money that may be most essential under more developed conditions have to be left out because they are not common to less developed forms, e.g. money as capital. By ignoring the fuller development of money the very relevance and potential of the fully developed function in earlier stages may be overlooked. For instance, if one abstracts the function of money as capital from the concept of money, as De Brunhoff does on the grounds that money capital retains its identity as money (the generic concept), one is ignoring one of the most significant aspects of the capitalist

71

development, past and present, i.e. the close connection between pre-capitalist forms of capital, e.g. interest-bearing capital and even merchant's capital, and the transformation of money into money capital under capitalism.

Even the 'traditional' functions of money that form the basis for the generic concept of money can be understood and analysed better from the vantage point of capitalist development. Thus money as a measure of value both quantitatively (in terms of the number of goods it covers) and qualitatively (the accuracy of such measurements, largely depends on the development of quantitative measures of both goods and the money object itself) functions more efficiently under capitalism than under previous economic systems. This is even more true about the function of money as a means of circulation (the development of banking and innovations in the financial sector, e.g. the use of computerized clearing of cheques by banks). Thus what seems to be posited in the generic concept as basic and primary, as cause and *premise* is in fact a derivative, a *result*. As we have demonstrated earlier in this chapter the common element captured by the generic concept is either empty or a particular. In the case under review here a general concept of money that abstracts from the functions of money in the most advanced conditions of economic development is either useless or, if anything, it is the concept of a particular subsumed under a totality. In terms of Marx's D-model, money as capital is the active, dominant monetary relationship. As a means of pure circulation, i.e. in the C-M-C circuit, it is passive and subordinate.

De Brunhoff's analysis is based on a fixed opposition between money and capital, for which she relies on quotations from Marx such as the following:

> It is wrong . . . to seek to ascribe the specific properties and functions that characterize money as money and commodities as commodities, to their character as capital . . . . (C.II. p.161)
> As money capital, it [capital] exists in a state in which it can perform monetary functions, in the present case the functions of general means of purchase and payment . . . . Money capital does not possess this capacity because it is capital, but because it is money. (C.II. p.112)

Both of these statements by Marx seem to support an analytical separation between money and capital. But another interpretation is possible: money by becoming capital does not lose its 'purely' monetary functions, but in this relationship these functions are subordinate to the capital

72

function. In a sense, to state that money remains money when turned into money capital is a tautology. How else can money capital perform its function without the ability to serve as means of circulation, e.g. to purchase labour-power (one of its most important functions)? But what is not a tautology is the dialectical relationship between money and capital. Money in the hands of the capitalist is capital if it is spent on purchasing labour power and the means of production. The same object when it reaches the pocket of the worker and is spent on consumer goods acts as pure money and not capital. Surplus-value invested productively by the capitalist is capital but if spent for his/her personal consumption it is no longer capital but a means of circulation. Thus if we interpret money and capital not as objects but as social relationships, the rigid opposition between them disappears.

We may conclude that De Brunhoff's approach to money is based on a particular interpretation of Marx's method, i.e. that scientific investigation begins with generic (S.1) concepts and not, as we have argued above, with S.3 concepts. The next case we examine below has a direct bearing on De Brunhoff's interpretation, as it deals with the question of whether Marx himself begins his analysis of capitalism with an S.1 or an S.3 concept of the commodity.

B. *The Question of the Beginning in Marx's* Capital

The problem of the beginning in Marx's Capital is based on the following question: why does Marx begin his work not with the concept of capital, which is the most fundamental relation in the capitalist mode of production (the object of Marx's Capital) and its *differentia specifia* from other modes of production, but with the commodity, which is presumably the common denominator of all commodity-producing economies?

There are a number of approaches to this question.[13] But from the point of view developed in the present work the following three are most relevant:

i) Marx begins with the commodity because it is the historically first form of human product that is produced for exchange, and since capitalism is a commodity economy *par excellence* it is only natural to begin with the commodity (the historicist approach). In this approach there is a presupposed identity of essence between the commodity in pre-capitalist conditions and the commodity under capitalism.

73

ii) Marx begins with the commodity because it is the basic, elementary structure of capitalist economy (the structuralist approach). In this approach the assumption of the historically first form is not necessary; rather the commodity is to be conceived as a substructure of capital.

This view can be interpreted in one of two ways: the commodity is either a) as a substructure consisting of non-capitalist commodity producers under capitalism or b) a general structure where the relations between capitalists and workers as well as relations among capitalists themselves are pure exchange relations. Clearly a) is not plausible as a beginning since the size of the non-capitalist commodity producing sector is relatively small under capitalism. b) is a more acceptable alternative as a point of departure. However its main deficiency is that it is based on a complete separation of the commodity relation and the capital relation among agents.

iii) Marx begins with the commodity, or with 'simple' commodity production, because such an approach abstracts from complicating features of capitalism such as the private ownership of means of production (the rationalist approach). In this pure model the value relation between commodities can be established without these 'complications', which can then be relaxed in more complex models of value determination. Although somewhat different from the structuralist approach, the rationalist interpretation is also ultimately based on a fixed opposition between the commodity and capital.

The latter point is one of the common grounds of all these approaches. In the historicist conception the commodity remains 'outside' of any capitalist relation; but it is historically accurate to say that capital, at least in the form of merchant's capital, was intimately bound to the commodity. Furthermore, in all these interpretations the commodity appears in the passive mode ready to be taken over by capital and dominated by it. Thus the question of the historical transformation of pre-capitalist forms of commodity production and of forms of capital into capitalist production of commodities is ignored. The commodity is treated as a thing rather than as a social relationship. The fact that capital lives only through the commodification of use values on a large scale and that therefore there is an intimate bond between the commodity and capital has no place in the analytical method of these three schools. In this method the commodity appears as a premise and not a result of capitalist production.

Marx's own approach is very different. First, he distinguishes between two concepts of the commodity:

> a) The commodity 'as the premise of the formation of capital'; 'the *historical* premise of the capitalist mode of production'; 'a *prerequisite*, the *starting-point*, of the formation of capital and capitalist production'.
> b) The commodity as 'the result, the product of capitalist production once it has become the universal elementary form of the product'.

What is the justification for this conceptual distinction? Marx explains:

> The commodity as it emerges in capitalist production, is different from the commodity taken as the element, the starting-point of capitalist production. We are no longer faced with the individual commodity, the individual product. The individual product manifests itself not only as a real product but also as a commodity, as a *part* both really and conceptually of production as a whole. Each individual commodity represents a definite portion of capital and the surplus value created by it. (TSV. III. pp. 112-13)

Marx's discussion can be elaborated further to make the distinction between (a) and (b) as sharp as possible. Commodity production and exchange is relatively small and isolated in pre-capitalist forms of production. Commodity production stands in a relation of dependence to other modes of production. Thus it does not exist 'for itself'. Capitalist production generalizes commodity production and as a result it acquires the character of independence and necessity. Thus the commodity, which is the result of capitalist production is 'enriched' and elevated to a higher level of social existence. It is clear that in this sense the concept of the commodity is an S.3 concept.

Thus if the second concept of commodity, i.e. the commodity as a result of capitalist production is considered, it is intimately bound up with capitalist production and, as such, it cannot be separated in an abstract way from capital as is done in the analytical method. By implication it is clear that it is this second concept that forms the beginning of Marx's *Capital*.

Notes to Chapter Two

1. "I said that Marx left us no *Dialectics*. This is not quite accurate. He did leave us one first-rate methodological text, unfortunately without finishing it: the *Introduction to the Critique of Political Economy*, 1859." (Althusser, 1969, p.182.) (Note that the author is referring to the *1857 Introduction* and not to the Preface to Marx's A *Contribution to the Critique of Political Economy*, 1859. The

75

confusion is due to the fact that the *1857 Introduction* appeared together with the former text in one volume after its discovery in 1903 [see Chapter One, Note 8, above]. In his later works Althusser refers specifically to *1857 Introduction*.) Compare with Lenin's statement: "if Marx did not leave behind him a 'Logic' . . . he did leave the *logic of Capital* . . ." (Lenin 1972, p.319).

2. We have already referred to Rubin's work in Chapter One. To mention just a few others, Althusser (1969) Chapter 6; Althusser and Balibar (1970); Colletti (1973) Chapter VIII; Della Volpe (1978, pp.186-204, 1980, Chap. IV); Ilyenkov (1982); Luporini (1975); Rosdolsky (1977); Sayer (1979-a), Chapter 4, all with varying degrees use this text as their major methodological source in interpreting Marx.

3. In spite of the fact that both Althusser and Colletti have used this text to turn Marx against Hegel, based on the analysis in the present chapter and Chapter Four below I claim that *1857 Introduction* is the most explicitly Hegelian text Marx ever wrote. In fact the influence of Hegel on this text is so strong that at times Marx weaves Hegel's words into his writing. Echeverria (1978), while recognizing Hegel's influence on Marx, does not think that this influence is reflected in the *1857 Introduction*. He, for instance, states: "This *Introduction* was written before Marx's appropriation of Hegel, and this will prove to entail important effects." (p.334) (See also note 9 below.)

4. In the Preface to this work Marx refers to *1857 Introduction* in the following words: "A general introduction, which I had drafted, is omitted, since on further consideration it seems to me confusing to anticipate results which still have to be substantiated, and the reader who really wishes to follow me will have to decide to advance from the particular to the general." (CR. p.19)

5. There are a few interesting points in section 4, including a discussion about the relationship between economic development and evolution of artistic forms.

6. For example a recent basic economics textbook starts with the following definition: "Every group of people must solve their basic problems of daily living: *what* goods and services to produce, *how* to produce these goods and services, and *for whom* to produce these goods and services. *Economics* is a study of how society decides what, how, and for whom to produce." (Begg, Stanley & Dornbusch 1984, p.1)

7. Jean-Baptiste Say (1767-1832) formulated the famous Say's Law according to which every producer brings his demand for goods to the market along with his supply of goods and thus supply creates its own demand, the implication being that no disparities between production and sale leading, for instance, to overproduction can ever occur. Marx criticizes this notion at a number of points in his writings (e.g. C.I. pp.208-9, TSV.II. p.493) and shows that it is based on the mistaken assumption that products exchange against products (a barter economy). The implications of Marx's critique of Say's Law for Marx's monetary theory are discussed in Shamsavari (1986).

8. It is this opposition that is the basis of Echeverria's dismissal of *1857 Introduction* as a misleading guide to Marx's method in *Capital*. According to Echeverria (1978) Marx finally decided to use 'general' concepts, i.e. S.1 concepts (see section II below) as his fundamental and primary concepts. That this is in fact not true will become clear in Part II of this book, but see also section III below, where we will try to show that the concepts of commodity and money in *Capital* are not generic.

9. For instance, Althusser locates the difference between Marx and classical economists not at the level of methodology, which he assumes to be identical, but the object (Althusser and Balibar, 1970). For more detail on Althusser's views see Chapter One.

10. Compare with Colletti (1973), where a two-way determination of concepts are suggested: '. . . exchange value presents itself to us in two different respects: on the one hand, as the most comprehensive and broadest *generality* from which all the other categories are *deduced* and from which a scientific exposition must begin; on the other hand, as an *objective characteristic*, as the last (in the deductive chain) and therefore most *superficial* and abstract characteristic (the most *generic* and indeterminate element, if taken by itself) of the concrete object in question.' (p.126) The first aspect discussed by Colletti roughly corresponds to S.3 and the second exactly to S.1. As opposed to the interpretation advanced in this chapter Colletti claims that S.1 forms the beginning for Marx (pp.127-9).

11. For Althusser this point in Marx becomes a dogma from which his structuralist approach is built up. For a critique of this approach to Marx's method see Chapter One.

12. See Einzig (1949), Dalton (1967), Polanyi (1968) and Drake (1980), Chapter 4 where he sums up numerous relevant research. Also see Leijonhufvud (1977), p.267.

13. See Banaji (1980) for a discussion and critique of the views of Meek (1973), Colletti (1973) and Nicolaus (1973) on the question of the beginning in *Capital*. Banaji's own approach derives basically from Lenin's view on the matter. In his *Philosophical Notebooks*, which was written after Lenin had studied Hegel's *Logic*, he makes the following statement about the concept of the commodity in *Capital*:

> In his *Capital* Marx first analyses the simplest, most ordinary and fundamental, the most common and everyday *relation* of bourgeois (commodity) society, a relation encountered billions of times, viz. the exchange of commodities. In this very simple phenomenon (in this "cell" of bourgeois society) analysis reveals *all* the contradictions (or the germs of *all* the contradictions) of modern society. The subsequent exposition shows us the development (both growth *and* movement of these contradictions and of this society in the Σ of its individual parts), from its beginning to its end. (Lenin 1972, Vol. 38, pp.360-1)

This interpretation is completely consistent with the one attempted in the present work. See also Zelený (1980, p.33), where a similar approach is adopted, although it falls somewhat short of the above interpretation.

CHAPTER THREE

MARX'S METHOD II: DIALOGUES WITH POLITICAL ECONOMY

In the present chapter we will examine Marx's specific criticisms of classical political economy on the basis of the results of our previous chapter. Through this examination we wish to demonstrate that Marx's specific comments on the method of political economy[1] reveal a single methodological perspective in spite of their enigmatic character. The enigmatic character of Marx's criticisms of political economy arises from the fact that we find Marx criticizing political economists on different and apparently contradictory grounds. Moreover, Marx often praises political economy for achieving what he elsewhere reserves for himself as his own achievement.

Our purpose here is first to problematize these apparent contradictions and gaps in Marx's commentaries on political economy and then to see if a coherent structure for Marx's critique arises from our textual analysis.

I. The Two Sides of Marx's Criticism of Political Economy

Marx often criticizes political economists on two opposing grounds:

1) Classical political economy is reproached for not analysing specific, concrete forms and thus for following an 'abstract' method of analysis, and,

2) Classical political economy, while praised for its 'analytical' approach, i.e. the reduction of phenomenal forms and appearances to their essences is criticized for not carrying abstraction far enough, for remaining at the level of specific and concrete forms.

Let us take these two points one by one.

1. At the end of his analysis of value in *Capital I*, Marx criticizes political economy's approach to value in the following words:

> Political economy has indeed analysed value and its magnitude, however incompletely, and has uncovered the content concealed within these forms.

78

But it has never once asked the question why this content has assumed that particular form, that is to say, why labour is expressed in value, and why the measurement of labour by its duration is expressed in the magnitude of the value of the product. (C.I. pp.173-4)

Marx is according credit to political economy for analysing value into labour, i.e. 'the content concealed' in various forms of value. Political economists have succeeded in reducing the phenomenal forms to their essences. Thus the various forms of value are analysed into and reduced to an essence common to them all, i.e. labour. This is a result of what Marx frequently calls the 'analytical method' of political economy. However, this analytic procedure, although historically justified as the first and primary stage of scientific work, falls short of a true and full scientific comprehension of economic phenomena. It seems that Marx expects the stage of 'analysis' to be followed by another stage in which the 'reduced' content or 'essence' has to account for the multiplicity of the specific and concrete forms it assumes.

In a footnote following the above-quoted words Marx goes into more detail. Here Marx points out that political economy has never problematized the particularity of the form of value: 'it has never succeeded . . . in discovering the form of value which in fact turns value into exchange-value', i.e., content or essence into phenomenal form. The explanation for this failure, Marx believes, should not be sought solely in the preoccupation of political economy with the quantitative side of value analysis. The reason 'lies deeper': The value-form being 'the most universal form of the bourgeois mode of production' defines, determines the specificity of that mode of production and thus escapes those who treat this mode as 'the eternal natural form of production' (C.I. p.174).

At this point we are not concerned with the validity of Marx's judgement about the reason for the failure of political economy to pose the question of value-form, but in the nature of Marx's criticism. Here political economy is criticized for failing to consider and analyse the form of value, a specific quality that 'stamps the bourgeois mode of production as a particular kind of social production . . .' Thus it is the specificity and the particularity of the value-form which remain unanalysed by political economy.

On the face of it, Marx seems to be blaming political economists for over-generalization and over-abstraction: by reducing value to labour, political economy has by-passed the specific character of value and thus has arrived at a concept valid for all forms of economy, namely labour, which is an eternal condition of all human production.

79

In the *1857 Introduction* we find many examples of this line of criticism by Marx. For example he mentions how economists reduce the concept of capital to means of production, i.e. a social relation to a mere object, which like labour, is an eternal condition of production:

> No production is possible without an instrument of production even if this instrument is only the hand. No production without stored-up, past labour, even if it is only the facility gathered together in the hand of the savage by repeated practice. Capital is, among other things, also an instrument of production, also objectified, past labour. Therefore capital is a general, eternal relation of nature; that is, if I leave out just the specific quality which alone makes 'instrument of production' and 'stored-up labour' into capital. (G. pp.85-6)

This form of criticism, conceived superficially, amounts to a call for 'concrete' (or specific) analysis, as opposed to an 'abstract' (or general) approach.

2. Side by side with the above line of criticism we find in Marx an apparently opposite line: political economy is to be reproached for not following an approach abstract enough, for not carrying 'abstraction far enough'.

Let us look at some examples.

On several occasions Marx objects to the analysis of value in the first chapter of Ricardo's *Principles*.[2] The main defect of that chapter, in Marx's view, is the insufficient degree of generality and abstraction accorded to the concept of value. After explaining the exchange values of commodities on the basis of the quantities of labour embodied in them, Ricardo moves on to consider exceptions to this general rule. For example he brings up the question of profits, which complicates the simple determination of value by labour: here, the difference in the amount of 'non-human capital' employed in various lines of production appears to be another, albeit secondary, cause explaining exchange values.[3]

Marx objects to Ricardo's procedure. He wants the law of value to be formulated and presented at such a level of abstraction and generality that enables it to subsume forms and circumstances apparently contradicting it in its general form — a formulation that does not admit of any 'exceptions'.

> One can see that though Ricardo is accused of being too abstract, one would be justified in accusing him of the opposite: lack of power of abstraction,

inability, when dealing with the value of commodities, to forget profits, a factor which confronts him as a result of competition. (TSV. II. p.191)

Compared to Smith, Ricardo

> consciously *abstracts* from the form of competition, from the appearance of competition, in order to comprehend the *laws as such*. On the one hand he must be reproached for not going far enough, for not carrying his abstraction to completion, for instance, when he analyses the *value* of the commodity, he at once allows himself to be influenced by consideration of all kinds of concrete conditions. On the other hand one must reproach him for regarding the phenomenal form as *immediate and direct* proof or exposition of the general laws, and for failing to *interpret* it. In regard to the first, his abstraction is too incomplete; in regard to the second, it is formal abstraction which in itself is wrong. (TSV. II. p.106)

The same point comes up in one of Marx's letters to Kugelmann (July 11, 1868):

> Science consists precisely in demonstrating *how* the law of value asserts itself. So that if one wanted at the very beginning to 'explain' all the phenomena which seemingly contradict that law, one would have to present the science *before* science. It is precisely Ricardo's mistake that in his first chapter on value he takes *as given* a variety of categories that have not yet been explained in order to prove their conformity with the law of value. (SC. p.196)

In short:

> Ricardo's method is as follows: he begins with the determination of the magnitude of the value of the commodity by labour-time and then *examines* whether the other economic relations and categories *contradict* this determination of value or to what extent they modify it. (TSV. II. p.164)

Thus Ricardo, unlike Smith, abstracts from competition to prove the law of value as such in its general and abstract form. But after formulating the law in its generality he proceeds to 'explain all the phenomena which seemingly contradict that law', and thus he 'allows himself to be influenced by consideration of all kinds of concrete conditions'. Here, Ricardo's power of abstraction suffers and stops short of achieving what it aimed for: he gets caught up in the intricate web of various concrete forms and conditions.

The above line of criticism seems to imply that Marx demands a more abstract and less concrete approach than that followed by political economy.

81

In the first of the above quotations we observe the rare occasion where Marx's double-edged sword of criticism is cutting both ways at the same time. He blames Ricardo on the one hand for lacking the power of abstraction (for letting himself be influenced by concrete conditions in treating the question of value), and, on the other, for 'formal abstraction' in taking a phenomenal form as 'direct proof' of the general laws and failing to 'interpret' it. In this quotation we have both points of view presented side by side.

Marx is criticizing political economy in two different terrains, fighting it on two opposing fronts. The ambiguous and enigmatic character of Marx's critique becomes all the more pronounced and puzzling when he praises political economy for achieving what he himself characterizes as his own major advance over political economy and one of the main points that distinguishes his work from that of political economists. For example he says:

> Classical political economy seeks to reduce the various fixed and mutually alien forms of wealth to their inner unity by means of analysis and to strip away the form in which they exist independently alongside one another. It seeks to grasp the inner connection in contrast to the multiplicity of outward forms. It therefore reduces rent to surplus profit, so that it ceases to be a specific, *separate* form ... (TSV. III. p.500)

We see, on the other hand, that Marx counts among the best points in *Capital* the fact that he treats '*surplus value independently of its particular* forms as profit, interest, rent, etc.' and comments that 'the treatment of the particular forms by classical political economy, which always mixes them up with the general form, is a regular hash' (Marx to Engels, Aug. 24, 1867, SC. p.180). The same point is reiterated in another occasion:

> That in contrast to *all* former political economy, which *from the very outset* treats the different fragments of surplus value with their fixed forms of rent, profit and interest as already given, I first deal with the general form of surplus value, in which all these fragments are still undifferentiated — in solution, as it were. (Marx to Engels, Jan. 8, 1868 SC. p.186)

We find the same point stated in the *Theories of Surplus Value*:

> All economists share the error of examining surplus-value not as such, in its pure form, but in the particular forms of profit and rent. (TSV. I. p.40)

In all the above quotations Marx is distinguishing himself from political economy on the basis of a point which for him constitutes one of the merits of political economy!

How are we to reconcile these seemingly contradictory judgements? In particular, how are we to reconcile the two above-mentioned lines of criticism we find in Marx?

II. A Synthesis of Marx's Opposing Lines of Criticism

Just as Marx did not leave behind a book of logic or dialectics, he never provided us with a general and comprehensive account of the methodological differences between himself and the political economists. As in his relation with Hegel, Marx's relation to political economy remains subject to divergent interpretations.[4]

However, there is one point where Marx comes closest to a 'grand summation' of his differences with the political economy. The occasion is a long passage in *Theories of Surplus Value*, which is well worth quoting in its entirety:

> Classical political economy seeks to reduce the various fixed and mutually alien forms of wealth to their inner unity by means of analysis and to strip away the form in which they exist independently alongside one another. It seeks to grasp the inner connection in contrast to the multiplicity of outward forms. It therefore reduces rent to surplus profit, so that it ceases to be a specific, *separate* form and is divorced from its apparent source, the land. It likewise divests interest of its independent form and shows that it is a part of profit. In this way it reduces all types of revenue and all independent forms and titles under cover of which the non-workers receive a portion of the value of commodities, to the single form of profit. Profit, however, is reduced to surplus-value since the value of the whole commodity is reduced to labour; the amount of paid labour embodied in the commodity constitutes wages, consequently the surplus over and above it constitutes unpaid labour, surplus labour called forth by capital and appropriated gratis under various titles. Classical political economy occasionally contradicts itself in this analysis. It often attempts directly, leaving out the intermediate links, to carry through the reduction and to prove that the various forms are derived from one and the same source. This is however a necessary consequence of its analytical method, with which criticism and understanding must begin. Classical economy is not interested in elaborating how the various forms come into being, but seeks to reduce them to their unity by means of analysis, because it starts from them as given premises. But this analysis is the necessary prerequisite of genetical presentation, and of the understanding of the real, formative process in its different phases. (TSV. III, p.500)

In the above passage Marx agrees with what he calls the 'analytical' method of political economy. This method involves a reduction of

83

'various fixed and mutually alien forms . . . to their inner unity' and a
stripping away of 'the form in which they exist independently alongside
one another'. Thus the analytical method 'seeks to grasp the inner
connection in contrast to the multiplicity of outward forms'. From
Marx's description it appears that the point of 'analysis' is the overcom-
ing of the independence, the mutual fixity and unrelatedness of various
external forms, and thus the introduction of unity and relatedness to
various apparently independent, external forms. It is clear that this form
of analysis is an indispensable ingredient of any form of theorizing and
conceptualization. Comprehension, in general, involves a unification of
various phenomenal forms into a common essence. Analysis, by introducing an inner connection, a principle of unification, overcomes the
opposition of external forms and leads to the comprehension, the 'grasping' of various phenomena.

Thus the 'general' form of analysis used by classical political economy
cannot be disputed. The point that Marx is raising does not concern this
general form but the particular form followed by political economy. In
other words the dispute is not over 'analysis' and 'abstraction' in general,
but over the *particular manner* of abstraction and analysis carried out by
political economists. This particular manner of analysis can only be
criticized on the grounds that it does not achieve its objective of complete
unification and abstraction, that it falls short of the aim it has set forth
for itself.

Let us now see what Marx perceives as the main defects of the
analytical method of political economy. We may distinguish three points:

a) Political economy carries out the reduction *directly*, by 'leaving out intermediate links' and seeking a *single* source for various forms.
b) Political economy 'is not interested in elaborating how various forms come
into being'.
c) Point (b) above follows from the fact that political economy 'starts from these
[various forms] as given premises'.

These points raise a few problems:

1) What does Marx mean when he says that political economy carries
out the reduction directly, leaving out intermediate links and seeking a
single source? More specifically, (a) what are intermediate links? (b) is
not the reductionism involved in any form of analysis a tracing to a single
source? (c) does not Marx himself reduce various forms of surplus-value
to surplus labour (a single source)?

84

2) What does he mean by saying that political economy is not interested in how various forms come into being? Does this mean that political economy is not interested in the history of forms? Is this a call for an historically determinate analysis? If so, why does Marx reserve this point for a special and separate treatment in the paragraph immediately following the above quoted passage?[5]

In what follows we will try to analyse these questions in the context of Marx's example of how the classical political economists handle the concept of 'profit'.

Political economy reduces various forms of 'non-labour income', e.g. interest and rent, into profit. But profit, for Marx, is merely another form of surplus-value alongside interest and rent under capitalism. Thus political economy has reduced certain forms of surplus-value into another 'single' form of surplus-value, i.e. profit. This procedure would seem to be vacuous and entirely useless if it were not for the fact that profit is not just any form of surplus-value, but a special form.

Let us look at this matter more closely. There are two crucial points raised by Marx's discussion:

a) Interest and rent, reduced to profit by classical political economists, happen to be precisely those forms of surplus-value that have had an historically prior existence, i.e. they are by no means the forms that have been created by capitalism. But at the same time they do subsist under capitalism.
b) Profit is a form of surplus-value that is exclusive to capitalism. It is the specific mode of surplus-value extraction in the capitalist mode of production and as such it is a creation of capitalism. This is not to say that profit had no pre-capitalist existence, as the example of merchant's profit demonstrates.

However, the pre-capitalist form of profit was by no means the dominant form of surplus labour extraction under pre-capitalist conditions. Furthermore, it was mainly restricted to the sphere of circulation rather than production (profit on mercantile capital). If we interpret profit under capitalism in this light, we may conclude that political economy has succeeded in the reduction of various pre-capitalist forms of surplus-value, such as interest and rent, which subsist under capitalism, into the most characteristic form of surplus-value under capitalism, i.e. profit.

Profit, from Marx's point of view, is the most developed form of surplus-value. But it is still distinct from the general form of surplus-value under capitalism. Political economy easily mixes up the analysis of this general form with that of profit.

> Because Adam [Smith] makes what is in substance an analysis of surplus-value, but does not present it explicitly in the form of a definite category, distinct from its special forms, he subsequently mixes it up directly with the further developed form, profit. This error persists with Ricardo and all his disciples. (TSV. I. p.89)

It is obvious that Marx is working with two distinct concepts of 'profit'. These two concepts are:

1) Profit as the general form of surplus-value under capitalism. As such it is identical with surplus-value itself.
2) Profit as a particular form of surplus-value alongside other forms, e.g. 'profit of the enterprise'.[6]

Classical political economy reduces 'non-wage' incomes into profit, but the profit to which these incomes are reduced is itself a particular form (number two above) and not the general form. This procedure is deficient because it 'leaves out the intermediate links' — the forms of retention and preservation of the pre-capitalist forms of surplus labour under capitalism or the forms of subsumption of the pre-capitalist forms under capitalism.

These transitional forms (pre-capitalist or subsumed by capitalism) or 'hybrid' forms are assumed as 'given' by political economy. They are not subjected to analysis. Thus the reasons for their 'coming into being' or 'coming to be' under capitalism are not explored.

Political economy is vindicated in its general approach of reducing forms into their essences. But these essences are bound to evaporate into mere 'existences' of forms if the analysis and abstraction is not carried far enough. In classical political economy, interest and rent are reduced to profit as the essential form of the capitalist extraction of surplus-value. But this form is not analysed in its general form, and therefore appears as a particular form of surplus-value alongside other forms and, thus, at par with them. As a result a manifold of forms is reduced to a single source or essence, but this essence rather than subsuming the multiplicity of forms itself reappears as a mere form alongside the other forms from which it was originally extracted.

The analytical method of political economy is based on the 'form-content' or 'appearance-essence' problematic in such a way that the result of analysis merely reproduces that problematic, i.e. it reproduces the opposition between essence and appearance rather than resolving it. This circumstance leads to a violation of the whole purpose of theorizing. The general laws, instead of explaining the phenomena completely, come to admit of exceptions.

It may be argued that Marx agrees with the analytical procedure of political economy, which involves a movement from phenomenal forms to essences, but that he considers this method as incomplete because it does not continue to advance from the resultant essences to an analysis of forms on the basis of these essences. According to this interpretation all that is required is a reverse movement from essences to forms (the synthetic method). After all, Marx himself approves of the analytical method of political economy as the first stage of scientific comprehension and a prerequisite for 'genetical' or 'dialectical' presentation. The problem with the above interpretation is that it assumes that the essences (or concepts) of political economy and those of Marx are identical and that therefore the whole question is simply a 'more concrete' or a 'more specific' or a 'more historically determinate' application of the concepts of political economy. But as the example we have analysed above demonstrates, the essence (e.g. profit) for political economy is reduced to a mere form by Marx's analysis. Profit as an essence is only an essence for Marx when it is interpreted in a more general way as surplus-value. However, when profit is interpreted as such it is already poles apart from the 'profit as essence' of political economy. Profit as essence has been sublated and subsumed under Marx's concept of surplus-value.

Let us now see if the methodological perspectives of the 1857 Introduction, developed in the previous chapter, shed any light on Marx's different and opposing judgements on political economy.

In the previous chapter we distinguished three concepts of the 'simple' category in Marx's 1857 Introduction, namely S.1, S.2 and S.3. Let us recall that S.1 represented 'simple' relations pertaining to historically original and elemental conditions or general conditions underlying every form of society, S.2 represented simple relations (whether original or carried over from the past) that are subsumed under larger wholes, and finally S.3 represented simple relations pre-supposing the highest degree of development.

For Marx, the classical economists never reach S.3 concepts; they are operating either at the level of S.1 or S.2 concepts. Here are some examples:

A. Ricardo's way of handling the value question clearly aims at S.3 but it does not advance beyond S.2. Ricardo finds in labour the key to the value-relation: he conceives labour as the content or essence of value. But this essence, when reflected back on the phenomenal forms from which it was 'extracted' is reduced to a mere form (although the most determining) alongside other forms: labour now becomes the *main* cause of value but not the *only* one. Thus, labour which seemed to advance to the level of S.3 is pushed back to the S.2 level: a *particular*, though admittedly dominant, form.

B. Adam Smith after stating the law of labour-value in a general form, a semblance of S.3, relegates the regulation of value by labour time to the primitive conditions of society where accumulation of land and capital is absent. Thus, although he aims at S.3, like Ricardo, he finally settles down at S.1. This shows the greater theoretical sophistication of Ricardo compared to Smith, a point Marx often highlights.

C. Ricardo analyses relative surplus value, which is the predominant and characteristic form of surplus labour extraction under capitalism. As in example A above he has discovered the essence. But this essence, by not being advanced to the level of absolute surplus-value (S.3), is reduced to a particular, although prominent, form alongside other forms.

D. Both Smith and Ricardo conceive of surplus-value as profit, i.e. they reduce all non-labour incomes under capitalism, such as rent and interest, to profit. But profit itself is only a particular, although characteristic, form of surplus-value in the capitalist system.

In these examples, the most drastic regression or backward movement occurs in B: the essence, instead of advancing to S.3, moves back to S.1. In the rest of the examples it is hard to see any regression. It seems that Ricardo discovers the essence of the phenomena and sticks to them at this level. After all, what is essence if not the predominant cause underlying diverse phenomena?

The point, as curious as it may seem, is that if essence does not advance beyond itself to the 'whole', a movement which will reduce the essence itself to a mere *moment* of the whole, it regresses to a level below the essence.

It is this regression that explains Marx's other front against political economists, i.e. the criticism by Marx based on political economy's 'false' abstractions, over-generalizations, etc.

What Marx means by lack of abstraction in political economy is the incomplete process of abstraction exemplified by the analytical method. Now it turns out that this same method is responsible for the opposite error of over-generalization and false abstraction.

Marx's criticism of political economy on this front approaches his criticism of 'vulgar economy'.[7] To the extent that political economists had to regress to S.1 they became part of the league of vulgar economists who reduced all determinate and specific economic relations to basic and fundamental principles underlying all forms of the economy.

Let us now summarize the above commentary:

i) Political economy begins from abstract concepts.

ii) Political economists attempt to move from these concepts to essence.

iii) When they succeed in this attempt (the culmination of the analytical method) they arrive at essences, but without form. These essences contradict appearances and phenomenal forms.

iv) In order to resolve this contradiction two paths are open:

iv-a) We may remain at the level of essence, in which case the essence which is in contradiction with phenomenal forms becomes a particular form and is ultimately identified as one of the phenomenal forms from which it was extracted. Or

iv-b) We may move from essence to S.3 which reduces form and content, concept and essence to mere moments of itself.

Steps (i) to (iv-a) constitute the analytical method of political economy. From (iv), thus, two different paths emerge. We will disregard the path moving onwards from (iv-b) and concentrate on the path issuing from (iv-a). This latter path can either lead to stagnation or represent a backward movement since it does not proceed forward. The analytical approach, not having gone far enough to achieve its aim (essence) or, after achieving it, unable to resolve the contradiction between essence and appearance, falls back on to S.1 or S.2.

From this perspective the apparent contradiction between Marx's two different frontal criticisms of political economy is resolved. But one question remains untouched in this argument, a question which we will deal with now by way of conclusion.

Marx often characterizes his method, in contrast to that of political economy, as having analysed surplus-value in its pure form, undisturbed by the phenomenal forms it takes under capitalism such as profit, rent and interest. We have quoted a number of passages from Marx in this chapter elaborating this point. We have also pointed out that there seems to be a contradiction between this judgement of Marx and his praise for political economy for reducing the fixed forms of wealth, and separate income categories, into one form (profit). To be more specific, Marx praises political economists for reducing rent and interest into profit. But he has a more general concept of profit in mind: he is interpreting political economy's profit as his 'surplus-value'. If profit and surplus value can be so identified then Marx's approval of political economy is quite reasonable. But the problem is that these two cannot be identified with each other. For Marx, profit is only one form of surplus-value alongside many others under capitalism.

Why does Marx pretend to be reading 'surplus-value' when the classics say 'profit'?

Profit is the main form of non-labour income under capitalism. By singling out this category political economists arrived at the most characteristic form of surplus-value under capitalism. They discovered the essence of non-labour income under capitalism. As the examples above show this procedure seems to be typical of the political economists: they always succeed in determining the most essential and characteristic form and are led to reduce all other forms to this one.

The political economists at their best discover concepts that capture the most essential and characteristic features of capitalism. Their concepts, far from being general, ahistoric and non-specific, carry all the marks of concrete, historically determinate and specific categories.

On the other hand, Marx himself may be blamed for reducing historically specific and concrete relations into general, ahistoric and fundamental conditions. For example, he reduces rent, interest and profit to surplus-value, and the latter to surplus labour. By trying to postulate an ahistorical category, i.e. surplus labour, is not Marx committing the same error as he attributes to political economists and, indeed, to vulgar economists? Marx reproaches political economists for not analysing the value-form, i.e. the form of labour as it appears in exchange. But in the case of surplus-value, is not Marx reducing all non-labour income to surplus labour? Is he not thus ignoring the form of surplus labour, i.e. the form that surplus labour assumes under capitalism?

The sharpest edge of Marx's criticism of political economy is now facing Marx himself. Does Marx meet this challenge? We cannot answer this question at this stage. Here we will limit ourselves to the following comments.

90

It is obvious that Marx objects to the tendency among political economists to rely on concepts that represent historically prior relations or fundamental conditions true for all times and places (a tendency that becomes the distinguishing mark of vulgar economy). At the same time he himself constructs some very generic concepts that can be construed as representing eternal conditions of production and economy. Is there a difference between the generality and abstractness of concepts in Marx and those of other economists?

There must be such a difference, or else the whole edifice of Marx's critique falls to the ground.

Footnotes to Chapter Three

1. There are many comments on the method and views of classical economists, particularly Smith and Ricardo, throughout the three volumes of *Capital*. But it is in Marx's *Theories of Surplus-Value* (TSV. I, II & III), the so-called fourth volume of *Capital*, that we find extensive commentary and criticism not only of classical political economy but also Mercantilism, Physiocracy and post-Ricardians. In this chapter we will rely on both *Capital* and *Theories* as well as other relevant texts such as the *1857 Introduction* and Marx's correspondence.
2. Ricardo, D., *On the Principles of Political Economy and Taxation*, Third Edn., published 1821 (Ricardo, 1951), pp.11-51.
3. In Chapter 1 of the *Principles* Ricardo develops his 'pure' labour theory of value in Sections 1 and III. In Section IV he considers the effect of fixed capital on the determination of values by pure labour quantities. His argument is fundamentally, that pure labour values determine exchange ratios only under the assumption of equal durability of capital in all branches of production and that if this durability is not the same, unequal rates of profit will accrue to different sectors. As a result price ratios cannot approximate labour ratios. For greater detail on these exceptions to the law of value and their connection with Marx's transformation problem see Shamsavari (1987), sec. IV; also see Chapter Twelve below.
4. See Chapter Two above.
5. Marx ends the above-quoted passage with the following sentence: "Finally a failure, a deficiency of classical political economy is the fact that it does not conceive the *basic form of capital*, i.e. production designed to appropriate other people's labour, as a *historical* form but as a *natural form* of social production; the analysis carried out by the classical economists themselves paves the way for the refutation of this conception." Marx devotes a few paragraphs to elaborate on this final point.
6. 'Profit of enterprise' is that portion of profit of an industrial capitalist that is left over after the deduction of the interest, assuming that the industrial capitalist uses borrowed money capital. According to Marx in relation to this capitalist 'property in capital is represented . . . by the lender. The interest that he pays to the lender appears therefore as a part of gross profit that accrues to property in capital as such. In contrast to this, the part of profit that falls to the active capitalist, now as profit of enterprise, appears to derive exclusively from the operations or functions that he performs with the capital in the reproduction process, especially therefore the functions that he performs as an entrepreneur in industry or trade.' (C. III. p.497)
7. Marx characterizes the work of 'vulgar economists' in contrast to the classical economists in the following terms:

". . . by classical political economy I mean all the economists who, since the time of W. Petty, have investigated the real internal framework of bourgeois relations of production, as opposed to the vulgar economists who only flounder around within the apparent framework of those relations, ceaselessly ruminate on the materials long since provided by scientific political economy, and seek there plausible explanations of the crudest phenomena for the domestic purposes of the bourgeoisie. Apart from this, the vulgar economists confine themselves to systematizing in a pedantic way, and proclaiming for everlasting truths, the banal and complacent notions held by the bourgeois agents of production about their own world, which is to them the best possible one." (C.I. pp.174-5, f.n.)

CHAPTER FOUR

THE HEGELIAN FOUNDATIONS

In this chapter we will attempt to lay bare the roots of Marx's methodological perspectives in Hegel's philosophy and logic. The exposition in this chapter aims not only to show the profound influence of Hegel on Marx but also to lay the foundations for the analyses in the rest of this work. This chapter, however, is not intended as an introduction to Hegel's thought, as it is strongly focused on those aspects of Hegelian doctrine that are particularly relevant for our purposes.[1]

I. THE DIALECTICS OF THE GENERAL AND THE PARTICULAR

In Chapter Two we have seen how Marx criticized generic concepts and argued for a deeper level of conceptualization in theorizing about social forms of production. Our conclusions were as follows:

1. The generic concept is empty or else it is not a true generality but a particular;
2. Production should be conceived as a totality, irreducible to general features that all social forms of production have in common (i.e. the so-called 'pre-conditions of production');
3. These pre-conditions instead of being *premises* are rather the historic products of concrete social forms of production. The process of social production converts both the natural and the historical pre-conditions into moments of the totality;
4. The moments of the totality can be conceived as having two modes of relationship to the totality: on the one hand they can function as passive ingredients of the whole and thus may be determined by the operation of the whole system; on the other hand they can have an active relationship with the totality, in which case they form determinant moments and, in a way, can be identified with the whole system.

In this section we will explore the roots of Marx's critique in Hegel's works. But before proceeding I wish to refer to the critique of the generic concept by a modern philosopher, Ernst Cassirer (Cassirer 1923).

According to Cassirer the only presumption in developing a generic

93

concept is 'the existence of things in their inexhaustible multiplicity, and the power of mind to select from this wealth of particular existences those features that are *common* to several of them' (Cassirer 1923, p.4). This process of determination of the essential features common to several particular objects 'leads of itself to *abstraction*'. This abstraction is pure and free from 'all admixture of dissimilar elements'. Cassirer believes that this mode of abstraction has its own 'peculiar merit'. This merit consists in that

> it never destroys or imperils the *unity* of the ordinary view of the world. The concept does not appear as something foreign to sensuous reality, but forms a *part* of this reality; it is a selection of what is immediately contained in it. (Cassirer 1923, p.5)

The pitfall of the generic concept, which 'forms a part of reality', is that it replaces the 'original sensuous whole' and in so doing 'claims to characterize and explain the whole'. However, according to Cassirer 'the traditional rule ... for the formation of generic concepts contains in itself no guarantee' that the features contained in the concept will be the *essential moments* of the living whole. The requirement of the 'act of negation' is to yield a higher concept that captures the essential moment and not an 'arbitrarily chosen part': 'the higher concept is to make the lower intelligible by setting forth in abstraction the *ground* of its special form' (Cassirer 1923, p.6). What is required of this higher level of conceptualization is thus to generate concepts which capture the essence of a concrete whole in such a way that the multiplicity of forms become mere moments or particular instances of the general concept:

> The ideal of *scientific* concept here appears in opposition to the schematic general presentation which is expressed by a mere *word*. The genuine concept does not disregard the peculiarities and particularities which it holds under it, but seeks to show the *necessity* of the occurrence and the connection of just these particularities. What it gives us is a universal *rule* for the connection of the particulars themselves. (Cassirer 1923, pp.19-20)

Let us now turn to Hegel. In both versions of the *Logic*, Hegel explicitly deals with the question of the generic concept.[2] At this point, however, I will only refer to a discussion on Aristotle in Hegel's *Lectures on the History of Philosophy*[3] where this question is discussed in most interesting and graphic terms. Hegel is discussing Aristotle's theory of 'soul'.[4] He begins by describing the latter's characterizations of the three determinations of soul, i.e. the nutrient or vegetable, the sensitive and the intelligent. The nutrient soul, when it exists by itself, is to be found among plants. When this soul is also 'capable of sense-perception, it is the animal soul; and when at once nutrient, sensitive and intelligent, it is the mind of man'. He then goes on to say:

> Man has thus three natures united in himself; a thought which is also expressed in modern Natural Philosophy by saying that a man is also both an animal and a plant, and which is directed against the division and separation of the differences in these forms. (LHP. v.2, p.184)

If these three 'souls' or natures were found *separately* and on their own in *three distinct* species, the question that Hegel is about to raise would not arise. In fact we find only one of these natures individualized in a distinct species, i.e. the nutrient soul (plant life). Both animal and human lives represent a combination of 'souls'. In particular, human life has all the 'three natures united' in it.

To conceive of, for instance, human life as a combination of these three natures raises the question of the articulation of these natures, i.e. the structured interrelations between them. Is human life a simple coexistence of these souls such that each has a separately defined function without any deeper *inner* connection? If not, the conception of human life as a combination of these three natures raises serious questions about the possibility of an 'analytical' approach which would involve complete separation of these souls:

> The only question (and it is Aristotle who raises it) is how far these, as parts, are separable. As to what concerns more nearly the relation of the three souls, as they may be termed (though they are increasingly thus distinguished), Aristotle says of them, with perfect truth, that we need look for no one soul in which all these are found, and which in a definite and simple form is conformable with any one of them. (LHP. v.2, p.185)

Aristotle's standpoint is profoundly anti-reductionist: there is no one 'soul' in which all the three natures are combined in such a way that any one component nature is conformable with the analytic (generic) determination of each nature, i.e. in abstraction from the combination, 'in a definite and simple form'. This means that, for instance, the sensitive soul as found in human life cannot be simply assimilated to the sensitive soul found in animal life. The existence of the intelligent soul in human life does change the nature of the sensitive soul, in other words the presence of the former cannot remain indifferent to the latter. Our sense experience, for example, cannot remain unaffected by our thoughts nor, of course, can our emotions be prevented from influencing our thinking. Thus the intelligent has always some presence in the sensitive and vice versa. Even the most abstract scientific concepts retain some degree of 'sensuousness'. For instance, any such scientific concept must be capable of being communicated at the very least to other scientists through one form or another of human communication, these forms all possessing a minimum of sense-content. Thus the sensitive soul found in human life cannot be 'simply' reduced to the one found in animal life.

This anti-reductionist view of Aristotle leads Hegel to characterize Aristotle's thought as truly 'speculative' as opposed to formal and logical when he says: 'This is a profound observation, by means of which truly speculative thought marks itself out from the thought that is merely logical and formal'.

He continues with a further example from Aristotle:

> Similarly among figures only the triangle and the other definite figures, like the square, parallelogram, etc. are truly anything; for what is common to them, the universal figure is an empty thing of thought, a mere abstraction. On the other hand, the triangle is the first, the truly universal figure, which appears also in the square, etc. as the figure which can be led back to the simplest determinations. Therefore, on the one hand, the triangle stands alongside of the square, the pentagon, etc. as a particular figure, but — and this is Aristotle's main contention — it is the truly universal figure. (LHP. v.2, p.185)

Hegel's above statement can be analysed into three points as follows: a) the generic concept of a geometric figure based on the common characteristics of such figures is empty ('a mere abstraction') and the triangle is definitely not this common denominator; b) the triangle, however, is the 'first, the truly universal figure' in the sense that other figures can be analysed back into it as their first building block; c) at the same time the triangle itself is a particular figure alongside other figures. Thus the triangle is said to have two separate existences, as a universal and as a particular. How are we to interpret this double determination of the triangle?

Immediately following this discussion of the triangle Hegel goes back to the example of 'souls'. He states that 'in the same way the soul must not be sought for as an abstraction'. Soul is not a generality, a common denominator: it exists as a particular. What is the nature of this particular which at the same time has a claim over universality? Hegel characterizes this in a variety of ways, as the following quotation shows:

> ... in the animate being the nutritive and the sensitive soul are included in the

intelligent, but only as its object or its potentiality; similarly, the nutritive soul . . . is also present in the sensitive soul, but likewise only as being implicit in it, or as the universal. Or the lower soul inheres only in the higher, as a predicate in a subject; and this mere ideal is not to be ranked very high, as is the case in formal thought; that which is for itself is, on the contrary, the never-ceasing return into itself, to which actuality belongs. (LHP. v.2, p.185)

However characterized it is clear that there is a double determination of the soul: i) the soul as object, potentiality, abstract universality, predicate in a subject, a lower form and ii) the soul as 'actuality', a truly universal principle. Soul in the first sense is an 'ideal' existence, or ideal 'moment'. Hegel points out that this 'ideal' must not be ranked very high. In the second sense soul is concrete, self-contained, actual as it 'is for itself', representing 'the never-ceasing return into self'. Here is how Hegel sums up his discussion:

Aristotle's meaning is therefore this: an empty universal is that which does not itself exist, or is not itself species. All that is universal is in fact real as particular, individual, existing for another. But that universal is real, in that by itself, without further change, it constitutes its first species, and when further developed it belongs not to this, but to a higher stage. (LHP. v.2, p.186)

Hegel's critique of the generic concept can be summarized in the following way. A generic concept is either empty or, if anything, it is a 'particular, individual, existing for another' — a condition of lack of independence, inwardness, completeness and, ultimately, necessity. Thus it does not have full 'reality', it is not 'actual'. That universal is real which by itself forms its 'first species' and upon further development no longer belongs to this first species but to a 'higher stage'. One may interpret Hegel as saying that, for instance, the nutritive soul as the common denominator of vegetable, animal and human life is an empty abstraction. As a reality, however, nutritive soul, i.e. plant life, is to be found as a particular 'existing for another', for animal or human life (e.g. to be used by them as food). Beyond this one can say that the nutritive soul in fact forms a first species, namely plant life. A development of this form of life into animal life, for instance, essentially preserves this soul, not as an appendage but as a transformed being in active relation with the sensitive soul. This relation, however, can be interpreted in two ways. The nutritive soul becomes part of animal or human life in the sense that both animals and human beings need to eat in order to reproduce themselves as living organisms. In this sense the nutritive soul stands in passive relationship to the sensitive or intelligent soul. As such it is an

97

ideal moment, still existing for another.

There is a second interpretation of this relationship, this 'belonging' to a higher order: the sensitive soul is itself a higher development of the nutritive soul in the same way as the intelligent soul is a development of the sensitive soul. In this relationship the lower form is no longer subordinate to a higher but through a process of development has become the very essence and principle of activity and subjectivity of the new form. Thus Hegel's critique revolves around two points:

> i) The generic concept, the common element is not a true universality as it refers to a particular that stands in passive relationship to universality.
> ii) True universality, which is a higher development of the generic concept, is the active essence, the principle of subjectivity, informing and determining the lower forms.

As this double determination of universality is closely related to the idea of development, I will briefly discuss Hegel's view of development.

> In order to comprehend what development is, what may be called two different states must be distinguished. The first is known as capacity, power, what I call being-in-itself . . .; the second principle is that of being-for-itself. (LHP v.1, pp.20-1)

Hegel elucidates the first state by the following example. If one claims that 'man is by nature rational' this means that he is so 'only inherently or in embryo'. 'In this sense, reason, understanding, imagination, will, are possessed from birth or even from the mother's womb'. In other words, the statement that 'man is by nature rational' is only true in an abstract, one-sided way, i.e. rationality exists in man only potentially, as being-in-itself. This abstractness, however, is crucial: 'But while the child only has capacity or the actual possibility of reason, it is just the same as if he had no reason . . .'. While the capacity to become rational is an essential feature of development, in itself and by itself it is not just incomplete, it is simply a 'nothing'.

The second state or principle of development refers to the actualization of what is potential or only implicit. Thus:

> . . . through the becoming objective of this implicit being, man first becomes for himself; he is made double, is retained and not changed into another. (LHP. v.1, p.21)

Although the first state of development is reduced by Hegel to a 'nothing' when it stands 'on its own' ('being-in-itself') in the second state this 'nothing' coming to 'its own' is, in effect, 'everything': 'he is made double, is retained and not changed into another'. Thus the transition from one state to another does not involve the suppression or replacement of the first state but its retention, its liberation from oblivion or 'nothingness'. On the other hand one may underestimate the significance of the second state by saying that 'it was all there in the first place' and thus there is no change or development. But this would be wrong:

> But even though man, who in himself is rational, does not at first seem to have got much further on since he became rational for himself — what is implicit having merely retained itself — the difference is quite enormous: no new content has been produced, and yet this form of being for self makes all the difference. The whole variation in the development of world history is founded on this difference. (LHP. v.1, p.21)

Following this passage Hegel refers to the existence of slavery in the East and its absence in the West, exploring the implications of this difference for the diverging patterns of development: the fact that in the West the freedom of man was explicit while in the East it was implicit (as in Eastern slavery) made 'an enormous difference in their condition'; he then continues:

> All knowledge, and learning, science, and even commerce have no other object than to draw out what is inward or implicit and thus to become objective. (LHP. v.1, p.22)

Hegel, however, does not lose sight of the importance of the 'implicit' in spite of all the significance he attaches to the second state:

> Because which is implicit comes into existence, it certainly passes into change, yet it remains one and the same, for the whole process is dominated by it. (LHP. v.1, p.22)

Here he gives the example of 'the plant'. He says that the plant 'does not lose itself in mere indefinite change'. From the germ to the fruit and thus the new germ, the process of development is dominated by 'the contradiction of being only implicit and yet not desiring so to be'. (LHP. v.1, p.22)

At this point Hegel makes an important distinction between the natural world and the mind, which will be a recurrent theme throughout this chapter. As the example of the plant shows, seeds lead to fruit and thus to new seed. In a way one may say that the result is a 'return to the first condition'. But surely the 'produced seed' is different from the 'sown seed'.

> With nature it certainly is true that the subject which commenced and the matter which forms the end are two separate units, as in the case of seed and fruit. The doubling process has apparently the effect of separating into two things that which in content is the same. Thus in animal life the parent and the young are different individuals although their nature is the same. (LHP. v.1, p.22)

This doubling process in nature produces two different entities. One can say that the internal contradiction between the implicit and the explicit in the organic world leads to an objective external differentiation and doubling.³ It is otherwise with Mind, according to Hegel.

> In Mind it is otherwise: it is consciousness and therefore it is free, uniting in itself the beginning and the end. As with the germ in nature, Mind indeed resolves itself back into unity after constituting itself another. But what is in itself becomes for Mind and thus arrives at being for itself. The fruit and the seed newly contained within it on the other hand, do not become for the original germ, but for us alone; in the case of Mind both factors not only are implicitly the same in character, but there is a being for the other and at the same time a being for self. That for which the "other" is, is the same as that "other". The development of Mind lies in the fact that its going forth and separation constitutes its coming to itself. (LHP. v.1, pp.22-3)

The above discussion clearly shows that Hegel puts the dialectic of the general and the particular in the context of development, particularly historical development and the progress of Mind. This same dialectic lies at the root of Marx's D-model as developed in Chapter Two above. The following quotation from Hegel's *Philosophy of Right* should clarify this point:

> Every self-consciousness knows itself (i) as universal, as the potentiality of abstracting from everything determinate, and (ii) as particular, with a determinate object, content, and aim. Still, both these moments are only abstractions; what is concrete and true (and everything true is concrete) is the universality which has the particular as its opposite, *but the particular which by its reflection into itself has been equalized with the universal.* (Ph.R. p.23, Additions, emphasis added)

Let us recall that in the D-model each element or part of a totality exists in two different modes, a passive and an active one. In their passive role

100

these elements are subordinate to the whole, are 'moments', 'particulars'. In their active mode, by contrast, these elements determine the totality and although in this mode they are still particulars they rise above particularity and become universal.

Let us examine this question more closely. Since the nineteenth century, sociology has gradually come to accept the view that a society is bigger than the sum of its constituent elements, i.e. individuals. One can characterize this viewpoint as holistic causality or determination by wholes. As opposed to this we have determination by parts. Now the very idea of determination by wholes is very abstract but has the advantage of being non-reductionist. On the other hand determination by parts is more concrete, more intuitive but has the disadvantage of being mechanistic and reductionist. But these two principles are direct opposites only on the assumption that wholes and parts are conceived in absolute separation from each other, a separation which is at the foundation of analytical method. If instead wholes and parts are defined in relation to each other, then the fixed opposition between the two forms of causality disappears.

If parts are defined non-mechanistically as parts of a whole (as Marx defines production and distribution in *1857 Introduction*, for instance), the possibility of a one-way determination by any part (e.g. production or economy) is ruled out, because such a mechanical system of causality is based on the separability of parts from wholes and their unambiguous definition purely on their own. In other words if, for instance, distribution is not defined in isolation from production and in fact is conceived as 'inside' it, then it is nonsensical to say that, for instance, distribution determines (in the sense of one-way causation) production or vice versa, since such a statement amounts to saying distribution determines 'itself'.

Thus the notion of mechanical causality fails to make sense when parts are not defined in complete separation from wholes. On the other hand a form of holistic causality (e.g. Althusser's 'structural causality') that gives the supreme power of determination to the abstract whole remains as mechanistic as classical causality since it is an empty whole or structure that is engaged in a one-way determination.

It is only when the whole is concrete in the sense defined by Hegel, i.e. a concrete defined in relation to particularity (but not in absolute opposition to it) that we may conceive of a form of causality that overcomes the problems of mechanical as well as holistic causality. The D-model represents a particular approach to the resolution of the fixed opposition between the two forms of causality.

101

The interchange between cause and effect, parts and wholes, content and form, particular and universal is at the heart of Hegel's dialectics, though not in an interactionist, transactionist sense which keeps these pairs in self-external existence and merely allows a two-way form of causation.

II. HEGEL ON THEORIES OF KNOWLEDGE

For Hegel truth is a universal and not a particular, although it does contain particularity — a particularity 'which by its reflection into itself has been equalized with the universal'. In the same way truth is also concrete and not abstract although it contains abstraction as a moment. Similarly truth is immediate as opposed to mediate, although it involves mediation to the highest degree. Finally truth is necessary but it contains maximum freedom.

These ideas are fully explored in Hegel's *Logic*, which is the subject of the next two sections in this chapter. But in order to appreciate Hegel's concerns we need to know how Hegel evaluates the alternative approaches to the question of knowledge existing in his time. Hegel devotes considerable space in his (Encyclopaedia) *Logic* to this question (EL. pp.50-121). There he distinguishes three 'attitudes of thought towards the objective world'. The first attitude is the *metaphysical* method. The second is discussed in two sections, the first of which refers to the *empirical* school and the second to the *critical* philosophy of Kant. We will shortly see why Hegel classifies these two otherwise quite different approaches to the problem of knowledge together, but since 'analysis' is common to both I will refer to the second attitude as the *analytical* method. Finally the third attitude is the *intuitive* (or immediate) method. In what follows I will give a brief description of the first and the third method and a more detailed account of the analytical method.

A. The Metaphysical Method

The first attitude to knowledge refers to metaphysical thinking — an attitude whose method involves 'no doubts and no sense of contradiction in thought . . . ' It is based on the belief that 'reflection is the means of ascertaining the truth . . .' (EL. p.50). In other words thinking about an object is the sole means of obtaining knowledge about that object. A faith in the transparency of the external world to reflection is the fundamental assumption of the metaphysical approach. According to

Hegel 'philosophy in its first stages, all the sciences, and even the daily action and movement of consciousness, live in this faith' (EL. p.50). Hegel identifies three problems in this method:

1. The laws and forms of thought are in a state of isolation from each other, they are 'cut off from their connexion, their solidity'. Each such law or form is considered to be 'valid by itself and capable of serving as a predicate of truth' (EL. p.51). Thus truth is to be established by supplying a series of predicates that are distinct and separate from each other, without internal cohesion.

> But attribution is no more than an external reflection about the object: the predicates by which the object is to be determined are supplied from the resources of picture-thought and are applied in a mechanical way. (EL. p.53, Additions)

Pictorial thinking is the lowest level of thought: distinct and discrete objects are perceived on the basis of sensation. No necessary connections apart from the ones directly supplied by the senses (e.g. a temporal succession of distinct events) are established between objects. This is why when an object becomes the subject of examination this process does not take the form of concept-formation, i.e. the examination of the object in its own self without external additions; rather it uses the method of attribution and external reflection.

2. 'The metaphysical system adopted a wrong criterion'. Hegel states that the object of the metaphysicians were totalities which belong to reason but that 'they were derived or assumed from popular conception' (EL. p.54). This criterion was wrong because it sought validation of truth not from reason itself but from popular ideas which thus remained uncriticized.

3. The metaphysical system 'turned into Dogmatism'. This dogmatism was based on the following foundation:

> When our thought never ranges beyond narrow and rigid terms, we are forced to assume that of two contrary assertions . . . the one must be true and the other false. (EL. p.54)

In spite of these faults the metaphysical school had an advantage compared to the later empiricist school and critical philosophy: in the metaphysical approach thought and reality are united, i.e. there is no unbridgeable gulf separating the subjective and the objective.

> The metaphysical systems took the laws and forms of thought to be the fundamental laws and forms of things. They assumed that to think a thing was the means of finding its very self and nature: and to that extent they occupied a higher ground than the Critical Philosophy of later times. (EL. p.51)

Yet in spite of the fact that their lack of awareness of the 'antithesis of subjective and objective' led them to make statements 'possessing genuinely philosophical and speculative character' they never managed to go beyond 'finite categories, or the stage when the antithesis is still unresolved' (EL. p.50).

Hegel's view of the 'advance' in knowledge is by no means 'linear-progressive' — he recognizes the fact that although the analytical method proved to be superior to the metaphysical, the latter had a higher intuition of truth. Marx's evaluation of Mercantilism, Physiocracy and the classical political economy also follows the same pattern, as we shall see (Chapter Ten).

B. The Analytical Method

Hegel discusses both the empirical school and critical philosophy under one heading. However, as mentioned earlier, we will discuss these two schools in separate sections.

1. The Empirical School

Hegel praises the empirical school in the following way:

> In Empiricism lies the great principle that whatever is true must be in the actual world and present to sensation. This principle contradicts that everlasting 'ought to be' which puffs up reflection to treat the actual present with scorn, and to point to a scene beyond — a scene that has no existence or locality except in the understanding of those who talk of it. (EL. p.65)

Thus as opposed to the metaphysical and the common-sense approach, the empirical school is concerned with 'reality' and not with 'imagined worlds'. Hegel affirms that philosophy has this much in common with empiricism — it 'recognizes only what is; having nothing to do with what merely ought to be and what is thus confessed not to exist' (EL. pp.65-6).

> On the subjective side, too, it is right to notice the valuable principle of freedom involved in Empiricism. For the main lesson of Empiricism is that man must see for himself and feel that he is present in those facts of knowledge which he has to accept. (EL. p.66)

104

Empiricism represented a powerful antidote to the metaphysical view, which was caught up in the 'vain world beyond' with its 'mirages and phantasms of the abstract understanding'. Therefore empiricism succeeded in gaining 'a fully, self-sufficing phase of truth' — 'that firm and fast support so much missed in the old metaphysic' (EL. p.66, Additions).

Following the above positive evaluation of empirical school he deals with the problems of this school.

Empiricism 'being in its facts limited to the finite sphere' denies the existing of anything outside the senses. It uses the metaphysical categories of matter, force, etc. and forms conclusions on their basis 'all the while unaware that it contains metaphysic'. It uses metaphysical categories 'in a style utterly uncritical and unconscious' (EL. p.66). In this school sensations represent the medium through which concepts are generated and this is what Hegel considers to be the 'failure of empiricism'. This failure arises from the way empiricism uses sensations to obtain knowledge. The method employed is that of 'analysis'.

> In sensation we have a group made up of many elements or attributes which we are expected to peel off one by one, like the coats of an onion. Now, what is the meaning of this process? We disintegrate and take to pieces these attributes which have coalesced, and we add nothing but our own act of disintegration. Yet analysis is the process from the immediacy of sensation to thought: those attributes, which the object analysed contains in perfect union, receive the form of universality by being separated. Empiricism labours under a delusion, if it supposes that, while analysing the objects, it leaves them as they were: it really transforms the concrete into an abstract. And as a consequence of this change the living thing must die: life can exist only in the concrete unit. (EL. p.67, Additions)

Hegel's dispute with empiricism is not over the relevance of analysis for knowledge but its function in the empiricist method. He emphasizes that analysis starts from the concrete and that this represents a 'considerable advantage' over the metaphysical method.

> Not that we can do without this division [abstraction, separation], if it is our intention to comprehend. Mind itself is an inherent division. The error lies in forgetting that this is only one-half of the process, and that the main point is the reunion of what has been divided. (EL. p.67, Additions)

Thus Hegel, in words strongly reminiscent of Marx's criticism of the analytical method of political economy, states clearly that analysis is essential for knowledge. The problem is not with analysis itself but with the way we deal with the results of analysis. The results of analysis (abstract concepts) are used in the empirical school in the same way as the discrete 'facts' are handled in the metaphysical school: they are related to each other in an 'external' manner without representing necessary connections:

> ... both modes of philosophising have the same method: both proceed from data or assumptions, which they accept as ultimate fact. (EL. p.68, Additions)

> ... Empiricism reaches so far as the perception of changes in succession and of objects in juxtaposition or co-existence; but it represents no necessary connexion. (EL. p.69)

The above is a criticism of Hume, as further discussion on the same page reveals:

> Hume founds his remarks on the truth of the empirical element, on feeling and sensation, and proceeds to attack universal truths and laws, because they do not derive their authority from sense-perception.

British classical empiricism from Bacon to Locke had laid a foundation according to which our sense experiences from the external world were the sole criteria for truth, for valid knowledge. Hume took over this idea and attempted to find a philosophical basis for empiricism. He tried to ground universal ideas and notions such as causality in sense experience. He conceived this relationship basically as a linear-temporal one in which the cause precedes the effect, and the effect follows the cause. He offered no criteria for establishing this relationship as a universal concept beyond the mere fact that repeated experience of an effect following a cause is the only basis for the idea of causality.

If sensation is made the sole criterion of truth then the certainty of an external world, which presumably is the source of these sense experiences, is put into doubt. If our knowledge of an external reality is based on subjective experience given by our senses, then how do we know that an external reality exists? What is the criterion for distinguishing between sensations that are presumably caused by external influences and those that are internally caused (e.g. feelings of hunger)?

Berkeley's philosophy was thus a logical culmination of this empiricist approach to knowledge. Berkeley, basing his work on the teachings of the empiricists in a manner that was more radical than Hume's scepticism, concluded that there was no way to establish an external reality from sense experience and therefore the certainty of an objective external reality was in doubt.

It is facile to dismiss Berkeley as a subjective idealist who does not believe in external world. I think he never doubted the existence of such a world. His views must be looked at in the context of the development of British classical empiricism. The truth contained in his philosophy, I believe, is that the objectivity of any reality cannot be established independently of the experiencing subject.[6]

This is precisely the point where Kant's critical philosophy finds its justification.

2. Critical Philosophy

Kant's greatest contribution was to shift the emphasis of the theory of knowledge from the source of knowledge to the knowing subject itself.[7] In his first Critique i.e. Critique of Pure Reason[8] Kant, in opposition to empiricism, which conceived of thinking as a passive process, emphasized the activity, the spontaneity of human consciousness. Whether at the level of intuition or comprehension, human thinking has an innate ability to organize and construct the object of experience in a way that it becomes capable of being experienced. The object of experience is by no means an immediate reality given to thought but is essentially a product of thought. At the level of pure intuition, for instance, to intuit anything is to intuit it in space and time. If we consider spatial intuition, things are intuited as either 'inner' or 'outer'. The ability to distinguish between these two must be inherent in human mind in order to lead to the experience of something as external to the mind, or internal. In other words what is assumed in the popular conception as an obvious fact — that we can distinguish between a cat that we 'see' climbing a tree and the idea of a cat that may spring to our mind without seeing an actual cat — is based on the fact that it is our mind that makes such distinction possible. What we perceive as a simple distinction between the inner and the outer is not a self-evident fact imposed by the objective world but is based on our ability to distinguish between the inner and the outer.

Similarly when we think of categories such as identity, difference, causality, etc. we may conceive them as being objectively given to thought. This was the error of empiricism which led to Hume's agnosticism and Berkeley's idealism. It was in fact these two philosophies that highlighted the inherent contradiction of an empiricist approach to knowledge and exposed the falsity of the starting point: the passivity of the mind. Kant attempted to show that these categories are innate in

107

human mind. Thus Kant's response to Hume, who asserted the contingency of causality, was that the latter had adopted a wrong criterion: causality is not deduced from the observation of external events but is inherent in human mind. The ability of human mind to order things in time accounts for its conception of causality.

Kant's position, however, was inherently faulty. Being a radical response to Hume and Berkeley it drifted to the other extreme and ultimately reproduced the classical dualism in another form. For Hume, for instance, causality could only be based on sense perception. For Kant it was innate in the mind. Hume and especially Berkeley ended up with an uncertainty of the knowability of the objective world. Kant ended up by assuming that we can only know phenomena, i.e. the very appearances that are capable of organization by human thought, and not 'things-in-themselves'.

Hegel, while praising Kant for his emphasis on the activity of thought, reproaches him for not carrying his critical analysis one step further to the knowledge of things-in-themselves, for stopping short at the level of phenomena.

This is how Hegel assesses the contribution of critical philosophy of Kant:

> If . . . it is characteristic of free thought to allow no assumptions to pass unquestioned, the old metaphysicians were not independent thinkers. They accepted their categories as they were, without further trouble, as a sort of *a priori datum*, not yet investigated by reflection. The Critical Philosophy reversed this. Kant undertook to examine how far the forms of thought were capable of assisting the knowledge of truth. In particular he demanded a criticism of the faculty of cognition as preliminary to its exercise. That is a fair demand, if it mean[s] that the forms of thought must be made an object of knowledge. Unfortunately there soon creeps in the misconception of seeking knowledge before you know, — the error of refusing to enter water until you have learnt to swim. (EL. p.71, Additions)
>   In common with Empiricism the Critical Philosophy assumes that experience affords the one sole foundation for cognitions. But a cognition, as it holds, does not express the truth, and means only a knowledge of the phenomenon or appearance. (EL. p.69)

The empirical and critical schools also share aspects in common with the analytical approach. Let us recall that Marx's main quarrel with political economy is about the latter's so-called 'analytical method'. Marx's characterizations of this method directly correspond to Hegel's pronouncements on what he calls 'analytic cognition'. Before presenting Hegel's summary of analytic cognition, let us discuss an example from Hegel, where he criticizes Kant for his analytical method.

Hegel criticizes Kant for the way in which the latter deduces the concept of matter from the forces of attraction and repulsion. In Kant, these forces 'conceived as forces' are 'regarded as self-subsistent and therefore as not connected with each other through their own nature; that is, they are conceived not as moments, each of which is supposed to pass into the other, but rather as fixed in their opposition to each other' (LL. pp.178-9). 'Kant's method in the deduction of matter from these forces, which he calls a *construction*, when looked at more closely does not deserve this name . . .' (LL. p.179).

Hegel goes on to say:

> For Kant's method is basically analytical, not constructive. He presupposes the idea of matter and then asks what forces are required to maintain the determinations he presupposed. (LL. pp.179-180)

Thus Kant 'presupposes the idea of matter' and does not criticize it. He relates matter to elements, 'forces' outside matter. He does not conceive of matter as having these forces '*contained in it*'.

> It is evident that this is the method of a cognition which reflects on experience, which first *perceives* the determinations in a phenomenon, then makes these the foundation, and for their co-called *explanation* assumes corresponding *basic elements* or *forces* which are supposed to produce these determinations of the phenomenon. (LL. p.180)
>
> . . . Kant's exposition of the opposed forces is analytic; and whereas matter is supposed to be derived from its elements, it is presented throughout the entire discourse as already formed and constituted. (LL. pp.183-4)

Thus matter, in this conception, is presented 'as already formed and constituted', whereas it is 'supposed to be derived from its elements'. The forces attributed to matter are not immanent, internal to matter. Therefore, matter cannot be truly derived from these forces.

Marx criticizes the approach of political economy to value on similar grounds. Political economy takes the concept of value and relates it to an element, a force outside value, i.e. labour. Value is presented 'as already formed and constituted', whereas it is 'supposed to be derived from' labour. Political economy takes value as a 'give premise' and then seeks its cause in labour. Throughout the entire analysis of value the value-relation is presupposed. Political economy does not, and is not able to, derive value from labour, as witnessed by Smith's wavering on this question and Ricardo's 'exceptions' to the law of value.

Let us now see how Hegel characterizes 'analytic cognition':

The distinguishing feature of analytic cognition is already defined in the fact that as the first premise of the whole syllogism, analytic cognition does not as yet contain mediation; it is the immediate communication of the Notion and does not yet contain otherness, and in it the activity empties itself out of its negativity.... The determination, therefore, brought about by this relation, is the form of simple *identity*, of *abstract universality*. Accordingly, analytic cognition has in general this identity for its principle; and transition into an other, the connexion of different terms, is excluded from itself and from its activity. (LL. p.787)

If we look now more closely at analytic cognition, we see that it starts from a *presupposed*, and therefore individual, *concrete* subject matter.... (LL. p.787)

Now since analytic cognition is the transformation indicated above, it does not pass through any further *middle term*; the determination is in so far *immediate* and has just this meaning, to be peculiar to the object and in itself to belong to it, and therefore, to be apprehended from it without any subjective mediation. (LL. p.788)

It has been remarked that analysis becomes synthetic when it comes to deal with *determinations* that are no longer *posited* by the problems themselves. But the general transition from analytic to synthetic cognition lies in the necessary transition from the form of immediacy to mediation, from abstract identity to difference.... It has already been remarked that even when analytic cognition goes on to deal with relationships that are not an externally given material but thought determinations, it still remains analytic, since for it even these relationships are *given* ones. (LL. p.793)

We may summarize Hegel's description as follows:

a) Analytic cognition does not contain mediation, otherness; it is immediate, simple identity; it contains no transition to otherness.

b) 'It starts from a *presupposed*, and therefore individual, *concrete* subject matter'.

c) 'It does not pass through any further *middle term*': determination is immediate; no subjective determination is involved.

d) 'Analysis becomes synthetic when it comes to deal with *determinations* that are no longer *posited* by the problems themselves'. The transition from analytic to synthetic is a transition from immediacy to mediation. 'Even when analytic cognition goes on to deal with relationships that are not externally given material, but thought determinations, it still remains analytic, since for it even these relationships are *given* ones'.

110

These points are strongly reminiscent of Marx's criticism of the analytical method of political economy. Marx talks about political economy's method in such terms as: it leaves out intermediate links (the middle term or mediation in Hegel, points [a] and [c] above), it begins with various forms as given premises (points [b] and [d] above) etc. Furthermore, Marx's point about political economy's lack of interest in how various forms come about is related to the fact that in political economy, on the basis of its analytical method, concepts do not pass through a 'middle term' — they do not make a transition to 'otherness'.

Hegel supplements his discussion of 'analytic cognition' by an analysis of what he calls the 'synthetic cognition'. The latter is a 'reverse' movement compared to the former and is supposed to overcome its deficiencies.

This is how Hegel characterizes synthetic cognition:

> Analytic cognition is the first premiss of the whole syllogism — the *immediate* relation of the Notion to the object; *identity*, therefore, is the determination which it recognizes as its own, and analytic cognition is merely the *apprehension* of what is. Synthetic cognition aims at the *comprehension* of what is, that is, at grasping the multiplicity of determinations in unity. It is therefore the second premise of the syllogism in which the *diverse* as such is related. Hence its aim is in general *necessity*. The different terms which are connected, are on the other hand connected in a *relation*; in this relation they are related and at the same time mutually indifferent and self-subsistent; but on the other hand, they are linked together in the *Notion* which is their simple yet determinate unity. Now synthetic cognition passes over, in the first instance, from *abstract identity* to *relation*, or from *being* to *reflection*, and so far it is not the absolute reflection of the Notion that the Notion cognizes in its subject matter. The reality it gives itself is the next stage, namely, the stated identity of the different terms as such, an identity therefore that is at the same time still *inner* and only necessity, not the subjective identity that is *for itself*; hence not yet the Notion as such. Synthetic cognition, therefore, has indeed the Notion determinations for its content, and the object is posited in them; but they only stand in *relation* to one another, or are in *immediate* unity, and just for that reason, not in the unity by which the Notion exists as subject. (LL. pp.793-4)

Thus synthetic cognition attempts to relate concepts yielded by the analytical method to each other, thus to overcome 'otherness'. Its aim is to overcome external or unrelated diversity by establishing, for instance, causal relations between phenomena. Thus it makes the transition 'from abstract identity to relation, or from being to reflection'. Its objective is to achieve the concreteness of Notion by subsuming diverse phenomena under a single law or concept. But it does not achieve this objective because these diverse phenomena 'only stand in relation to one another, or in immediate unity, and just for that reason, not in the unity by which the Notion exists as subject'. In other words the phenomena, the forms or concepts, although related according to some principle, still stand in external opposition to each other. They retain their 'original' identity and, thus, are not truly reduced to 'moments' of the true unity, the Notion. Synthetic cognition is a necessary movement that should follow analytic cognition but the former is not, in itself, sufficient for arriving at Notions.

The elements, or concepts, related to each other in synthetic cognition can easily be analysed (reduced) back to their original existence because their relation to each other is external, i.e. they have not been fully subsumed under a unitary concept of which they should form dependent movements. Thus political economy can not only be characterized by its analytic method but also by its synthetic approach. Political economists not only arrive at abstract concepts but relate these concepts to each other.

Let us look at Ricardo's treatment of value as a way of illustrating the pitfalls of analytic and synthetic cognition.

Ricardo, according to Marx, states the principle of value determination by labour time in its full generality in the first chapter of his *Principles*. But in the same chapter he qualifies the general principle by referring to a variety of circumstances that violate the determination of value by labour (see Chapter Three above). Ricardo followed the analytical method in reducing value to labour. But the way in which he conceived labour made it impossible to explain the circumstances under which prices deviated from labour-values. He thus had to make 'exceptions' to the law of labour-value based on empirical situations. His procedure, therefore, represented a compromise of theory with 'facts'. He defended the general principle of value-determination by labour as the main and most typical form while accounting for deviations from the norm by invoking external, empirical and accidental causes.

Marx's critique of Ricardo in this context involves his demand for the subsumption of the 'external' causes, the exceptions under the general law so that these causes do not stand as factors external to the main cause but are reduced to its moments. Such a procedure would obviously involve a transformation of the concept of the value-determining element (labour) itself.

In the following quotation from Hegel we can see clearly the basis of Marx's critique. The method preferred by Marx, i.e. what Hegel calls the 'method of the absolute', while containing both phases of analysis and

112

synthesis, effectively overcomes their opposition:

> The essential point is that the absolute method finds and cognizes the *determination* of the universal within the latter itself. The procedure of the finite cognition of the understanding here is to take up again, equally externally, what it has left out in its creation of the universal by a process of abstraction. The absolute method, on the contrary, does not behave like external reflection but takes the determinate element from its own subject matter's immanent principle and soul. This is what Plato demanded of cognition, that it should *consider things in and for themselves*, that is, should consider them partly in their universality, but also that it should not stray away from them catching at circumstances, examples and comparisons, but should keep before it solely the things themselves and bring before consciousness what is immanent in them. The method of absolute cognition is to this extent *analytic*. That it finds the further determinations of its initial universal simply and solely in that universal, is the absolute objectivity of the Notion, of which objectivity the method is the certainty. But the method is no less *synthetic*, since its subject matter, determined immediately as a *simple universal*, by virtue of the determinateness which it possesses in its very immediacy and universality, exhibits itself as an other. (LL. p.830)

The above quotation gives a terse and succinct critique of the essence of Ricardo's analytic-synthetic method. This method, which Hegel characterizes as the 'finite cognition of the understanding', consists of taking up 'equally externally, what it has left out in its creation of the universal by a process of abstraction'. The analytic mode of abstraction involves the extraction of an element common to a variety of forms. This common element, or generality, is unable to explain the variety of external forms from which it is abstracted. Thus when compared with these forms it appears as 'too abstract'. In order to achieve a full and adequate explanation, 'what is left out' in the process of abstraction has to be brought back. But this bringing back is as external ('equally external') as the original extraction or abstraction.

Let us note that in the above quotation Hegel characterizes his method as analytic and synthetic at the same time.

C. The Intuitive Method

The intuitive school, whose most important representative was Jacobi,[9] may be considered as a philosophical revolt against the advances of physical sciences in seventeenth and eighteenth century on the one hand and the emergence of the empirical and the critical philosophy on the other. The result of all these scientific and methodological advances tended to imply that truth is always finite, partial and mediated. The physical sciences led to the knowledge of *specific* natural forces and the formulation of *particular* laws. The empirical school, based on its claim that only sense perception can lead to knowledge, could not conceive of knowledge as anything but partial and finite. Finally, critical philosophy, having declared that things-in-themselves cannot be known claimed that only *phenomena* may be objects of knowledge.

The ideal of knowledge for Jacobi was at a higher level than the achievements of science, empiricism and critical philosophy. For him Reason was the sole principle by which men live and that 'this Reason is the knowledge of God' (EL. p.105).

Now God is anything but partial, finite and mediated. Being perceived as total, infinite and unmediated, God cannot be known by methods and philosophies that claim knowledge to be always partial, finite and mediated. Jacobi thus proposed the intuitive or immediate method as the means of obtaining truth.

> With what is here called faith or immediate knowledge must also be identified inspiration, the heart's revelations, the truths implanted in many by nature, and, in particular, sound judgement or Common Sense, as it is called. All these forms agree in adopting as their leading principle the immediacy, or the self-evident way, in which a fact or body of truths is presented in consciousness. (EL. p.107)

Hegel's criticism of this school is that the full knowledge of universals such as God cannot be simple or immediate nor can it be obtained at the level of intuition. All knowledge is mediated and the knowledge of God must be the most mediated of all.

> The theory of which we are speaking is not satisfied when it has shown that mediate knowledge taken separately is an inadequate vehicle of truth. Its distinctive doctrine is that immediate knowledge alone, to the total exclusion of mediation, can possess a content which is true. This exclusiveness is enough to show that the theory is a relapse into the metaphysics of Understanding, with its pass-words 'Either — or'. (EL. pp.109-10)

From his criticism of these three methods the nature of Hegel's ideal of truth is clear. For Hegel Truth is infinite, total, concrete and immediate, but not to the exclusion of all finititude, particularness, abstractness and mediation. As opposed to these methods Hegel calls his own method the 'speculative' or 'absolute' method, fully exposed in his *Logic* at a pure theoretical level and applied to the study of forms of human consciousness (e.g. his *Phenomenology of Mind*) and social institutions (e.g. his *Philosophy of Right*).

We are now in a position to explain in fuller detail what Hegel's 'absolute method' is all about.

III. APPROACHING HEGEL'S LOGIC

In the previous section we reviewed Hegel's appraisal of three alternative theories of knowledge, i.e. the metaphysical, the analytical and the intuitive methods, with particular emphasis on the analytical approach. We have seen how Hegel, while praising each school for a particular strength possessed in revealing truth, criticizes each for their limitations as guides to true knowledge. The metaphysical school, by assuming an identity between forms of thought and the laws of objective reality had a higher intuition of truth than the later analytical method; at the same time its reliance on pictorial thinking and its lack of power of analysis and criticism prevents it from achieving true knowledge — it ultimately leads to flights into the supernatural and dogmatism. The empirical school makes a major improvement over the metaphysical method by bringing the subject of scientific inquiry down from the heavens above to earth. However, this method remains limited, as it makes sense perception the sole foundation of truth and does not probe deeper into the fundamental causes of things. Critical philosophy overcomes the naïvety of the empirical school by denying the passivity of thought and investigating the very nature of the thinking organ. None the less critical philosophy introduces the same limitations to the scope and possibility of knowledge as exist in the empirical method. Both the empirical and critical schools rely exclusively on the method of analysis (this is the reason, I believe, why Hegel discusses these two schools under one heading). Finally, the intuitive method, in reaction to the analytical method, attempts to extend the scope of knowledge to those universals such as God that escape the analytical method. It chooses intuition or immediate knowledge as a means towards that end. According to Hegel immediate knowledge falls considerably short of its objective, as true knowledge always involves mediation and therefore cannot be immediate.

I believe there is a unity in Hegel's critique of these three methods, based on the common problematic shared by all three. This problematic, what I call dualism, consists of a system of fixed oppositions: activity and passivity, objectivity and subjectivity, immediacy and mediation, abstract and concrete are in rigid opposition to each other. All three

115

methods either in their methodology or in their fundamental assumptions are captive to this dualism. For instance, in the empirical method it is assumed as a matter of course that our thoughts are based on sense perceptions received from some external source quite independently of the receiving subject. Here the dualism consists of a rigid opposition between an 'active' external world and a passive receiving subject. Similarly Kant's first *Critique* leads to a dualism between the world of phenomena (appearances) and things-in-themselves (essences), as he fails to extend his critical analysis of the human experience beyond phenomena.

These methods move in a vicious circle determined by these dualisms of fixed oppositions. They swing from one pole to another without criticizing this polarity itself. When they aspire to universality, particularity or concreteness is sacrificed. When they aim at concreteness, this concreteness is to be achieved without mediation (the intuitive method). When abstraction is the objective (critical philosophy), it is achieved at the cost of concreteness. When, for instance, the empirical method bases its knowledge of reality on sense perception (i.e. something presumably concrete) it ends up by using metaphysical concepts to describe reality.

None of these methods really yield concepts that conform to Hegel's ideal of a true concept (Notion),[10] in which the fixed oppositions mentioned above are fully resolved. Of course this does not mean that the terms of these oppositions, e.g. concrete and abstract, disappear in Notion. Quite the contrary. What does disappear is rather the *rigidity* of these oppositions.

For Hegel, Notion is determinate (because clearly specified), concrete (since it is a union of diverse elements and determinations) and mediate (because it cannot exist apart from its conditions of being). But at the same time it is universal (since it cannot be reduced to particular determinations), abstract (since it is a thought and not an object) and immediate (because it is internally consistent and necessary).

The movement from abstract, immediate, determinate and contingent to concrete, mediate, universal and necessary in such a way that this process does not abolish but retains the departure points governs the entire development of Hegel's categories in the *Logic*.

As an example I will now discuss the relationship between the ideas of 'abstract' and 'concrete'.

We saw in Chapter Two how Marx criticized the generic concept and in the first section of the present chapter we looked at some of the ideas Hegel expressed on the same issue. From the context of the relevant discussions one can conclude that in fact Hegel and Marx have two levels of abstraction and therefore two levels of comprehension in mind. Let us now see how Hegel approaches the distinction between these two levels of abstraction.[11]

This is how Hegel judges the place and function of the universal as the common element:

> Universality, when related to these individuals as indifferent ones . . . is merely their *common elements*. When one understands by the universal, what is *common* to several individuals, one is starting from the *indifferent* subsistence of these individuals and confounding the immediacy of *being* with the determination of Notion. The lowest conception one can have of the universal in its connection with the individual is this external relation of it as merely a *common element*. (LL. p.621)
>
> The notion is generally associated in our minds with abstract generality, and on that account it is often described as a general conception. We speak of notions of colour, plant, animal, etc. They are supposed to be arrived at by neglecting the particular features which distinguish the different colours, plants, and animals from each other, and by retaining those common to them all. This is the aspect of the notion which is familiar to understanding . . . (EL. pp.251-2, Additions)

As is clear from the above quotations, Hegel characterizes the conception of Notion as the 'common element' (the 'generic' concept) as the lowest possible conception that one may have of Notion. He also relates this particular conception to 'understanding'. Finally he calls it 'abstract' universal or abstract generality. Why does Hegel call the generic concept 'abstract' generality?

Before answering this question let us look at the way Hegel characterizes abstract generality:

> Thought, as Understanding, lives in a world where every term or product of thought preserves a stereotyped distinction from each other. Each of these limited abstractions the Understanding believes to be and exist on its own account. (EL. p.122)

Here we have the first characteristic of abstract generality, i.e. that it is isolated, independent and not in active relationship with other such concepts. The second characteristic of abstract generality is that it is conceived in such complete opposition to particularity that it becomes a particular itself. We have already concluded that the generic concept is either empty or, if anything, it is a particular. Here is how Hegel expresses this idea in the *Logic*:

117

In our ordinary usage of the term thought, and even notion, we often have before our eyes nothing more that the operations of Understanding. And no doubt thought is primarily an exercise of the Understanding — only it goes further, and the notion is a term not limited to the Understanding merely. The action of the Understanding may be described as investing its subject-matter with the form of universality. But this universality is an abstract universal: that is to say, its opposition to the particular is so rigorously maintained, that it can scarcely be defined in other terms than as a particular itself. In this separating and abstracting attitude towards its objects the Understanding is the reverse of immediate perception and sensation, which, as such, never get beyond their native sphere of action in the concrete. (EL. pp.122-3, Additions)

The third characteristic of abstract generality is its inherent instability, its constant tendency to turn into its opposite:

. . . the abstract thinking of the Understanding is so far from being either ultimate or stable, that it has evidently a perpetual tendency to work its own dissolution and swing round into its opposite. Rational thinking, on the contrary, is secured by making these opposites enter as unsubstantial elements into itself. (EL. pp.131-2, Additions)

In other words, if the concept is unable to become fully internal to thought, to establish internal relations with other concepts and thus be transformed into a wholly concrete concept (Notion), it is bound to remain isolated not only in relation to reality but also in relation to thought. Thus a universality of this nature, in which the opposition between the universal and the particular is rigidly maintained, degenerates into a particular existing side by side with other particulars. Thus the concepts of Understanding, or concepts of analytic cognition, are bound to dissolve and degenerate into their opposites (into particulars) if they do not advance to the level of rational thought, for example if they do not make the transition to Notion (through the intermediate stage of 'Essence').

Let us now go back to our original question as to why Hegel calls the concepts of understanding *abstract* generality. In our normal way of thinking we usually refer to ideas, concepts, theories and in general all products of thought as abstract as opposed to concrete. 'Concrete' normally refers to objects external to thought, as in expressions such as the 'concrete situation' or 'concrete fact'. In this context a term such as abstract generality may seem inappropriate since generality is by our standards abstract and therefore does not have to be specified as abstract generality.

Hegel, however, uses the term abstract in a different, though not entirely opposite sense. For Hegel the term abstract refers to one-sidedness, separateness (lack of interrelation) and contingency. In this sense the term 'abstract' can characterize both our thoughts as well as real objects and relations. For instance we may describe a man's relationship to the bourgeois legal system as abstract since it is a one-sided relationship (in which 'all men are equal'). In the same way a worker's relationship to the capitalist mode of production is one-sided because in this relationship he is not considered from any other point of view save his activity as a worker.[12] Similarly an abstract idea is an idea that is one-sided in the sense that it is not adequate to its object, it is not a complete idea. Thus although we are not entirely wrong to use the term abstract to refer to ideas since the latter are detached from reality and therefore are separate from it, our use of this term remains limited to the realm of thought only.

In the same way the term 'concrete' is used by Hegel to describe both reality and thought. A concrete reality is one that exhibits a system of necessary relationships between a diversity of elements. A concrete idea is one that is rich in content and expresses necessity and the highest level of mediation. Hegel's view of the Notion is that it is concrete universality as opposed to the abstract generality of the concepts of Understanding.

> For the truth is concrete; that is, whilst it gives a bond and principle of unity, it also possesses an internal variety of development. Truth, then, is only possible as a universe or totality of thought; and the freedom of the whole, as well as the necessity of the several divisions, is only possible when we distinguish the several elements, and give a precise expression to these differences. (EL. p.19)

Hegel says: 'in itself the Idea is really concrete, for it is the union of the different determinations' (LHP. v.I, p.24). And Marx simply reformulates Hegel in saying: 'The concrete is concrete because it is the concentration of many determinations, hence unity of the diverse' (G. p.101).

We have seen (Chapter Two) how Marx wrestled with the concepts of 'abstract' and 'concrete' and how he was at pains to explain that, for example, the outcome of scientific work is concrete, but not in the sense of a reality outside of thinking (he called it concrete-in-thought or thought — concrete, to distinguish it from 'real concrete'). We have also seen how he tried to establish that proper scientific work begins with abstract concepts.

In ordinary thinking the distinction between the two terms 'abstract' and 'concrete' is based on the dichotomy between the objective world and subjective thought. Hence 'concrete' refers to the former while 'abstract' is reserved for the latter. In Hegel's philosophy both of these terms come to refer to thought and ultimately (due to the complex unity of thought and being, consciousness and reality to be found in Hegel) to objective reality. It is this complex unity which distinguishes Hegel's theory of knowledge from those reviewed in the previous section.

Hegel's doctrine attempts to overcome the dualism present in the theories of knowledge criticized by him. Hegel achieves this by adopting a developmental and historical (but not necessarily 'historicist') perspective on the question of knowledge and truth. In most theories of knowledge prior to Hegel knowing is conceived of as a relationship between a fixed external reality and an equally static knowing subject. This approach leads to a fixed opposition between reality and thought, object and subject. This dualism is resolved by Hegel not through a denial of dualism (in fact he emphasizes that difference and contradiction are the basis of all activity, movement and life) but by asserting that if there is a duality it is not between reality and thought but *within both*. This, I believe, is the key to understanding Hegel's philosophy in general and his *Logic* in particular.

Hegel was not the first modern philosopher to go beyond dualism. It was Kant, who in spite of the analytical approach in his first *Critique*, opened the way to Hegel's philosophy in his second and particularly his third *Critique*. In the latter work Kant comes to consider artistic and biological form,[13] in which Kant had to abandon the dualism of his earlier work since these forms vitiate consideration of a dualistic separation between objective and subjective, abstract and concrete, means and ends, etc., i.e. the very stuff that forms the stock in trade of both empiricism and critical philosophy. For instance, in an artistic work one cannot easily distinguish between the objective and subjective, as the two merge together in a harmonious unity. In the same way in a biological form, e.g. an organism, the objective (the 'material' from which the organism is made up, the organs, etc.) and the subjective (the unity of parts, the end and purpose) rather than being in opposition to each other form a complete whole.

Hegel evaluates the contribution of Kant's third critique in the following way:

The salient feature in the Critique of Judgement is, that in it Kant gave utterance to a general image, perhaps even the thought of Idea. Such an approximate image, of an Intuitive Understanding, of an adaptation within things themselves, suggests a universal which is at the same time apprehended

120

as being in its own nature a concrete unity. It is in these approximations to thought alone that the Kantian philosophy rises to the speculative height. Schiller, and others, have found a way of escape from the abstract and separatist understanding in the idea of artistic beauty. In that idea the thought and the sensuous conception have grown together in one. (EL. p.95)

One of the Kant's greatest services to philosophy consists in the distinction he has made between relative or *external*, and *internal* purposiveness; in the latter he has opened up the Notion of life, the Idea, and by so doing has done *positively* for philosophy what the *Critique of Reason* did but imperfectly, equivocally, and only *negatively*, namely, raised it above the determinations of reflection and the relative world of metaphysics. (LL. p.737)

As we have seen, for Hegel the truth is universal and not particular, although it does contain particularity 'which by its reflection into itself has been equalized with the universal'. Similarly truth is also concrete and not abstract, although it contains abstractness as a moment. In the same way truth is immediate although it involves mediation to the highest degree. The structure of Hegel's *Logic* consists of a complex dialectic of these apparently opposed concepts.

Hegel's *Logic* is subdivided into three major parts: the Doctrine of Being, the Doctrine of Essence and the Doctrine of Notion. Each of these parts in turn are subdivided into three sections exploring various logical categories. For example, the Doctrine of Being has the categories of Quality, Quantity and Measure. Under each category three subcategories are discussed: for instance under Quality we have pure being, determinate being and being-for-self.

Each part, category or subcategory essentially goes through three phases and follows the same structure — the structure that governs the whole of the *Logic*. Since it is impossible to do justice to this complex and intricate work within the scope of the present study I will not attempt an exposition of it. Instead I will discuss a number of interpretations of this work which will give the reader a flavour of its rich content.

Approaches to Hegel's Logic

There are at least three ways in which the *Logic* can be interpreted:

1. As a critical analysis of the evolution of human knowledge (in historical stages or in a logical sequence).
2. As a positive exposition of a new theory of knowledge and methodology.
3. As a pure exposition of the identity of reality and thought

121

through the revelation of a common rational principle.

There is no necessary conflict between these three approaches. In fact, if these views are not held exclusively and in absolute opposition to each other, with some modification, they are all present in the *Logic*.

In what follows I will discuss the first two approaches, leaving the third one to the final section of this chapter.

1. According to the first interpretation the structure of the *Logic* follows some form of historical order in the evolution of knowledge:

At the level of Being concepts simply 'are'; they do not bear any intrinsic relation to each other. The categories of Being, such as 'pure' being, determinate being, quantity, quality and measure exist side by side, or, rather, cancel each other out. These categories maintain an external existence in relation to each other.

Thought at the level of understanding, ultimately, moves in the sphere of 'being'. Its concepts maintain an external relation not only with objective reality but with each other. Each of them maintains an independent existence 'on its own account'.

G. R. G. Mure, for instance, states the following:

> The categories of Being are in fact thought at the level where it is almost bare intuition below discursion. (Mure 1950, p.28)

He also states that the categories of being belong to understanding (which 'excludes sense but includes intuition').

At the level of Essence, concepts of Understanding enter into relations with each other. At this level a principle of unity or relation or distinction is introduced among concepts. This relation or distinction is supposed to be wholly internal to thought.

> ... with Essence the emphasis passes from intuition to discursion, and so from thought which self-perception illustrates to thought which finds its illustration in empirical thinking. (Mure 1950, p.80)

The transition to Essence, although absolutely necessary for the ultimate transition to Notion, is ravaged by contradictions that can easily cause a regression to the level of Understanding.

The specificity of concepts at the level of Essence consists in this: these concepts, although related to each other according to a law or formula, still remain external to each other. For one thing, the identification of one concept as 'essence' reduces other related concepts to forms or appearances of this essence. In this process, the forms lose their identities and are easily reduced to the essence. Thus the distinction of concepts that served as the basis of a system of relationships between concepts is readily evaporated into the single concept of essence. As a result, the various concepts either lose their distinctness and identity by being fully subsumed under essence or else they maintain their external opposition to essence and can thus become easily polarized into abstract and unrelated concepts.

These contradictions arise from the fact that the level of Essence is characterized by 'dialectical opposition', by mere equilibration and the external coexistence of concepts without the existence of an inherent bond that relates various concepts to each other such that both essence and appearance become moments of a single unity.

The contradictions of Essence are fully resolved in Notion.

In contrast to the level of Essence, in Notion the contradiction between essence and appearance, form and content, is fully resolved. Thus unlike the level of Essence in which these oppositions are resolved by one pole becoming fully absorbed in the other pole, at the level of Notion opposite poles come to form essential moments of the whole such that no one of them can be reduced to the other.

> In Notion the emphasis is not upon cancellation, as it was in Being; nor, as it were in Essence, upon equilibrium in contradiction; but upon preservation. (Mure 1950, p.157)

Thus according to this interpretation, there is a correspondence between the stages in the evolution of human thinking and knowledge and in the three doctrines of the *Logic*. This is how Hegel himself states this relationship. In Chapter VI of the *Encyclopaedia Logic*, before announcing the three subdivisions of the *Logic*, he says:

> In point of form Logical doctrine has three stages or aspects: α the Abstract Stage, or that of Understanding: β the Dialectical, or that of negative reason: γ the Speculative, or that of positive reason. (EL. p.122)

This correspondence is exhibited in Diagram 5.

According to this view Hegel's *Logic* represents two movements:

i) an historical movement in which the three successive doctrines of the *Logic* correspond to three successive stages in the evolution of human knowledge; and ii) a linear-progressive movement from Being to Essence to Notion in the following sense: each succeeding doctrine reveals

DIAGRAM 5

Theories of knowledge	Stages of evolution	Doctrines of Logic
Metaphysical reason Empiricism	Understanding	BEING
Analytical or negative reason (Kant)	Dialectics	ESSENCE
Positive reason (Hegel)	Speculative method	NOTION

itself as the truth of the preceding one. Thus Essence is the truth of Being, and Notion is the truth of Essence.

This interpretation, as we have seen, finds some support in Hegel. Let us recall that Hegel in the above quotation precedes his observation by saying that 'in point of form Logical doctrine has three stages or aspects', i.e. this is only the formal aspect of the structure of the *Logic*. It would thus be a mistake to emphasize this aspect too strongly. In fact this view if held strictly and to the exclusion of other aspects would amount to an *analytical* approach to Hegel's *Logic* — a work that is precisely conceived as a critique of analytical reason.

2. In the second approach to the *Logic*, the stage view is retained, but it is given a different interpretation.

For instance John G. Hibben, while recognizing that the three divisions of the *Logic* 'represent the successive stages in the progressive unfolding of our knowledge', sees these stages in a different light:

> They are to be regarded as successive stages only in the sense that by our analysis we separate them in our thoughts, and think of one as following the other. But in reality we should conceive of these elements of knowledge in such a manner as to regard one as lying within the other, and this in turn within the third. The progress indicated in their development is one not of advance so much as a deepening insight into more and more fundamental attributes and relations. (Hibben 1902, pp.68-9)

124

Thus the stages are not to be conceived of as representing an 'advance' but basically a 'deepening' process. Thus Being already contains Notion so that the transition from Being to Notion is not a linear advance but a return to Being whereby Notion represents a deepened concept of Being. Interpreted in this way the analytical approach to the *Logic* breaks down because (i) the stages no longer represent succeeding phases of a linear-progressive movement; and (ii) these phases cannot be separated in a rigid manner from one another.

However, Hibben is not able to adhere to this interpretation consistently. In the following quotation, while interpreting the *Logic* as a positive methodology of knowledge he attempts an analytical separation of the three divisions of the *Logic*:

> The doctrine of being is the result of an answer to the question as to *what* a thing is.
> The doctrine of essence, an answer to the question *by what* is it constituted.
> The doctrine of the notion, an answer to the question, *to what end* is it designed and is it capable of progressing.
> The complete knowledge of a thing, therefore, embraces the categories of its being, the ground of its being, and the purpose of its being. (Hibben 1902, p.69)

While I sympathize with the interpretation of the *Logic* as a positive theory of knowledge, the way Hibben presents this view Hegel's methodology is hardly distinguishable from any other (empirical or analytical) methodology: in Hibben's analytical approach the three questions corresponding to the three divisions of the *Logic* are treated separately and in isolation from each other.

We now turn to Hegel's own interpretation of the three doctrines of the *Logic*:

> The Notion has exhibited itself as the truth of Being and Essence, which both revert to it as their ground. Conversely it has been developed out of being as its ground. The former aspect of the advance may be regarded as a deepening of being in itself, the inner nature of which has been truly laid bare: the latter aspect as an issuing of the more perfect from less perfect. When such development is viewed on the latter side only, it does prejudice to the method of philosophy. (EL. p.244)

In the above passage Hegel is presenting two viewpoints about the transition from Being-Essence to Notion.

The first aspect is a deepening of Being, i.e. Notion represents a deepening of Being. This means that Being already had the character of Notion (if only implicitly), and further development has made what is implicit more explicit. In this respect development is a necessary self-moving process. It is logical necessity that develops Being through Essence into Notion.

The second aspect refers to a development that lacks necessity. The transition from less perfect to more perfect may be subverted by external influences. This is why Hegel says that this view of development compromises the method of philosophy, as it must show an internally consistent and necessary self-movement.

If we take the second view of development only, Being would appear as a pre-condition of Notion, as temporally or historically first, as a formative or causative element.

> If the formative element therefore be called the imperfect, then the notion, or the perfect, is at any rate a development from the imperfect, since its very nature is thus to absorb or suspend its pre-supposition. At the same time it is the notion alone, which, when it lays itself down, makes the pre-supposition ... (EL. p.244)

It is clear that for Hegel the first view of development is the most significant and dominant one. Notion is the pre-condition, pre-supposition of Being rather than vice versa.

The first view is probably most clearly stated when Hegel deals with the question of the beginning in science, which is the subject of the next section.

IV. THE QUESTION OF THE BEGINNING

The nature of the beginning in the *Logic* goes through a deepening process as we move from the doctrine of Being to the doctrine of Notion. Its first determination in the doctrine of Being is in the form of pure or simple immediacy leading to the definition of the beginning as 'pure being'.

1. *The Beginning as 'Pure Being'*: The first and the simplest determination or characterization of the beginning takes the form of an immediate, self-contained entity. As such it is devoid of any mediation, any distinction.

> Now starting from this determination of pure knowledge, all that is needed to ensure that the beginning remains immanent in its scientific development is to consider, or rather, ridding oneself of all other reflections and opinions whatever, simply to take up, *what is there before us.*
> Pure knowing as concentrated into this unity has sublated all reference to

an other and to mediation; it is without any distinction and as thus distinction-less, ceases itself to be knowledge; what is present is only *simply immediacy*.

Simple immediacy is itself an expression of reflection and contains a reference to its distinction from what is mediated. This simple immediacy, therefore, in its true expression is *pure being*. Just as *pure* knowing is to mean knowing as such, quite abstractly, so too pure being is to mean ... nothing but *being* in general: being, and nothing else, without any further specification and filling. (LL. p.69)

Thus the beginning must be an *absolute*, or what is synonymous here, an *abstract* beginning; and so it *may not presuppose anything*, must not be mediated by anything nor have a ground; rather it is to be itself the ground of the entire science .... The beginning therefore is *pure being*. (LL. p.70)

The determination of the beginning as 'simple immediacy' or 'pure being' is essential for any science. The commencement and establishment of the latter as distinct from not only 'non-science' but also from other sciences must be based on a total break with 'the other' of the science.

Any science as a self-contained and independent whole must have its own specific foundation. To attain such a foundation one must rid 'oneself of all other reflections or opinions whatever' (reflections and opinions brought into the science from outside and thus alien to the science) and 'to take up, what is there before us' i.e. the unique object of the science in 'absolute' break with and 'abstraction' from what is external to science. Thus:

> the very fact that science must begin with what is absolutely simple, that is, with what is most general and of least import, would restrict the exposition solely to these same quite simple expressions of the simple without any further addition of a single word; all that could be properly admitted would be negative considerations intended to ward off and banish any heterogeneous elements which otherwise might be introduced by pictorial thought or unregulated thinking. (LL.p.40)

Thus Hegel's first characterization of the beginning as 'pure being' is dictated by the necessity of a break with 'pictorial' or 'unregulated thinking' (non-science or pre-science). Hegel's procedure here is to ensure that the beginning is wholly internal to the science and unmediated with other forms of thought.

However, after this first definition or determination of the beginning, i.e. after securing an abstract and absolute foundation for science, Hegel problematizes the nature of this beginning in view of the total process of scientific development. The determination of the beginning as simple immediacy has ensured the break of the science with non-science. But the question is now to relate the beginning thus secured as an internal foundation to the process and the result of the internal development of the science.

2. *The Circle of the Scientific Advance:* The beginning, once established as internal to science cannot be separated from the process and the end-product of the scientific advance.

This meaning of the beginning arises throughout the discussion of the nature of progress in philosophy in Hegel's *Science of Logic:*

> . . . progress in philosophy is rather a retrogression and a grounding or establishing by means of which we first obtain the result that what we began with is not something merely arbitrarily assumed but is in fact the *truth*, and also the *primary truth.* (LL. pp.70-1)
>
> It must be admitted that it is an important consideration . . . that the advance is a *retreat into the ground,* to what is *primary* and *true,* on which depends and, in fact, from which originates, that with which the beginning is made. Thus consciousness on its onward path from the immediacy with which it began is led back to absolute knowledge as its innermost truth. This last, the ground, is then also that from which the first proceeds, that which at first appeared as an immediacy. . . . The essential requirement for the science of logic is not so much that the beginning be a pure immediacy, but rather that the whole of the science be within itself a circle in which the first is also the last and the last is also the first. (LL. p.71)

Hegel thus identifies the beginning with the result. As a consequence scientific advance forms a circle. The activity of science constantly brings the fruits of development back to its foundation and thus enriches the beginning with the results of its highest achievement.

This identity of the beginning and the end-product is essential to science not only because it gives the scientific process a sense of continuity but also because it establishes the science as a self-contained and self-propelling process.

> We see therefore that, on the other hand, it is equally necessary to consider as *result* that into which the movement returns as into its *ground.* In this respect the first is equally the ground, and the last a derivative; since the movement starts from the first and by correct inferences arrives at the last as the ground, this latter is a result. Further, the *progress* from that which forms the beginning is to be regarded as only a further determination of it, hence that which forms the starting point of the development remains at the base of all that follows and does not vanish from it. The progress does not consist merely in the derivation of an other, or in the effected transition into a genuine other; and in so far as this transition does occur it is equally sublated again. Thus the beginning of philosophy is the foundation which is present and preserved throughout the entire subsequent development, remaining completely immanent in its further

128

determinations. (LL. p.71)

Through this progress, then, the beginning loses the onesidedness which attaches to it as something simply immediate and abstract; it becomes something mediated, and hence the line of scientific advance becomes a *circle*. (LL. pp.71-2)

The idea of the circularity of scientific advance can be easily reduced to an absurdity, i.e. it may be construed as implying a negation of the idea of advance. But Hegel's further specifications of the beginning runs counter to such an interpretation. I believe that the notion of the circularity of scientific advance expresses the idea of the closure, the internality or the self-movement of science on the one hand and the non-linear nature of progress in science on the other. The circularity here does not imply a 'vicious circle' or a 'bad infinity' but simply self-identity and internal movement. This internal movement can be characterized as such only if an invariant structure is specified throughout the entire process. What unites the beginning and the end result is the very logic of the movement. Thus if the beginning and the end are to be conceived as moments of a single process they must have something in common. This communality accounts for the identity of the beginning and the end result.

However, there are deeper reasons for Hegel's identification of the beginning and the end. Although Hegel figuratively characterizes advance in science as 'retreat' and talks about 'the closed circle of a science', there exists a crucial difference between the beginning and the end that accounts for the movement or progress from one to the other.

3. *The Beginning as Abstract Universality:* Hegel returns to the question of the beginning in Book Three of the *Science of Logic*, i.e. after having completed the exposition of the doctrines of Being and Essence. It is here that the idea of the beginning acquires its complete form as a concept no longer identifiable as 'pure being'.

Because it is the beginning, its content is an immediate, but an immediate that has the significance and form of *abstract universality*. (LL. p.827)

The immediate of sensuous intuition is a *manifold* and an *individual*. But cognition is thinking by means of notions, and therefore its beginning is *only in the element of thought* — it is a *simple* and a *universal*. (LL. p.828)

Hegel, in contrasting sensuous intuition with cognition, claims that in the former the immediate is a manifold (a concrete) and an individual while in the latter it is simple (abstract) and universal.

The beginning of cognitive thinking stands in sharp contrast with that of sensuous intuition — they are complete opposites. The end result of cognitive thinking for Hegel, i.e. the concept ('notion'), absolute idea, etc. is a universal (like the beginning) but it is no longer 'simple' or abstract. Rather it is a concrete, a manifold, a unity of diverse determinations.

Thus the advance from the beginning (simple or abstract universality) to the end result (concept, notion, absolute idea) while still forming a closed circle is an advance from simple universality to concrete universality. (It is still a circle since the beginning of cognition 'is only in the element of thought', i.e. it is fully subsumed under the process of cognitive thinking and is not an object alien or external to the latter.) In fact it is the deficiency (the simplicity, the abstractness, the onesidedness) of the beginning compared with the end-result that explains the movement from one to the other. This process, of course, presumes the presence of the end-result in the beginning. The result here acts as an Aristotelian 'final cause'.

> Hence the beginning has for the method no other determinateness than that of being simple and universal; this is itself the *determinateness* by reason of which it is deficient. Universality is the pure simple Notion, and the method, as consciousness of the Notion, knows that universality is only a moment and that in it the Notion is not yet determined in and for itself . . . . Since however it is the objective immanent form, the immediate of the beginning must be *in its own self* deficient and endowed with the *urge* to carry itself further. (LL. pp.828-9)

We may ask — what is it that accounts for the presence of this 'urge' in the simple universal beginning that carries it forward to Notion. The answer lies in Hegel's peculiar method (i.e. what he calls the Absolute Method). The meaning of universality in this method is different from the meaning it acquires in 'finite cognition' (e.g. in the empirical method). The universal in 'Absolute Method' is not 'subjective' but 'objective', it is not external to the object but internal to it. As an abstract universal it does not (as in 'finite cognition') lead a life of its own isolated from the elements and forms from which it has been abstracted and generalized. It represents a 'concrete totality'. However, it is not yet Notion since it still exists in itself and not for itself, it 'is not yet posited'.

Hegel continues the above-quoted passage in the following way:

> But in the absolute method the universal has the value not of a mere abstraction but of the objective universal, that is, the universal that is *in itself* the *concrete*

130

totality, though that totality is not yet *posited*, is not yet *for itself*. Even the abstract universal as such, considered in its Notion, that is in its truth, is not merely the *simple*, but as *abstract* is already *posited* as infected with a *negation*. For this reason too *there is* nothing, whether in *actuality* or in *thought*, that is as simple and as abstract as is commonly imagined. A simple thing of this kind is a mere *presumption* that has its ground solely in the unconsciousness of what is actually present. (LL. p.829)

Thus considered in its Notion or truth, the beginning as an abstract universality contains 'a negation'. Obviously Hegel is here problematizing the idea of the 'simple' and the 'abstract': 'There is nothing, whether in *actuality* or in *thought*, that is as simple and abstract as is commonly imagined'.

Let us recall that Hegel defined the beginning at the early stages of the development of his *Logic* as 'pure being', as simple immediacy. This determination was essential in view of the necessity of securing the beginning as a moment wholly internal to science. But at a later stage this determination is negated and the beginning is characterized as simple or abstract universality. Further, this determination is qualified by a distinction that Hegel makes between objective (concrete) universality and subjective (abstract) universality.

Above, that with which the beginning is made was determined as the immediate; the *immediacy of the universal* is the same thing that is here expressed as the *in-itself* that is without a *being-for-self*. Hence it may indeed be said that every beginning must be made *with the absolute*, just as all advance is merely the exposition of it, in so far as its *in-itself* is the Notion. But because the absolute is at first only *in itself* it equally is *not* the absolute nor the posited Notion, and also not the Idea; for what characterizes these is precisely the fact that in them the *in-itself* is only an abstract, one-sided moment. Hence the advance is not a kind of *superfluity*; this it would be if that with which the beginning is made were in truth already the absolute; the advance consists rather in the universal determining itself and being *for itself* the universal, that is, equally an individual and a subject. Only in its consummation is it the absolute. (LL. p.829)

Thus the universal that makes the beginning is characterized by the fact that in it the absolute is only in itself. The advance consists in the development of the beginning to a point where the absolute becomes for-itself. This is the essence of the advance from the beginning to the end-result. The absolute is present from the very beginning but it exists only in-itself. It becomes for-itself as a result of scientific advance which consists of an internal development in which the universal determines itself as a universal and thus is universal for-itself.

131

The concrete totality which makes the beginning contains as such within itself the beginning of the advance and development. As concrete, it is *differentiated within itself*; but by reason of its *first immediacy* the first differentiated determinations are in the first instance merely a *diversity*. The immediate, however, as self-related universality, as subject, is also the *unity* of these diverse determinations. (LL. p.830)

The beginning as 'pure immediacy' (its first characterization) can be conceived as differentiated; but this differentiation will take the form of mere diversity (i.e. diversity without an internal bond, as pure externality) unless it is imbued with the element of universality. It is only when the immediate acquires the character of a self-related universality that it becomes concrete totality and thus the 'unity of diverse determinations'.

Let us now summarize the main points of the above discussion before proceeding further.

Hegel first defines the beginning as 'simple immediacy' (pure being). In our interpretation this first determination is crucial since it secures an internal (immediate) basis for the science. This step helps to establish the distance between any science and non-science or other possible sciences. However, in itself, this determination is deficient in that a mere break with non-science does not establish science as a self-contained and internal process. Hegel, at this juncture, introduces the idea of the circularity of scientific progress, the fact that the end-result of scientific advance is a return or retreat to the beginning. This characterization ensures that scientific advance is an independent, self-related and reproductive process. We have claimed that the idea of circularity of science in Hegel cannot be reduced to a vicious circle. There is advance in science but it is wholly internal to the latter. In order to show the advance Hegel attempts a further determination of the beginning as simple or abstract universality. With this definition of the beginning, the latter is endowed with the general, abstract, or simple form of Notion which constitutes the apex of scientific advance. The beginning is a universal (like Notion) but it is such only in itself and not for itself. When the beginning determines itself as a universal then it is turned into Notion, i.e. the universal for itself.

For Hegel the beginning and the end (Notion) share this much: both are immediate and universal. The universal of the beginning is a universal 'in-itself', while Notion is a 'for-itself' universal. Hegel is using two concepts of universality here. But this applies to the idea of immediacy as well. The beginning is immediate in one sense and the end (Notion) in another sense. Before we elaborate on this point let us see how Hegel uses the concept 'simple'.

132

Let us recall that when Hegel characterized the beginning as abstract (or simple) universality he identified the notion of 'abstract' with that of 'simple'. In this identification both words mean 'isolated' and 'one-sided'. But this definition of simple as abstract (and both as 'isolated', 'one-sided' or external) is problematic. For Hegel this is a primitive determination of 'simple'. Thus 'simple' in its first determination is defined as an abstract and isolated relation. But, as we have shown above, Hegel problematized this concept of 'simple' by stating that both in actuality and in thought things are neither as simple nor as abstract as is commonly thought. We cannot conceive of anything which is unrelated to other things, and which stands isolated, purely on its own.

Thus there must be a further determination of the concept of 'simple' in Hegel that overcomes the deficiency of the first definition.

> As *universality* is the utterly *simple* determination, it does not seem capable of any explanation; for an explanation must concern itself with definitions and distinctions and must apply predicates to its object, and to do this to what is simple, would alter rather than explain it. But the simplicity which constitutes the very nature of the universal is such that, through absolute negativity, it contains *within itself* difference and determinateness in the highest degree. *Being is simple as immediate* being; for that reason it is only something *meant* or *intended* and we can not say of it what it is; therefore, it is one with its other, with *non-being.* Its Notion is just this, to be a simplicity that immediately vanishes in its opposite; it is *becoming. The Universal,* on the contrary, is that *simplicity* which, because it is the Notion, no less possesses *within itself* the *richest content.*
>
> First, therefore, it is the simple relation to itself; it is only *within itself.* *Secondly*, however, this identity is *within itself*, absolute *mediation*, but it is not something *mediated.* (LL. pp.601-2)

Clearly Hegel is here operating with two distinct concepts of the 'simple' and the 'immediate'. Furthermore, at this level the concept 'simple' is no longer to be identified with the concept 'abstract' but with 'immediate'.

The distinction between the primitive concept of 'simple' and its more developed one consists in the fact that in the former meaning it denotes an abstract, one-sided and isolated relation while in the latter sense it is a concept that 'possesses *within itself* the *richest content*'.

The same distinction is made for the concept of the 'immediate'. Immediate can mean negation of all mediation. But it could also represent (as in Notion) 'absolute mediation'.

The simplicity that characterizes 'pure being' vanishes since it only makes sense in relation to 'an other', i.e. non-being. Thus this simplicity is, ultimately, a mediated one (it refers to an other). But the simplicity that characterizes Notion is a pure or 'simple' relation to self.

The first concept of simplicity, by its nature, refers to an 'other'. But this defies the nature of simplicity. The higher concept of simplicity overcomes this deficiency by subsuming its 'other'. Thus 'the simplicity which constitutes the very nature of the universal is within itself difference and determinateness in the highest degree'. And the universal 'is that simplicity which, because it is the Notion, no less possesses within itself the richest content'.

We may conclude that the concept of 'simple' in Hegel acquires two determinations:

1) *Simple as an isolated and one-sided moment: in this meaning 'simple' is used as synonymous with 'abstract'.*

2) *Simple as a characteristic of universal, or indeed as universality itself, as Notion. As such it has 'the richest content'. In this meaning, 'simple' is pure self-relation, immediacy (not simple, abstract immediacy, but immediacy that is based on 'absolute mediation').*

We are now in a position to sum up Hegel's ideas about the question of the beginning.

The beginning of science for Hegel has two forms or determinations. However, these two forms are not in conflict with each other but simply represent two essential moments of scientific development.

Hegel first defines the beginning as simple (abstract) immediacy. As we have seen above, this determination is essential in order to secure an internal and immanent foundation for science. Any new scientific discipline begins with a break with non-science or other sciences. The beginning, thus, must be 'simple' and 'abstract' in the sense of a total abstraction (break) with any elements alien to the science. But such a simple and abstract beginning cannot be a moment of science unless it is imbued with the intent of the science. Thus the break (abstraction, simplicity) has to be combined with a union, unity or identity ensuring the belonging of this beginning to the said science. The beginning as an isolated moment (simple, abstract) separated from the environment alien to the science remains isolated (and thus abstract and simple) unless it is united with the process and the end-result of scientific development. However, should the abstract beginning be united with the end-product it would lose its abstractness and simplicity.

In the process of the winning over, i.e. the internalization of the simple beginning, the latter loses its simple-abstract identity. It was

134

simple-abstract (isolated, one-sided) in relation to elements outside the science. But now it is internal to science and, therefore, is no longer external or isolated (thus no longer 'simple' or abstract). The beginning is thus transformed in the process of its internalization. This leads to the second or higher determination of the concept of the beginning.

In this higher level, the beginning is simple-immediate universality. "The beginning acquires the character of universality and the meaning of its simplicity is transformed from simplicity as abstractness (one-sidedness) into simplicity as immediacy and self-relation. But it is an immediacy that is based on absolute mediation, possessing the richest content."

The question that may be legitimately raised at this juncture is whether there is any difference between the beginning and the end. A simple answer supported by Hegel's idea of the circularity of the scientific advance is 'no'. But as we elaborated above, circularity in Hegel expresses the idea of internal development and does not negate true advancement. Thus there must be a difference between the beginning and the end. What unites the beginning and the end is the idea of simplicity as self-relation, as immediacy. The difference lies in that the beginning is only potentially the end, it is an end 'in itself' and not 'for itself'. The beginning is in need of self-development to grow into the end.

The identity or unity of the beginning and the end-product in Hegel's *Logic* cannot be fully explained by the idea of simplicity as immediate or as self-relation. What we have said so far about this identity is purely formal and does not expose the roots of this identity. After all, our exposition so far has been based on Hegel's *Logic* alone. For Hegel, the *Logic* is the ultimate form of philosophy, which in its turn is the highest form of absolute knowledge. The treatment of the fundamental questions of Hegel's philosophy in his *Logic* necessarily takes on a highly abstract and pure form. Towards the end of this chapter we will attempt to reveal more fully the logic of the identity of the beginning and the end based on Hegel's *Philosophy of Mind*.

Before advancing any further in our analysis of Hegel's *Logic* we need to look back and see how far we have advanced in tracing Marx's perspectives on the question of the beginning to Hegel's *Logic*.

In Chapter Two we demonstrated that Marx, in his *1857 Introduction*, while first approving the general procedure of the beginning with simple concepts — an approach followed by political economy — subsequently embarked on an extensive critique of the concept 'simple'. Marx's elaboration of the concept 'simple' yielded three distinct interpretations of the latter:

135

S.1. 'Simple' as the concept of an elementary, historically prior relation.
S.2. 'Simple' as the concept of an elementary relation co-existing with, but subsumed under, a complex and developed whole.
S.3. 'Simple' as the concept of a relation that presupposes a more concrete development.

We concluded that only S.3 qualifies as proper beginning for Marx.

We may claim that S.1 and S.2 satisfy the first determination of the beginning in Hegel as simple (abstract) immediacy since both of these 'simples' express abstract, isolated and one-sided relations. S.3, however, cannot be described as simple immediacy because it is based on the highest development and presupposes the 'richest content'. S.3 is, therefore, simple universality. The simplicity of S.3 refers to self-relation and thus cannot be reduced to the simplicity of S.1 or S.2, which refers to abstractness. It is only S.3 that satisfies Hegel's full determination of the beginning in science.

The simplicity of S.3 is of a higher order compared to the simplicity exhibited by S.1 and S.2. The progress from S.1 and S.2 to S.3 in Hegel is described by Charles Taylor in the following way:

> We start off with simple Being, in which we have in a sense an image of the totality, for it is self-related. It suffers diremption into *Dasein*, but returns to itself in Infinity and *Fursichsein*. This is richer inwardly. Finally we get to the Idea which is the richest of all. But in achieving this inner complexity we have also achieved greater inwardness, greater intensity of inner unity, hence in a sense greater interpenetration and hence higher simplicity. When we come to the end we have subjectivity, self-consciousness, which is the most complex unity, but at the same time the most simple, because it is totally transparent. It is a unity where the separation of parts, the mutual exteriority is totally overcome. We come to the greatest articulation of our concept, but also the most intense unity and hence clarity and simplicity. (Taylor 1975, pp.343-4)

Let us recall that Hegel's first determination of the beginning as simple immediacy was justified on the basis of the necessity of a break with elements external to science. From this perspective the method of beginning with simple concepts which are abstracted and detached from the external world (e.g. the method followed by classical political economists in the constitution of the science of political economy) is fully justified. However, this beginning, in order to serve as the foundation of a science, must not only be detached and abstracted from elements

136

outside the science but must also become fully internal to the latter, i.e. it must be transformed from 'simple immediacy' to 'simple universality'.

Classical political economy succeeded in taking the first step (beginning with simple concepts) but failed in taking the second step (that is, the internalization of simple concepts and their elevation to the level of simple universality). Political economists started from simple concepts as given premises and thus did not transform them. They left those concepts hanging by themselves while trying to explain them by extraneous factors.

We have already referred to the 'analytical' approach to Hegel's *Logic*. According to this approach (i) the movement of categories in the *Logic* is linear-progressive in an historical time scale or a logical sequence; and (ii) the categories represent distinct and separate stages. We have shown that while Hegel recognizes this 'stage' view (the progress from less perfect to more perfect), he at the same time proposes an alternative view (which does not necessarily negate the first view but basically enriches it) according to which progress in the *Logic* exhibits a deepening process.

What are the consequences of this 'dialectical' approach to the *Logic*? First there is no linear-progressive movement of the categories. As we have seen in the present section Hegel characterizes the movement and transition from one phase to another by circularity and retreat. Secondly, the separation between categories is not fixed and rigid. For instance, Being which is often described as the beginning and the first doctrine (which it is) is characterized by Hegel as a derivative of Notion as well. Thus the fixed opposition between the three doctrines as well as the categories breaks down.

This idea of the derivative nature of Being and the absolute priority of Notion has often been interpreted in a way which corresponds to the third approach to Hegel's *Logic*, as mentioned in the previous section. According to this approach it is thought, Idea and ultimately God that lie at the root of all reality. This view is extensively discussed in the next section. However as a background to the next section as well as further clarification of the subject of the present section I will end here with the following remarks.

Concluding Remarks

Let us recall that Hegel's discussion of development involves three basic ideas:

137

1. Development is a process in which what is merely implicit (or in-itself) becomes explicit (for-itself) and that this becoming explicit is the crucial factor in the process.
2. The developing being does retain its identity throughout the process; the implicit does not disappear but appears again (in other words development is not linear-progressive but involves a return into self).
3. There is a major difference between development in nature and the development of thought in that in thought there is a genuine internal return to self while in nature the beginning and the end are physically distinct objects.

This is how Hegel attempts to apply these ideas to the stages of development in the *Logic*:

> The onward movement of the notion is no longer either a transition into, or a reflection on something else, but Development . . .
> Transition into something else is the dialectical process within the range of Being: reflection (bringing something else into light), in the range of Essence. The movement of the notion is development: by which that only is explicitly affirmed which is already naturally and, properly speaking, present. In the world of nature, it is organic life that corresponds to the grade of the notion. Thus, e.g. the plant is developed from its seed. The seed virtually involves the whole plant, but does so only ideally or in thought: and it would therefore be a mistake to regard the development of the root, stem, leaves, and other different parts of the plant, as meaning that they were *realiter* present, but in a minute form, in the germ. That is the so-called 'box-within-box' hypothesis; a theory which commits the mistake of supposing an actual existence of what is at first found only as a postulate of the completed thought. The truth of the hypothesis on the other hand lies in its perceiving that in the process of development the notion keeps to itself, and only gives rise to alteration of form, without making any addition in point of content. (EL. pp.248-9)

The above quotation while confirming the basic aspects of development in Hegel, as described above, at the same time provides a greater insight into the complexity of the *Logic*. It is clear that the presence of Notion in Being, for instance, is an implicit one and that therefore the development leading up to Notion is a process by which the Notion-implicit becomes the Notion-explicit or simply Notion. Furthermore, Hegel by rejecting the 'box-within-box' hypothesis, essentially refutes the idea that the process of development can be reduced to the point of departure. In effect those who interpret Hegel as believing that the entire reality —

past, present and future can be reduced to a simple beginning that contains all reality in miniature form ignore the very enrichment that the process of development itself brings to the world. This error amounts to a backward projection of a 'completed thought', the apex of the most complete development, to the origin and beginnings of all reality. That Hegel need not be so mystically and even mysteriously interpreted becomes evident if we look at a few examples from Marx.

As we have seen in Chapter Two the concept of the commodity which forms the beginning of *Capital* is not the concept of the commodity as it appears in pre-capitalist conditions. This concept is based on a commodity that results from capitalist production rather than on a commodity that is the premise and the historical starting point of this form of production. If the idea of capital is already presupposed in the concept of the commodity then the commodity implicitly contains the more developed notion of capital. Further development makes this implicit aspect more explicit.

In the Introduction we discussed Marx's distinction between the method of inquiry and the method of presentation. As we interpreted this distinction the method of presentation was not merely a formal process but the essence of theoretical comprehension. Marx says that only upon the completion of the inquiry can the real movement be presented: this presentation, if successful, involves a reflection 'back in the ideas' of the 'life of the subject-matter' in such a way that it appears as an 'a priori construction'. He refers here to the same structure as we find in Hegel's *Logic*. Any scientific work starts from certain premises and ends up with certain conclusions about the subject-matter investigated. To say that the conclusions are already implicit in the premises is nothing mystical, mysterious or unusual and does not negate the crucial step of development from premises to conclusions. In general, apart from works that are unusually spontaneous or utterances of deranged minds, all acts involving human consciousness have the structure of the unity of the beginning and the end.

Our final example from Marx shows that human action (and, by analogy, all forms of human creativity, artistic as well as scientific) has a Hegelian structure. Here, Marx elegantly states the principle of the ideal presence of the end result in the beginning in discussing the specificity of human labour.

> We presuppose labour in a form in which it is an exclusively human characteristic. A spider conducts operations which resemble those of the weaver, and a bee would put many a human architect to shame by the construction of its

honeycomb cells. But what distinguishes the worst architect from the best of bees is that the architect builds the cell in his mind before he constructs it in wax. At the end of every labour process, *a result emerges which had already been conceived by the worker at the beginning, hence already existed ideally.* (C.I. pp.283-4, emphasis added)

V. MARX'S CRITIQUE OF HEGEL'S IDEALISM: A RECONSIDERATION

We have already attempted to demonstrate that Marx's methodological perspectives in the *1857 Introduction* as well as his criticisms of the classical economists have strong roots in Hegel's philosophy and logic. In this concluding section I wish to expose these roots even more deeply by examining a major critical comment by Marx on Hegel's idealism in the above-mentioned text (already quoted without elaboration in Chapter Two). Here is the quotation again:

> ... Hegel fell into the illusion of conceiving the real as the product of thought concentrating itself, probing its own depths, and unfolding itself out of itself, by itself, whereas the method of rising from the abstract to the concrete is only the way in which thought appropriates the concrete, reproduces it as the concrete in mind. But this is by no means the process by which the concrete itself comes into being. (G. p.101)

This critique in fact corresponds to the third approach to Hegel's *Logic* mentioned without further elaboration in Section III above. Now we are in a position to discuss this interpretation in conjunction with Marx's comment above.[14] We will see below that there is no basis for such an extreme and sweeping criticism of Hegel's philosophy.

Marx's criticism contains three closely related points:

i) For Hegel reality is a product of thought — a product created in a process which amounts to an unfolding of thought as a result of an *internal* self-development ('out of itself, by itself').
ii) What is described in (i), rising from abstract to concrete, is only the method by which thought 'appropriates' (comprehends) reality.
iii) Reality itself does not come about in the same way that concrete-in-thought is produced.

(Note that Marx is conflating various conceptions of thought — human thought in general, products of human thought, e.g. science, Hegel's Mind, etc.)

140

Let us take the first point above. I believe it is based on a misreading of Hegel. We have already observed in section I of this chapter how Hegel makes a distinction between mind and nature when discussing the question of return-into-self. To reiterate:

For Hegel, Nature is characterized by externality or self-externalness. As such, it stands in sharp contrast to Mind which shows a high degree of internalness or self-relation. In Mind (Spirit) higher phases of development do not simply replace lower phases but preserve and contain them as moments. We thus have a fully internal self-development in which different phases or aspects do not stand in an external relation to each other but form the moments of a single whole. Each succeeding phase of the spirit sublates the preceding phase and thus the higher development reduces the lower form to a moment of itself.

The following quotations from Hegel's *Philosophy of Mind* and *Philosophy of Nature* should amply clarify these points:

> The 'concrete' nature of mind involves for the observer the peculiar difficulty that the several grades and special types which develop its intelligible unity in detail are not left standing as so many separate existences confronting its more advanced aspects. It is otherwise in external nature. There, matter and movement, for example, have a manifestation all of their own — it is the solar system; and similarly the *differentiae* of sense perception have a sort of earlier existence in the properties of *bodies*, and still more independently in the four elements. The species and grades of mental evolution, on the contrary, lose their separate existence and become factors, states, and features in the higher grades of development. As a consequence of this, a lower and more abstract aspect of mind betrays the presence in it, even to experience, of a higher grade. (Ph.M. p.7)[15]

I believe that this passage contains a precise answer to Marx's criticism. First we find Hegel distinguishing between Nature and Mind on the basis of the principles of inwardness and internal self-development found in the latter but not in the former. Secondly, the essence of this self-development is progress through the integration of lower forms into higher forms. Thirdly, the higher form has an 'ideal' presence in the lower as a potentiality. Thus there is no hint of the presence of this internal self-development from lower to the higher, which is a characteristic of the Mind, in this complete fashion in all spheres of reality.

> In time nature comes first, but the absolute prius is the Idea. This absolute prius is the finis, the true beginning, alpha is omega. Men often consider that which is immediate to be superior to that which is mediated, because the latter seems to imply dependence. The Notion has both aspects however, it is mediation

through the sublation of mediation, and therefore immediacy. (Ph.N. v.1, p.211)

Here, when Hegel talks about an 'absolute prius' he does not mean that the Idea is first in the order of natural history (having already said that in fact nature is first). As we will see later he is objecting to a naturalist philosophy that gives primacy in thought to what is historically first, to the linear-causal explanation that limits causation and conditioning to 'first causes'. Following the above assertion Hegel offers another formulation. He states that Nature can be conceived of as a *system of stages, the one proceeding of necessity out of the other'* in such a way that the truth of each stage lies in the higher, succeeding one. But this, in fact, is not true in the nature of real evolution but only in the 'inner Idea which constitutes the ground of nature' (Ph.N. v.1, p.212). Here again the word 'ground' should not be interpreted in a naturalistic way to mean first or original causes. One does find in Hegel places where an identity between a real, historical beginning and a beginning in thought is intimated, for instance in the following statement (already quoted in Chapter One above):

> The thinking or figurate conception which has before it only a specific, determinate being must be referred back to the previously-mentioned beginning of the science made by Parmenides who purified and elevated his own figurate conception, and so, too, that of posterity, to *pure thought*, to being as such and thereby created the element of science. What is the first in the *science* had of necessity to show itself *historically* as the first. (LL. p.88)

This perspective, however, cannot be sustained consistently and systematically in view of Hegel's specific pronouncements to the contrary. But it is precisely this formulation that lies at the basis of Marx's and Engels's views of the relationship between simple commodity production and the capitalist production of commodities (both of them tend to conflate the historical development from the first to the second with the conceptual development from labour-values to production prices, as we have shown in Chapter One above). To show that this does not exhaust Hegel's total viewpoint we quote a specific commentary that appears in the *Science of Logic*:

> A capital misunderstanding which prevails on this point is that the natural principle or the beginning which forms the starting point in the natural evolution or in the history of the developing individual, is regarded as the truth, and the first in the Notion. Now in the order of nature, intuition or being are undoubtedly first, or are the conditions for the Notion, but they are not on that account the absolutely unconditioned; on the contrary, their reality is sublated in the Notion and with it, too, the illusory show they possessed of being the

conditioning reality. When it is a question, not of truth but merely of history, as in pictorial and phenomenal thinking, we need not of course go beyond merely narrating that we start with feelings and intuitions and that from the manifold of these the understanding extracts a universality or an abstraction and naturally requires for this purpose the said substrate of feelings and intuitions which, in this process of abstraction, remains for representation in the same complete reality with which it first presented itself. But philosophy is not meant to be a narration of happenings but a cognition of what is true in them, and further, on the basis of this cognition, to comprehend that which, in narrative, appears as a mere happening. (LL. p.588)

Let us recapitulate the main points made by Hegel in the above passage:

1) What constitutes the beginning of natural evolution or history (the first in 'time') is not the 'first' (or the beginning) in Notion.
2) In the order of nature, i.e. natural or historical evolution, feeling and intuition are first and conditioning (absolute necessity, the supposition, premise) for Notion; but,
3) Notion does not take these 'beginnings', these absolute premises, as given, as it finds them; rather it sublates and subsumes them. Thus,
4) The 'way' of Notion in dealing with these 'substrates', these elemental but necessary pre-conditions, is essentially different from the way Understanding deals with them. The difference consists in that the action (operation) of the latter leaves them untouched in their pristine existence while the action of Notion transforms and absorbs them into itself.

Based on the above interpretation I believe that there is no ground for identifying the 'beginning' or 'first' of Notion with the 'first' in time. And, therefore, there is no ground for Hegel's alleged 'historicism'.[16]

But the question still remains as to why Hegel sometimes identifies the 'first' in history with the 'first' in thought.

I think that the above-quoted passage contains the answer. In this passage the whole question of the first (the beginning) is problematized. The question is the very nature of the first.

For Understanding, the beginning is an external existence that remains outside thinking — an existence that not only conditions thinking but also retains an external existence in relation to thought. Such a beginning, being wholly external to thought, cannot form the beginning of thought.

Thus the beginning of thought cannot be identified with any 'real'

143

beginning. Thought begins with thought and not with 'unthought'. Thus, posing the question of the beginning is not separate from the object with whose beginning we are concerned (the beginning of what?). Thus, the beginning is only meaningful in relation to an object. The point is that the 'naturally' or 'historically' first never exists or can exist 'purely' or 'simply'. It is always 'mixed up' with other things: it is always part of a concrete existence. Therefore the 'first' can never be identified 'concretely' or in reality. The first can never be a 'concrete' reality. It has always to be sorted out of concrete reality. Therefore, it does truly belong to thought. Thus, the beginning is necessarily 'abstract'.

Furthermore, when we consider Hegel's 'absolute method' in his *Logic* this beginning is not even abstract; rather it is based on the richness of concrete development (S.3).

'First' as a temporal concept, i.e. the first in time, the natural-historical beginning, has no significance apart from the question of what is it that the beginning is the first of. 'First' or 'beginning' finds its meaning only in relation to a system that has evolved naturally or historically. As such it represents the original 'shoots' of the system. Its full meaning and significance becomes apparent only in relation to the system in its fully developed form. Conceived in this light, the 'beginning' loses its external existence as the natural-historical first, as a temporal concept and becomes fully internal to the system. The conception of the beginning as something external to thought makes sense only in the discourse of Understanding.

We have already seen that for Hegel the beginning is a) wholly internal to thought and b) abstract-simple in one sense but concrete in another sense, i.e. it is based on Notion and is not a generic concept. We also have seen in Chapter Two that Marx problematizes the whole question of the 'simple' beginning and arrives at S.3. Based on these observations, Marx's assertion above that thought moves from the abstract to the concrete is at best a simplification of the process of thought. Now it may be true historically that science begins first by analysis, by classification and then in the course of its historical evolution progressively moves towards synthesis and theorizing. But this is not necessarily the course taken by scientists when they develop and present a new theory or recast old findings in a new form of exposition.

When Marx accuses Hegel of the illusion of identifying the movement of thought with that of real history, it is in fact only an illusion of Marx himself, a misinterpretation of Hegel that, of course, is not limited to Marx. This illusion can arise from a projection of Hegel's conception

144

of Mind, which represents the highest level of development, back to the lower layers of the entire order of reality.

Marx's criticism of Hegel's idealism can also be interpreted as implying a complete correspondence between the course of history and the process of scientific theorizing. I will argue later in this section that this is not the case. At this point I wish to show that this idea is the root of the 'copy theory of knowledge' professed to be the basis of the Marxist theory of knowledge.[17] According to the latter, the 'correspondence of thinking to objective reality' is the criterion of truth. This clearly leads to a virtual identification of true thoughts with objective reality.

In all the three approaches to Marx's method reviewed in Chapter One we find a similar identification:

In the historicist approach knowledge follows reality from the historically first to the highest development. In the structuralist approach knowledge starts from basic simple relations at the bottom of the existing social totality and moves up the ladder to reach the complex structure at the top. In the rationalist school knowledge starts from simple models corresponding to simple realities and moves on to more complex models corresponding to complex systems.

In all three approaches we find thought following the order of reality in a linear fashion. There is an explicit or implicit correspondence between theory and reality.

In Hegel the relationship between thought and reality is more complex. The activity, subjectivity and negativity of thought has the ability to rise above reality. If this is possible then there may be a disjunction between being and thinking, theory and reality. Thinking will not reflect being in a simple, linear and subordinate way but will advance beyond it and in fact reach a situation where reality reflects thinking (through the prediction of future events by scientific methods, the production of new 'facts',[18] etc.) Knowledge is not a reproduction of concrete reality in the form of concrete-in-thought, as Marx claims. Why reproduce reality if we have the reality at hand, present in knowledge in a non-problematic manner? Why is such a reproduction needed if there is a perfect correspondence between thought and reality? The need for knowledge exists precisely because reality is not present in knowledge, and thought cannot simply reflect reality as in a mirror. If such reflection were possible the need for theorizing would not arise. In fact knowledge does not simply reproduce reality but, in a sense, 'produces' it.

For Hegel the activity and creativity of the human mind do not remain indifferent to 'objective' reality but proceed to interpret it. This interpretation does not alter reality but puts it in a new context. It does, however, change the significance of the objective reality, especially in relation to the knowing subject. From this perspective it would appear that it is Mind that creates the objective world and this would lead to an interpretation of Hegel's view of knowledge as 'idealistic'.

The correspondence thesis discussed above is not, however, completely dismissed by Hegel. In the first place, for Hegel truth is an idea that is 'adequate' to its 'object'. The latter, however, should not be interpreted as a 'real' object. Secondly the correspondence is a special case and not the general rule. The fact that except in a most fully developed form there is a real disjuncture between the order of reality and the order of thought is most clearly expressed in the following quotation from Hegel's *Philosophy of Right*:

> In a more speculative sense, a concept's determinacy and its mode of existence are one and the same thing. But it is to be noticed that the moments, whose result is a further determined form of the concept, precede it in the philosophical development of the Idea as determinations of the concept, but *they do not go in advance of it in the temporal development as shapes of experience*. Thus, for instance, the Idea determined as the family, presupposes the determinations of the concept from which family will later on in this work be shown to result. But the explicit existence of these inner suppositions as shapes of existence also, e.g. as the right of property, contract, morality, and so forth, is the other aspect of the development, and it is *only in a higher and more complete civilization* that the development has gone so far as to endow its moments with this appropriately shaped existence. (Ph.R. p.35)

Hegel's view as expressed in the above quotation can be summarized in three points:

a) The determinations of a concept (Notion, Idea) such as the family involves a number of moments, determining characteristics, or even 'pre-conditions'. This is the subjective side of the development of the concept of family.

b) There is also 'the other aspect of development', i.e. the objective, real development of the concept of the institution of family in history. The forms taken by this development are what Hegel calls the 'shapes of experience'.

c) There is no necessary correspondence between moments in the concept of family and the real forms that this institution takes in the course of its historical development (the latter 'do not go in advance of it [the concept] in the temporal [real, historical] development as shapes of experience'). In fact there may be a real disjunction between the temporal and objective development and the order of moments in the idea. It is only 'in a higher and more complete civilization' that development 'goes so far' as to give all the moments in the Idea the 'shape of experience', i.e. an objective form.

Thus to insist on identity of thought and being is to assume that a higher and more complete form has already been achieved.

There are many examples of this dialectical relationship between conceptual development and historical development in both the *Grundrisse* and *Capital*. As I have quoted many relevant passages from the *1857 Introduction* in Chapter Two (Section II) I shall confine myself here to an example from *Capital I*.

The mobility of labour under capitalism has often been upheld not only as an essential feature of capitalism but also as a necessary pre-condition for capitalism. This view seems to be based on Marx's characterization of labour under capitalism as free labour — free in a double sense: (i) free from servile relations of production and (ii) free from ownership of means of production. The historical experience of capitalist development not only in England (which served as Marx's model) but also in other countries shows that to interpret 'free' labour as labour that 'freely' moves between jobs and to interpret this freedom as the quintessence of capitalism is a gross exaggeration. This kind of freedom is only tangentially present in the logic of capitalist development and, according to Marx himself, it becomes a 'law of social production' only under socialism. For instance, Marx says:

> Thus large-scale industry, by its very nature, necessitates variation of labour, fluidity of functions, and mobility of the worker in all directions. But on the other hand, in its capitalist form it reproduces the old division of labour with its ossified particularities. (C.I. p.617)

For Marx 'mobility between jobs' is a requirement of *large-scale industry* and not of capitalism in itself; in fact, the capitalist mode of production, to the extent that it involves large-scale production, meets this necessity in a 'negative' form and only partially. Thus Marx comments that in its capitalist form the mobility of labour means a complete lack of 'all repose, all fixity and all security as far as the worker's life situation is concerned.' It leads to threatening the means of subsistence of the worker by 'snatching' away his means of production and to his superfluity through suppression of 'his specialized function'. But in spite of this negative form

147

'large-scale industry . . . makes the recognition of variation of labour and hence the fitness of the worker for the maximum number of different kinds of labour into a question of life and death.' He goes on to say:

> This possibility of varying labour must become a general law of social production, and existing relations must be adapted to permit its realization in practice. (C.I. p.618)

Thus for Marx 'perfect mobility of labour' although present partially and as a tendency in large-scale industry under the capitalist mode of production is really never perfect due to its negative form. Existing social relations 'must be adapted' before this mobility achieves perfection. What this adaptation involves is made clear in Marx's subsequent elaboration:

> That monstrosity, the disposable working population held in reserve, in misery, for the changing requirements of capitalist exploitation, must be replaced by the individual man who is absolutely available for the different kinds of labour required of him; the partially developed individual, who is merely the bearer of one specialized social function, must be replaced by the totally developed individual for whom the different social functions are different modes of activity he takes up in turn. (C.I. p.618)

Thus perfect mobility of labour between jobs cannot be justified on the basis of Marx's writings as an 'absolute' law and condition of capitalist production. Nor can 'freedom' of labour in an absolute sense be considered as a hallmark of capitalism. That is why Marx often refers to the 'free' worker of the capitalist mode of production as a 'wage-slave'.

We can see from the example above that Marx approaches the question of the mobility of labour under capitalism in a truly Hegelian manner: the mobility of labour exists under capitalism only 'negatively' and imperfectly: it achieves perfection only in a more advanced form of society.

I wish to conclude this chapter by some comments on the specific nature of Hegel's theory of knowledge that makes it especially suitable for those branches of knowledge, such as the social sciences, that deal with developing and dynamic realities.

Hegel's position avoids the dualism that characterize both idealism and materialism, especially in their extreme or unsophisticated forms. In idealism, reality reflects thinking and in materialism it is the other way round. A rigid and fixed opposition between reality and thought is the common ground of both. In idealism, it is thinking that is most secure and capable of order and certainty while reality represents an uncertain, unordered and, ultimately, unknowable world. In materialism, it is thinking that lacks the qualities of order and certainty while reality is assumed to be orderly and thus capable of being known.

Hegel avoids this dualism. What is different in Hegel compared to European philosophers of the modern age who came before him, from Descartes to Kant, is what Engels describes as 'the tremendous sense of the historical', or the developmental perspective, in Hegel.[19]

Both idealism and materialism take reality and thought as *given*, as fixed in time and space. They do not question the nature of the reality or thought. In opposition to materialism, Hegel maintains that what it considers as properties of the objective world, order and certainty for instance, also belong to thought and they belong there in an even stronger sense compared with reality. As opposed to idealism he claims that the properties of thinking, the ability to differentiate and distinguish for example, also exists in nature, e.g. the differentiation of species.[20]

Thus neither reality nor thought are devoid of order. Order is neither copied by thought from reality nor is it imposed by thought on reality. The question is not order as opposed to disorder, organization as opposed to chaos but varying kinds and degrees of order and organization.

If reality is conceived of as consisting of different levels and degrees of order and this reality is also perceived to include thought, then we do not have a rigid dichotomy between a thought-ordering reality or a reality-ordering thought. Thus the classical dichotomy disappears and is replaced by a system in which there is neither complete harmony nor rigid disjunction between thought and reality or, still better, between all levels of reality including thought.

For Hegel it is only in religion, art and philosophy that object and subject, reality and thought merge to form a perfect harmony, where the notions correspond to or are adequate to their object and where thought is most concrete and least abstract.

Thought in its concrete forms is a reality most capable of order. But since other realities are also differentiated, ordered and organized in various degrees and levels, thinking based on its own order and organization is capable not only of discovering order in reality but also of ordering reality in the image of thought. This is the basis for theorizing, predicting and also action in the external world.

1. For a basic introduction to Hegel see Singer (1983). G. R. G. Mure's two introductory texts on Hegel can be consulted for more detailed treatment (Mure, 1940 & 1965). Taylor (1975) represents a much more detailed and comprehensive exposition. On the *Logic* the following sources may be consulted:
William Wallace's *Prolegomena* accompanying his translation of Hegel's (Encyclopaedia) *Logic* (Hegel, 1873) is a useful introduction. John G. Hibben's early work (Hibben, 1902) is a very lucid treatment of Hegel's *Logic*. More detailed and complex treatments can be found in Harris (1890) and Mure (1950). Taylor (1975) gives extensive treatment to the *Logic*.
MacIntyre (1972), Weiss (1974) and Inwood (1985) are very good collections of scholarly papers on various facets of Hegelian philosophy.
MacGregor (1984) represents a rather unconventional but interesting interpretation, proposing a very close relationship between all aspects of the doctrines of Hegel and Marx.
2. Hegel's *Logic* exists in two versions: i) *The Science of Logic* published in three volumes (1812-1816), which represents the more detailed treatment and therefore is referred to as the Larger *Logic* (LL.); ii) the second version, which is a smaller work, appeared as the First Part of the *Encyclopaedia of the Philosophical Sciences* first in 1817 and subsequently went through two further editions (1827 & 1830); this is referred to as the Encyclopaedia *Logic* (EL.). In this chapter we will be drawing on both versions.
3. In this first section I am using Hegel's *Lectures on the History of Philosophy* (LHP.), in preference to the *Logic*, for the following reason:
LHP. along with his Lectures on *Aesthetics* and *Philosophy of Religion* were published posthumously based on his notes and the notes taken by his students during 1818-1831 when he lectured at the University of Berlin. According to J. Glenn Gray, although these notes 'were never intended for publication in their present form, there are definite advantages to their informal lecture style. As spoken words they are more easily comprehensible than are Hegel's published works. Goethe was one of the first to remark, after a long visit from Hegel, the great difference between reading Hegel's books and talking to him: "that which seems unclear and abstruse in the writings of such a man — because we cannot directly apply it to our own needs — becomes in vital conversation with him very soon our own property".' (Hegel, 1970, pp.5-6)
4. See Ilyenkov (1977), pp.348-50, for a short discussion of Hegel's evaluation of Aristotle's theory of the soul.
5. Compare with what Marx says about the division between commodities and money in *Capital I*:
"Money necessarily crystallizes out of the process of exchange, in which different products of labour are in fact equated with each other, and thus converted into commodities. The historical broadening and deepening of the phenomenon of exchange develops the opposition between use-value and value which is latent in the nature of the commodity. The need to give an external expression to this opposition for the purposes of commercial intercourse produces the drive towards an independent form of value, which finds neither rest nor peace until an independent form has been achieved by the differentiation of commodities into commodities and money. At the same rate, then, as the transformation of the products of labour into commodities is accomplished, one particular commodity is transformed into money." (C.I. p.181)
6. Hegel discusses British empiricist philosophers in some detail in LHP. (V.3): Bacon (pp.170-88), Locke (pp.295-313), Hobbes (pp.315-19), Berkeley (pp.364-9) and Hume (pp.369-75).
See also his discussion of Scottish philosophy (pp.375-9), where he compares it to Kantian philosophy. For instance, he states at the beginning of his discussion:
"In Scotland quite another school of thought developed, and the Scotch are the foremost of Hume's opponents; in German Philosophy, on the other hand, we have to recognize in Kant another opposing force to that of Hume. To the Scottish school many philosophers belong . . . . To the scepticism of Hume they oppose an inward independent source of truth for all that pertains to religion and morality. This coincides with Kant, who also maintains an inward source or spring as against external perception; but in the case of Kant this has quite another form than which it possesses with Scottish philosophers." (LHP. p.375)
Note that my discussion of the empiricist philosophers and Kant involves formulations that

(except when Hegel is quoted and commented upon) may not necessarily coincide with Hegel's judgements, as I have not attempted to summarize Hegel's arguments at all points in this chapter.

7. See Cassirer (1981) for a detailed and sympathetic account of Kant's life and work. For a basic exposition see Körner (1955). Hegel discusses Kant in great detail in LHP. (pp.423-78).

8. Kant (1929).

9. See also LHP. (pp.410-23) for a discussion of Jacobi.

10. 'Notion' is another word for concept (*Begriff* in German). The term Notion has been preferred to concept by many English translators and interpreters of Hegel (Taylor, 1975 is an exception) in order to distinguish Hegel's ideal view of what concepts should be like from the idea of concept in Understanding. However this procedure, which I too prefer for practical reasons and have followed in this work, has the pitfall of implying an absolute opposition between the concepts of Understanding and the Hegelian Notions. As we shall see the whole thrust of Hegel's Philosophy is to overcome these fixed oppositions.

11. The lowest form of thinking for Hegel is what he calls 'pictorial thinking', which is at the level of mere sensation or perception. At this level thinking is quite involved and mixed up with the concrete (real) content of sense experience. Therefore no pure thought-form, for example a form completely detached from the objective reality, a form that is pure thought in itself, can arise at this stage.

'Understanding' overcomes this limitation by generating 'concepts', i.e. abstractions, universals, etc. At the level of understanding concepts are 'abstract universalities'. The decisive step taken by understanding is to create universals, that is, thought determinations in themselves, general concepts that cannot be identified with any particular 'real' instance. This step represents the birth of pure thought forms. But the new-born bears the birth-marks of its progenitor. It is afflicted by a curious kind of materiality and primitive reality.

The example of the concept or universal as the 'common element' is typical of the level of understanding. Concept in this sense is universal (it is a thought-form) but it still bears the mark of the real individuals from which it is extracted. It has a 'thing-like' character. Thus while it is abstract (universal) in the sense that it cannot be reduced to any real instance, it is not abstract (universal) enough. That is to say it is abstract in the sense of its detachment from reality (it is abstract in itself) but it is not abstract enough because it is still based on the duality between the thought-form it represents and the concrete (real) instances on which it is based.

Let us look at the question of 'abstractness' at the level of Understanding more closely. In Hegel, the abstraction at this level has a double significance. There is first of all the 'good' sense of abstraction which is identical to Hegel's concept of universality. Secondly, we have the 'bad' sense of abstraction, which arises precisely from the nature of abstraction at this level. The act of abstraction here amounts to a 'surgical' operation in which the concept is 'stripped' from the concrete circumstances of its existence. In this process the concept is emptied out of its concrete content. The concept thus bears the marks of its birth. It is abstract in the sense of being deprived of concrete relations. Thus although the concept has gained its 'independence', it is only 'formally' independent. Its 'abstractness' implicitly refers to the external conditions from which it has been 'severed'. Thus it is still external in the sense of not being fully internal to thought.

In Notion, concept comes into its own. As Notion, concept is no longer 'abstract' because it is no longer a concept 'abstracted' from an external system. Rather it is fully internal to the system to which it belongs.

That is why Hegel brands concepts of Understanding as abstract universality. They are universals and thus thought-forms, but because they retain a certain relationship with their concrete (real) counterparts they remain abstract — abstract not in the sense of detachment from their real instances but in relation to thought.

Let us see how Hegel evaluates concepts as they appear at this level. 'Philosophy has to do with Ideas, and therefore not with what are commonly dubbed "mere concepts". On the contrary, it exposes such concepts as one-sided and false, while showing at the same time that it is the concept alone (not the mere abstract category of the understanding which we hear called by the same) which has actuality, and further that it gives this actuality to itself. All else, apart from this actuality established through the working of the concept itself, is ephemeral existence, external contingency, opinion, unsubstantial appearance, falsity, illusion, and so forth. The shapes which the concept assumes in the course of its actualization are indispensable for the knowledge of the concept itself. They are the second essential moment of the Idea, in distinction from the first, i.e. from its form, from its mode of being as concept alone.' (Ph.R. p.14)

From the above quotation it is clear that Hegel conceives of concepts in two different ways: 1) Concept at the level of Understanding. Here the concept is a mere form. It is the first moment of something higher: it is the Idea's 'mode of being as concept alone'. Thus concept in its first meaning is the first essential moment of the Idea.

2) Concept as Idea, or 'Notion'. It is a unity of form and content. This result presupposes what Hegel calls 'the second essential moment of the Idea'.

This second essential moment consists of the transition from being to essence in Hegel's *Logic*. In this transition the shapes that the concept takes in its process of actualization become prominent.

Hegel arrives at a conception of Notion through the contradictions of the concept at the level of Understanding.

The concept in its elementary, empirical form (as, for example, obtained by abstracting common elements of the objects of experience) is deficient but at the same time it points towards a higher form, the Notion.

The elementary concept is based on what is common to a variety of individuals. But even at this level it is a universal. In it, we have a reality that is distinct from empirical facts: it is 'abstract', for example detached from reality and, thus, is not bound up with the empirical existence of objects. It is its 'ideality' that constitutes its essential nature. But this ideality is in contradiction with the 'thing-like' character of the elementary concept. The concept at this level retains a certain reality and familiarity: we recognize each particular object of sense-experience as a particular instance of the universal concept. Thus the universal finds a natural ground in every particular instance. Hence the particular and the universal correspond unambiguously to each other. Obviously the concept cannot be identified with any particular instance. In concept, we have a reality which cannot be identified with any specific particular.

The Notion resolves the contradiction inherent in the elementary concepts (for example concept at the level of Understanding). This resolution takes the form of the internalization of external differences. In Notion, the differences of form that exist externally and deprive the concept of its concreteness become forms and moments that are internal and necessary for the concept (Notion). Thus the contradiction between the general concept (universal) and its specific instances is resolved in Notion. These instances as forms of existence are subsumed under Notion.

The contradiction is resolved because the Notion has achieved the concreteness it was deprived of in the ordinary concept of 'Understanding'.

12. For example Marx in his *Critique of the Gotha Programme* discusses how in the first phase of communist society workers are rewarded on the basis of their work rather than their needs. He asserts that this 'equal' treatment of 'unequal' workers implies that bourgeois right (as equal right) still exists in this phase of development. Like equality before law the equality in distribution is based on a common standard, i.e. labour. In this relationship workers 'are regarded *only as workers*, and nothing more is seen in them, everything else being ignored' (Marx 1972, p.16).

13. On the deep impression made by Kant's *Critique of Judgement* on Goethe see Cassirer (1981), pp.273-4.

14. Taylor characterizes Hegel's *Logic* in the following terms:

'The *Logic* thus presents the chain of necessarily connected concepts which give the conceptual structure of reality . . . . The *Logic* shows a necessary conceptual structure of reality based on contradiction . . . What the *Logic* gives us therefore is the basic formula of rational necessity which embodies itself and thus is manifest in the universe . . . . Thus the formula presented in *Logic* is in a sense the inner kernel of *Geist's* self-knowledge, God's inner intellectual life . . .' (Taylor 1975, p.231)

15. Here is an alternative and more recent translation of this important passage:

'Observation of the concrete nature of spirit is peculiarly difficult, in that the particular stages and determinations in the development of its Notion do not remain behind together as particular existences confronting its profounder formations. In the case of external nature they do however: matter and motion have their free existence as the solar system, the determinations of the senses also exist retrogressively as the properties of bodies, and even more freely as elements, etc. The determinations and stages of spirit occur in the higher stages of its development essentially only as moments, conditions, determinations, so that what is higher already shows itself to be empirically present in a lower and more abstract determination, all higher spirituality, for example, being already in evidence as content or determinateness within sensation. Superficially, it might therefore seem necessary to regard that which is religious, ethical, etc. as having its essential placing and even root as the content of the simply abstract form of sensation, and to regard the determinations of it as particular kinds of sensation. If lower stages are regarded with reference to their empirical existence however, higher stages will have to be simultaneously recollected. Since they are only present within these higher stages as forms, this procedure gives rise to the anticipation of a content which only presents itself later in the development. Consciousness is anticipated in natural awakening for example, the understanding in derangement, etc.' (Hegel 1978, pp.23-5)

16. Hegel's *Phenomenology of Mind*, which attempts to chart out the historical development of human social consciousness, can easily be construed as representing the profile of the growth of the consciousness of the thinking human individual. Hegel himself is aware of the possibility of such an interpretation and warns against it in his Preface to the *Phenomenology*:

'The task of conducting the individual mind from its unscientific standpoint to that of science had to be taken in its general sense; we had to contemplate the formative development (*Bildung*) of the universal [or general] individual, of self-conscious spirit. As to the relation between these two [the particular and general individual], every moment, as it gains concrete form and its own proper shape and appearance, finds a place in the life of the universal individual. The particular individual is incomplete mind, a concrete shape in whose existence, taken as a whole, one determinate characteristic predominates, while the others are found only in blurred outline. In that mind which stands higher than another the lower concrete form of existence has sunk into an obscure moment; what was formerly an objective fact (*die Sache selbst*) is now only a single trace: its definite shape has been veiled, and become simply a piece of shading. The individual, whose substance is mind at the higher level, passes through these past forms, much in the way that one who takes up a higher science goes through those preparatory forms of knowledge, which he has long made his own, in order to call up their content before him; he brings back the recollection of them without stopping to fix his interest upon them. The particular individual, so far as content is concerned, has also to go through the stages through which the general mind has passed, but as shapes once assumed by mind and now laid aside, as stages of a road which has been worked over and levelled out. Hence it is that, in the case of various kinds of knowledge, we find that what in former days occupied the energies of men of mature mental ability sinks to the level of information, exercises, and even pastimes, for children; and in this educational progress we can see the history of the world's culture delineated in faint outline. This by-gone mode of existence has already become an acquired possession of the general mind, which constitutes the substance of the individual, and, by thus appearing externally to him, furnishes his inorganic nature. In this respect culture or development of mind (*Bildung*), regarded from the side of the individual, consists in his acquiring what lies at his hand ready for him, in making its inorganic nature organic to himself, and taking possession of it for himself. Looked at, however, from the side of universal mind *qua* general spiritual substance, culture means nothing else than that this substance gives itself its own self-consciousness, brings about its own inherent process and its own reflection into self.' (PM. pp.89-90)

Thus for Hegel, while any process of development passes through certain necessary stages, the exact profile of the passage is not a replica of an historically prior process of development. On the contrary, each new phase of development takes stock of the previous experience of development and no process of development can be assimilated exactly to a prior process or a general formula. To do so would amount to a virtual denial of any form of development or progress. For Hegel the forms of social consciousness or knowledge represented by religion, art and philosophy constitute forms of Absolute Mind or Spirit, i.e. the highest forms of human social consciousness. Yet if we look at historical development these forms make their appearance very early in human history and thus are not historically the end results of the development of human social consciousness. It cannot be denied, however, that Hegel on certain occasions proposes the identity of the beginning in thought or science with a historical beginning.

Based on the above observations I do not think that there is any ground for the charge of 'historicism', in a general sense, in Hegel. However, it may be legitimately claimed that Hegel was an historicist in a narrower sense. His philosophy of history shows that in fact he was indeed an 'historicist'. According to his philosophy of history, the historical process consists of the self-development of the Spirit. Thus an original and invariant essence, i.e. Spirit, is present from the very beginning of human history and that historical development is nothing but an unfolding and ever more self-revealing of this world Spirit.

It is in his philosophy of history that Hegel comes closest to mysticism and speculation (in its worst sense). Hegel, however, cannot be blamed for detecting a design of historical progression in history any more than Darwin for discovering the principle of natural selection that governs the evolution of species.

In any evolutionary process (the natural evolution of species or historical evolution of mankind) conceived as an organic development a predestined form or principle, an Aristotelian 'final cause' is presupposed. In this sense, Hegel's World Spirit and Darwin's 'natural selection' have comparable status. In both cases evolution follows a certain path or law that governs the process of evolution from the beginning; therefore, it must be present from the beginning. However, besides the justification given above, Hegel's philosophy of history finds a fuller justification in the context of his whole system and, especially, in relation to his Philosophy of Spirit (or Mind).

For Hegel, human history occupies a special place in his system because of the high degree of internal cohesion and self-relatedness that it exhibits compared with nature — a cohesion that comes closest to the self-relatedness of reason whose forms are explored in their fullest maturity in his *Logic*. In Hegel's system history, narrowly defined, corresponds to Objective Spirit. As such it is a phase of the development of spirit which comprises the three phases of subjective, objective and absolute spirit. Human history however, broadly defined, canvases the entirety of the development of spirit.

17. The 'copy' theory of knowledge finds its most explicit and crudest form in Lenin's *Materialism and Empirio-criticism* (Lenin, 1970). For a more sophisticated modern treatment see Cornforth (1976).

18. See Lakatos (1978), where he claims that 'in a progressive research programme, theory leads to the discovery of hitherto unknown novel facts'. He gives the following examples: 'Halley, working in Newton's programme, calculated on the basis of observing a brief stretch of a comet's path that it would return in seventy-two years' time; he calculated to the minute when it would be seen again at a well-defined point of the sky. It was incredible. But seventy-two years later, when both Newton and Halley were long dead, Halley's comet returned exactly as Halley predicted. Similarly, Newtonian scientists predicted the existence and exact motion of small planets which had never been observed before. Or let us take Einstein's programme. This programme made the stunning prediction that if one measures the distance between two stars in the night and if one measures the distance between them during the day (when they are visible during an eclipse of the sun), the two measurements will be different. Nobody had thought to make such an observation before Einstein's programme.' (p.5)

19. Engels states this in his 1859 review of Marx's *Critique*. See Chapter One above for the exact reference and a detailed discussion of Engels's views on Marx-Hegel relationship.

20. See, for instance, Hegel's discussions of organic nature in his *Phenomenology* (PM. pp.284-327).

PART II

MARX'S CONCEPTS IN *CAPITAL*

CHAPTER FIVE

THE CIRCLE OF CIRCULATION

The concepts of 'circulation' and 'simple circulation' of commodities play a key role in Marx's *Capital* and in interpretations of this work, as is evident from the debates concerning the theoretical status of the concepts of 'simple circulation of commodities', 'simple commodity production' and 'simple exchange' in Marx's work. These concepts have also been important in debates concerning the transition from feudalism to capitalism, as well as in the dependency school of underdevelopment and the modes of production debate.[1]

Circulation is often conceived as a mere phase in the linear-teleological chain consisting of production, circulation, exchange, distribution and consumption. This is equally so in both mainstream and the Marxist economics.[2] An example from the latter should suffice to illustrate this mechanistic and one-sided view of circulation.

The standard Marxist approach to the determination of commodity values can be put in the following terms. Values are *created* in production and only *'realized'* in circulation. This approach is based on the following premises:

i) Production and circulation are analytically distinct spheres of the economy.
ii) Production is dominant over circulation in the sense that it is the origin and the creator of values.
iii) Circulation is merely an external constraint: it can help to realize the labour-value already contained in the commodity or it may only partially realize it (if not completely destroy it).[3]

157

Our purpose here is not to go into the intricacies of value theory[4] but to point out that while in some parts of Marx's exposition a one-sided view of circulation is presented, his overall treatment of the concept of circulation is much more complex.

That there is a terminological difficulty in *Capital* concerning these concepts cannot be doubted. Marx often uses the word 'circulation' with different meanings (sometimes in the same sentence or passage). Furthermore, 'circulation' and 'simple circulation' are sometimes used alternatively to designate one and the same concept. However, behind the terminological difficulty there lies a much more formidable problem. There is a conceptual complexity underlying the terminological confusion.

In what follows we will try to show that in Marx's *Capital* there are three concepts of 'circulation', whether characterized as 'simple' or not — that need to be clearly distinguished from each other. These concepts can be identified as follows:

C.1 *Circulation as a concept representing pre-capitalist forms of exchange and circulation of commodities.*
C.2 *Circulation as a concept representing commodity circulation and exchange under capitalism.*
C.3 *Circulation as a general form or foundation of the capitalist mode of production.*

The confusion of these meanings and concepts and their bracketing under the general concept of 'circulation' or 'simple circulation' — a confusion partially due to the lack of conceptual and terminological precision on the part of Marx himself — has led to many misinterpretations, with definite theoretical and practical consequences. The 'generic' concept of circulation is empty, as it does not distinguish between the various roles and functions of circulation under diverse forms of social production. Our distinguishing of three concepts of circulation is an attempt to overcome the generic concept and thus refute the view that circulation has a place and function which remains invariant in all economic systems.

The Two Concepts of Circulation in Capital

In the course of developing the concept of 'capital' Marx arrives at two

158

different concepts of circulation — concepts which are not explicitly distinguished from each other by him. This lack of terminological precision often leads to logical contradictions in Marx's discourse, as we will see below.

> To develop the concept of capital it is necessary to begin not with labour but with value, and, precisely, with exchange value in an already developed movement of circulation. (G. p.259)

What Marx means by 'exchange value in an already developed movement of circulation' is what he often calls the 'simple circulation of commodities', i.e. the exchange of commodities using a medium of exchange (e.g. money), and which is symbolically represented by the formula C-M-C. In this process a commodity is exchanged for money and then this money is used to buy another commodity by the person who sold the first commodity. This form of exchange is distinguished from barter by the fact that in the former the value of commodities has acquired a form that is independent of its material existence as exchange value, i.e. it has acquired the form of money or the monetary form, a form independent of the change of form or exchange of matter taking place in the process of exchange.

The monetary form of value, or money, has, it seems, achieved independence from the circulation of commodities. This independence, however, has its limits:

> We have seen that in money, as such, exchange value has already attained a form independent of circulation, but only a negative, transitory or, when fixated, an illusory form. It exists only in connection with circulation and as the possibility of entering into it; but it loses this character as soon as it realizes itself, and falls back on its two earlier roles, as measure of exchange value and as medium of exchange. (G. p.259)
>
> The independent form, i.e. the monetary form, which the value of commodities assumes in simple circulation, does nothing but mediate the exchange of commodities, and it vanishes in the final result of the movement. (C.I. p.255)

We see that exchange value in its monetary form attains an independence which is negative, transitory, etc. In the 'simple' circulation of commodities either money is exchanged for a commodity (i.e. M forms the point of departure), the M-C phase, or a commodity is exchanged for money (i.e. C forms the starting point), the C-M phase. In the first case, 'the exchange value of the commodity disappears in favour of its material content (substance)' and in the second case 'its content (sub-

159

stance) disappears in favour of its form as exchange value. In the first case, the form of exchange value is extinguished; in the second, its substance; in both, therefore, its realization is its disappearance' (G. p.260).

Money, as a form of exchange value, is independent of circulation only to the extent that exchange value in the form of money possesses a form which is not bound up with the material substance of commodities, i.e. it has an existence of its own. This independence, however, is transitory since in the exchange process, whose substance is a material change of form from one use-value to another, money serves only as an intermediary and moves outside the sphere of circulation as soon as it has served its function. We should not conclude that the 'simple' circulation of commodities C-M-C is, in the last analysis, barter and that money serves merely as an instrument which facilitates the exchange process without making a qualitative difference. First, without money or, generally speaking, the equivalent form, we do not have a movement of values in the circulation process, only a material exchange. Secondly, money as a medium of exchange transforms the simultaneity of the acts of sale and purchase by the parties involved in barter (C-C) into two distinct acts, C-M and M-C, that may be disjoint in time and space.

Let us now see how the full independence from circulation denied to money in its function as the medium of exchange is accorded to it when functioning as capital. In the form of capital, money is not only independent of circulation but also maintains and preserves itself through it. Indeed, the independence achieved by money as a mere medium of exchange in the circulation process was an 'external' independence; it was not rooted in the circulation process itself.

> As soon as money is posited as an exchange value which not only becomes independent of circulation, but which also maintains itself through it, then it is no longer money . . . but is *capital*. (G. p.259)

We see a crucial transition taking place here. Marx, in analysing money as capital, is transforming the concept of circulation. It is no longer a question of the 'simple' circulation of commodities in which money serves as the medium of exchange. We are facing a different kind of circulation now: the circulation of money as capital, i.e. the process symbolized by Marx as M-C-M.

> . . . in circulation M-C-M both money and the commodity function only as different modes of existence of value itself . . . . It is constantly changing from

one form into the other, without becoming lost in this movement; it thus becomes transformed into an automatic subject. (C.I. p.255)

Only with *capital* is exchange value posited as exchange value in such a way that it preserves itself in circulation. . . . It therefore always remains money and always commodity. It is in every moment both of the moments that disappear into one another in circulation. (G. p.260-1)

The only aspect in which capital is here posited as distinct from direct exchange value and from money is *that of exchange value which preserves and perpetuates itself in and through circulation*. (G. p.262)

The distinguishing mark of money in its role as capital — in contrast with its function as exchange value in 'simple' circulation — is that it achieves independence from the circulation process, not by running away from it (as in commodity circulation) but by settling down permanently in that process. This independence is no longer 'external' but 'internal'. This 'dialectic', this 'unity of opposites' (money as capital becoming independent of *circulation* while maintaining itself through *circulation*) breaks down if we note that the word 'circulation' is used in two entirely different ways and that it designates two concepts and not just one. If we do not make this distinction we face a logical contradiction.

Let us break down the above-quoted sentence from the *Grundrisse*:

a) 'money . . . as an exchange value which . . . becomes independent of *circulation* (emphasis added)

b) '. . . which also maintains itself through it' (i.e. *circulation*).

We can see that the word 'circulation' is used with two entirely different meanings in this sentence. Circulation in (a) is the 'simple' circulation of commodities; while in (b) it is the circulation of money as capital.

Before proceeding further let us consider a more glaring example of this 'dialectic' at a crucial point in *Capital* itself.

In *Capital* I, Marx after demonstrating that the circulation process of commodities cannot lead to any increase in the value of commodities and, therefore, surplus-value cannot originate in the exchange of commodities, goes on to show that no excess or surplus labour outside the sphere of, and without connection to, circulation can become surplus-value. He concludes his arguments with the following statement:

Capital cannot therefore arise from circulation and it is equally impossible for it to arise apart from circulation. It must have its origin both in and not in circulation. (C.I. p.268)

161

The assertion that capital 'must have its origin both in and not in circulation' obviously involves a logical contradiction. The only way to resolve (or rather remove) this logical contradiction is by recognizing that Marx is using two definitions of circulation, without explicitly admitting it.

An easy way out of this logical contradiction suggests itself from the foregoing discussion about the distinction between the 'simple' circulation of commodities, C-M-C, and the circulation of money as capital. Thus one may claim that Marx in saying that 'capital cannot therefore arise from circulation' is referring to the 'simple' circulation or commodities, C-M-C; and when he says that 'it is equally impossible for it [capital] to arise apart from circulation' he has the circulation of money as capital, M-C-M, in mind.

The fact that Marx calls both of these processes, the circulation of commodities and the circulation of money as capital, by the same name, i.e. circulation is obvious. What is not so obvious is that, apart from the circulation of capital, M-C-M, Marx conceives of the 'simple' circulation of commodities itself in two different ways. Thus, we not only have a distinction between commodity circulation on the one hand and the circulation of money as capital on the other, but also a distinction within the concept of the 'simple' circulation of commodities itself.

Before dealing with this question we consider another issue, which involves the idea of circularity in the concept of circulation.

The 'Circularity' of Circulation

In the *Grundrisse*, after introducing capital as a form of exchange value that preserves itself in circulation, Marx makes a distinction between the circulation of money as capital and 'that of simple exchange values as such'.

> Simple circulation is in fact circulation only from the standpoint of the observer, or *in itself*, not posited as such. It is not always the same exchange value — precisely because its substance is a particular commodity — which first becomes money and then a commodity again; rather, it is always different commodities, different exchange values which confront money. Circulation, the circular path, consists merely of the simple repetition or alternation of the role of commodity and money, and not of the identity of the real point of departure and point of return. Therefore, in characterizing simple circulation as such, where money alone is the persistent moment, the term *money circulation, money turnover* has been applied. (G. p.261)

There are two important ideas expressed in this passage, which may be put in the following way.

a) 'Simple' circulation is not properly *circular*; it is only circular relative to 'the observer', or in itself; circulation in this case consists merely in the simple repetition or alternation of the roles of money and commodities.[5]

b) *True circularity*, which is a characteristic of the circulation of money as capital, consists of '*the identity of the real point of departure and the point of return*'.

We will now explore these two points in detail.

a) The Circularity of Simple Circulation

The circuit of 'simple' commodity circulation, C-M-C, has the appearance of being circular in that the circuit begins with the commodity form C and ends with the same form.

> The two inverted phases of movement which makes up the metamorphosis of a commodity constitute a circuit: commodity-form, stripping off of this form, and return to it. (C.I. p.207)

Thus if we abstract from the material substances of commodities the whole movement C-M-C would appear as truly circular. In this abstraction, however, we are ignoring the material difference between the substances of the two commodity forms that open and close the circuit. But it is this difference between the beginning and the end of the circuit that constitutes its rationale and essence. In other words, the material difference between the commodity forms that figure at the beginning and at the end of the circuit C-M-C is the foundation of the 'simple' circulation of commodities. Without this difference the circuit would lose all meaning: we do not exchange materially identical commodities with each other. This must be true because the C-M-C circuit is geared to the exchange of use values for private (or internal) use or consumption (whether personal or productive). In 'simple' circulation 'it is always different commodities, different exchange values which confront money'.

Thus C-M-C lacks true circularity: there is no identity between the point of departure and the point of return. Even when a quantitative equality between the values of the first and the last C (which is the normal state of affairs in commodity exchange) is assumed, this assumption does not save the situation because in this circuit the object is not the acquisition of values but of use-values. The essence of this relationship consists of the qualitative incongruity between the two end-points whereas quantitative congruity is a secondary consideration.

Now that we have seen that the 'simple' circulation of commodities, C-M-C is not properly 'circular', the question arises as to why the term circulation is applied in this case. Marx provides us with some hints to answer this question. He mentions two reasons:

1. C-M-C is circulation 'only from the standpoint of the observer, or in itself, not posited as such.'
2. In C-M-C, circulation 'consists merely of the simple repetition or alteration of the role of commodity and money . . . .'

That in the C-M-C circuit, circulation consists of the repetition or alteration of the role of commodity and money can be seen if we break the circuit into the two inverted phases of which it is made up, i.e. C-M and M-C. These two phases represent two acts of sale and purchase in which, when compared with each other, commodity and money interchange roles. But what does Marx mean when he says that C-M-C is circulation 'only from the standpoint of the observer, or in itself, not posited as such'?

The answer to this question, I believe, lies in the following circumstances.

By its nature, C-M-C can very well represent any accidental, isolated and one-time recourse to the market by a 'person' who has a commodity to sell and who exchanges that commodity with some other commodity. The form C-M-C does not entail any necessity of the renewal or repetition of the act of exchange symbolized by it. This circuit, in the form it is presented, has a purely 'external' relation to the totality of exchange process in society.

This brings us to the circuit which overcomes this limitation and externality, the circuit which by nature has continuity, renewal and circularity engrained in it: the circuit of money as capital or M-C-M.

b) *The Circularity of* M-C-M

It is the circuit M-C-M, the circulation of money as capital, that involves true circularity. In this case, in spite of the fact that there must be quantitative incongruity between the M that opens the circuit and the M which closes it (without which the circuit would not make any sense at all, since it would mean that equal quantities of money are exchanged), there is qualitative congruity in the sense that both end-points represent the same object, i.e. money. In M-C-M we have true circularity in the sense of the identity of the point of departure and the point of return.

In this circuit, compared to C-M-C, the renewal of the process is a necessity rooted in the very form of the circuit itself. Money starts the circuit, changes into a commodity and returns as more money. But this point of return, except as an individual and isolated act, cannot vanish into private use. it comes back to begin a new circuit. The act of buying in order to sell, symbolized by M-C-M circuit, is different from the act of selling in order to buy (C-M-C), in that in the latter case the point of return (C) is likely to vanish into private use and its (circuitous) repetition requires an act independent of the circuit itself, while in the former case the end point (M) persists and thus the repetition of the circuit follows almost by necessity. That this must be so is evident from the fact that in the circuit M-C-M, M cannot be personally or productively consumed and a 'person' who buys in order to sell must continually do so.

Thus true circularity is achieved by the circulation of money as capital, where 'value suddenly presents itself as a self-moving substance which passes through a process of its own, and for which commodities and money are both mere forms'. (C.I. p.256)

> As the dominant subject of this process, in which it alternately assumes and loses the form of money and the form of commodities, but preserves and expands itself through all these changes, value acquires above all an independent form by means of which its identity with itself may be asserted. Only in the shape of money does it possess this form. Money therefore forms the starting-point and the conclusion of every valorization process. (C.I. p.255)

In the circulation of money as capital the concept of circulation finds its full meaning and achieves its full potential.

The discussion above may easily lead to the conclusion that the two concepts of circulation in *Capital* refer to the 'simple' circulation (the circulation of commodities, C-M-C) on the one hand and to the circulation of money as capital (M-C-M) on the other. This comfortable resolution of the enigmatic character of the concept of circulation in Marx, however, cannot be sustained if we probe deeper into the complicated structure of this concept as it actually functions in Marx's discourse.

That the concept of the circulation of money as capital does not fully exhaust the meaning of circulation will become clear after the following development. But an important point must be highlighted at this stage. Although the concept of the circulation of capital is not the highest point that the concept of circulation reaches in *Capital*, it is certainly an essential step on this ascent. It is only on the basis of this concept, which gives full meaning to the concept of circulation by being the perfect prototype of circularity, that the universal concept of the circulation of commodities as the general foundation of the capitalist mode of production could be developed.

The Three Concepts of Commodity Circulation

We have seen above how Marx analyses the circulation of commodities ('simple' circulation, C-M-C) and the circulation of money as capital (M-C-M, the general formula of capital). Now, the following comments by Marx cannot be reconciled with any interpretation with these two concepts.

> The capital relation arises only in the production process because it exists implicitly in the act of circulation, in the basically different economic conditions in which buyer and seller confront one another, in their class relation. (C.II. p.115)
> In the relation between capitalist and wage-labourer, the money relation, the relation of buyer and seller, becomes a relation inherent in production itself. But this relation rests fundamentally on the social character of production, not on the mode of commerce; the latter rather derives from the former. (C.II. p.196)

In these quotations the concept of circulation requires a new dimension. Marx talks about 'the act of circulation' or 'the money relation' as the foundation from which the capital relation arises or, alternatively, as 'a relation inherent in production itself'. That this view of circulation cannot be reduced to the concept of 'simple' commodity circulation is obvious. On the other hand, this view cannot be identified with the concept of the circulation of money as capital either, for the simple reason that the former is supposed to be the foundation of the latter.

If the above arguments are accepted, the point may still be raised about the preceding quotations that Marx simply means by circulation the relation of the sale (by labourers) and the purchase (by capitalist) of the commodity labour-power. This relation for Marx forms the basis of the capitalist form of exploitation and, therefore, of the capitalist mode

166

of production. Thus it may be argued that Marx does not advance a new concept of circulation: capitalist production rests upon circulation for the obvious reason that here by circulation he simply means the exchange of labour-power between labourers and capitalists from which the course of actual exploitation, via the labour process, commences.

That Marx explicitly refers to the exchange of labour-power as the foundation of the capitalist mode of production in the above-quoted passages cannot be doubted. This meaning is brought out in clear outline in Chapter Six of *Capital I* where Marx attempts to develop the capital relation from circulation, 'but without it'. The solution is found in the existence of a particular commodity, i.e. labour-power, which circulates like any other commodity, but one whose value in use (use-value), i.e. in the labour process, exceeds its exchange value in the market place.

The problem with the above conception is that it interprets the relation of circulation (here the exchange of labour-power; more specifically a moment of the circuit of money capital: M-LP-M) as something external to the production process. The capitalist buys the commodity labour-power in the labour market and the worker sells it, and this is the end of the process of exchange or circulation. After this stage the labour process takes over and turns out commodities that are offered for sale in the product market. Thus in this interpretation the sphere of production (the labour process) and the sphere of circulation (the labour and product markets) remain separated and external to each other.

But Marx views capitalist production in its entirety as embracing not only circulation and distribution but also the labour process ('production in the narrow sense'). It is the entirety of the capitalist mode of production that rests on circulation, has the 'form' of circulation, and not just certain moments of it such as the exchange of labour-power. This circumstance must definitely give rise to a concept of circulation that not only towers above the concept of 'simple' commodity circulation and of the circulation of money as capital but goes a long way past the circulation of the commodity labour-power.

If we refer back to the above quotations from Marx we see that he relates the act of circulation to 'the basically different economic conditions in which buyer and seller confront each other, in their class relations'. He also clearly distinguishes this relation from the 'mode of commerce' which depends on the 'mode of production' ('the social character of production'). Here arises a concept of circulation that somehow characterizes the capitalist mode of production and which cannot be reduced to the mode of exchange or commerce (circulation in the sense of commodity exchange). On the contrary, the latter can be explained only on the basis of the former.

This point is made most clearly and forcefully by Marx in the following passage in the context of his discussion concerning the status of merchant's capital under capitalism and in pre-capitalist forms of production.

Capital can be formed in the circulation process, and must be formed there, before it learns to master its extremes, the various spheres of production between which circulation mediates. The circulation of money and commodities can mediate spheres of production with the most diverse organization, in which their internal structure are still oriented principally to the production of use-values. When circulation process becomes independent in this way, as a process in which spheres of production are linked together by a third party, this expresses a double situation. On the one hand, that circulation has still not mastered production, but is related to it simply as its given precondition. On the other hand, that the production process has not yet absorbed circulation into it as a mere moment. In capitalist production, on the contrary, both these things are the case. The production process is completely based on circulation, and circulation is a mere moment and a transition phase of production, simply the realization of a product produced as a commodity and the replacement of its elements of production produced as commodities. The form of capital that stems directly from circulation — commercial capital — now appears simply as one of the forms of capital in its movement of reproduction. (C.III. p.445-6)

Let us now analyse this passage into the three main ideas expressed in it.

1) 'Capital can be formed in the circulation process, and must be formed there . . .' Circulation here means 'simple' commodity circulation, C-M-C. In fact, historically the first form of capital, i.e. merchant's capital is formed in the circulation process — 'before it learns to master its extremes'.

2) 'The circulation of money and commodities can mediate spheres of production with the most diverse organization, in which their internal structure are still oriented principally to the production of use-values'. This characterization expresses the characteristics of the general form of circulation as a 'primitive' form. These characteristics are:

i) Circulation between different spheres of production with different types of organization (different 'modes of production').

ii) The common feature of these different modes of production is that they are all geared primarily to the production of

168

use-values and not exchange values.

In this context circulation is 'independent', which means that it is isolated from, and external to, different modes of production between which it takes place; it is related to them 'as its given precondition'.

In these circumstances, compared to the situation under capitalism, the role of circulation is a limited one since on the one hand it 'has still not mastered production' and on the other hand 'the production process has not yet absorbed circulation into it as a mere moment'. This 'negative' characterization of the function of circulation in pre-capitalist conditions points directly to the characteristics of circulation under capitalism.

We have a double movement between pre-capitalist modes and the capitalist mode of production: the 'simultaneous' movement of the absorption of the production process by circulation *and* the reduction of circulation to a mere phase of production. This truly dialectical movement has to be justified without getting entangled in logical contradictions.

3) Under the capitalist mode of production, circulation relates to production in two different ways:

 i) 'The production process is completely based on circulation . . .'

 ii) '. . . circulation is a mere moment and a transition phase of production . . .'

Based on the preceding analysis of the passage from *Capital III* under discussion we can now fully explore the three aspects of, or concepts of, circulation to be found in *Capital*.

I. Circulation as an historically prior form is a process that occurs between differently organized spheres of production (different modes of production) which are principally oriented to the production of 'use-values' (i.e. products destined for internal consumption, whether personal or productive). This does not mean that no products find their way outside the limited circle of internal use (otherwise no circulation could take place), but it means that exchange does not absorb the entire product of these modes of production: only 'surplus' products are exchanged. Thus, under these conditions circulation has a merely external relation to production. Since products are not produced primarily for exchange but for internal use, circulation does not reach anywhere near the 'interior' of production — it is not 'internalized': it only scratches the 'surface' of the production process.

It is on this basis that merchant's capital, the historically first form of capital, arises. What is true of circulation under pre-capitalist conditions applies equally to merchant's capital, i.e. this 'primitive' form of capital remains external to production and does not touch the roots of the spheres of production between which it mediates.

II. Circulation as a mere phase of the capitalist mode of production is wholly absorbed by production. In this form its function is similar to (I): it basically mediates between different units of production and to this extent remains external to production. However, it is quite unlike (I) in that its mediation is not between different spheres of production which are not already absorbed by capital. The units between which it mediates, whatever their internal principle of organization, capitalist or not, function in relation to capital.

The same observation applies to merchant's capital: this form which historically develops 'directly out of circulation (C.1) appears here (under capitalism) merely as one form of capital . . .'

III. Circulation as the foundation of the capitalist mode of production explains the internal principles of organization under capitalism. Capitalist units of production produce primarily for market, for circulation. Circulation thus has taken over all the production processes and reorganized them in its own image.

In terms of Marx's D-model which was developed in Chapter Two above, circulation in the latter sense is an *active* moment governing the entire movement including circulation itself as a *passive* phase (C.2).

Making the distinctions between the concepts of circulation expounded above is the only way to remove the logical contradictions that abound in Marx's discourse. However, it is the unity of these concepts that ultimately explains Marx's use of the same word (circulation) for these entirely different concepts, however unjustifiable it may seem.

The Unity of the Three Concepts of Circulation

Marx's commentary implies that, under capitalism, an historically prior and primitive form of circulation (C.1) which had an external existence in relation to the different modes of production between which it mediated under undeveloped conditions of production is transformed into the internal principle of the organization of production (C.3). But this is not all. In the course of this historical evolution or transformation of C.1 into C.3, C.1 does not simply disappear but retains an existence under C.3, subordinate to it (C.2). Thus, by being internalized into production, C.1 does not drop completely out of the picture but leaves a trace (C.2). The transition from C.1 to C.3 does not annihilate C.1 but preserves it as a necessary moment of C.3.

The picture that arises from this discussion is that of a complex hierarchy of forms in which:

i) One form, C.3, dominates the whole complex.

ii) C.3 cannot be reduced either to its historic predecessor (C.1) or to a subordinate moment of itself (C.2), which is a partial transformation of C.1.

iii) The original form (C.1) is preserved in a double sense: a) it is preserved in the form of C.3, and thus elevated to a universal form, and b) it is preserved in the shape of C.2 as a subordinate moment.

iv) C.2 serves as a transitional form between C.1 and C.3 but not in the historic sense of a transition from a pre-capitalist mode of production to the capitalist mode. C.2 functions continually under capitalism and mediates between different spheres of production, whether organized capitalistically or not. It is the medium through which capitalism taps the resources of non-capitalist or pre-capitalist forms of production without completely absorbing them. C.2 represents the historic continuity between the past and the present. And it is this continuity that presents the greatest obstacle in way of the conceptual separation of C.1, C.2 and C.3 from each other.

Summary

We have shown above that unless we make precise distinctions between the various concepts of circulation that are present in Marx's discourse the latter suffers from logical contradictions.

We have shown that Marx distinguishes very clearly between two kinds of circulation, C-M-C and M-C-M. Only the latter form is recognized as truly circular. The concept of circularity embodied in M-C-M serves as a bridge from the 'simple' circulation of commodities (C.1) to circulation as the foundation of the capitalism system (C.3). But in this transition C.1 itself is preserved in the form of a relation subordinate to capitalism (C.2).

171

With these distinctions Marx's discourse becomes more intelligible and is no longer bogged down in logical contradiction. For example, when Marx says that the capital relation cannot arise from circulation nor can it arise apart from it, that it 'must have its origin both in and not in circulation' he is saying that capital cannot arise from circulation (C.1 or C.2) (since this type of circulation is external to production) but it cannot develop on any other foundation (C.3).

The vital function that the exchange of labour-power plays under capitalism was shown to be inadequate in itself to provide the basis for C.3. The generalization of the exchange of labour-power (and the process of commodification of use-values that accompanies it) to the whole economy transforms the meaning and function of C-M-C.

We have shown above that C-M-C, in itself, lacks continuity: to sell in order to buy can be a one-time and isolated event. There is no necessity for its renewal inherent in this form. However, when this relationship becomes generalized in such a way that all products are made for exchange, then the seller has to return to the market continually. This is most obvious in the case of labourers who have to sell their labour-power continuously in order to survive. But every commodity producer from the capitalist to the petty commodity producer has to have constant recourse to the market. Thus under capitalism the C-M-C circuit acquires a new dimension: here sale and purchase are necessary functions for production. The 'simple' circulation of commodities (C.1) has become the vital principle of the organization of production (C.3). As such it has the character of circularity and continuity.

In the historic movement from C.1 to C.3 there is a middle term C.2 which represents C.1 under C.3. C.3 does not eliminate C.1 but preserves it as a subordinate moment. This preservation allows the capitalist mode of production to coexist with a diversity of other modes of production without ceasing to absorb them under its own rule.

Notes to Chapter Five

1. For an extensive discussion of the various interpretations of 'simple' commodity production see Chapter One. Debates on the transition from feudalism to capitalism and problems of economic development and underdevelopment will be explored in the concluding chapter.
2. See Chapter Two. This linear view of circulation derives primarily from *Capital II*, where Marx's treatment of the circulation process in some chapters supports this view (e.g. Chapters 5 and 6). But as we shall see in Chapter Ten below Marx's discussions of the various circuits of capital cannot be easily reconciled with a linear view.

Although this linear view had been dominant in interpretations of Marx there is an important exception, i.e. Rubin's view. For instance, in his discussion of abstract labour Rubin at one point deals with the question whether value arises from exchange or directly from the production process. The problem is that in Marx statements are found to support both points of view. Rubin clearly notes that Marx uses 'exchange' in two different senses: i) as exchange of products and therefore a phase in the entire reproduction process and ii) as the general social form of the capitalist economy.

The problem is that in treating the question of the relation between exchange and production two concepts of exchange are not adequately distinguished. We must distinguish exchange as a social form of the process of reproduction from exchange as a particular phase of this process of reproduction, alternating with the phase of direct production.

At the first glance it seems that exchange is a separate phase of the process of reproduction. We can see that the process of direct production comes first, and the phase of exchange comes next. Here exchange is separate from production and stands opposite from it. But exchange is not only a separate phase of the process of reproduction; it puts its specific imprint on the entire process of reproduction. It is a particular social form of the social process of production.

Since exchange is actually the dominant form of the process of production, it leaves its imprint on the phase of direct production. (Rubin 1972, p.149)

This brilliant comment, however, remains isolated in Rubin's work and he is unable to rescue Marx's theory of value from its 'productionist' foundations (see Chapters Eleven and Twelve below).
3. The following quotation from Michel De Vroey highlights the problems of the standard approach to Marx's theory of value:
"I dislike the expression 'realization of value' precisely because it suggests that value already exists before being realized and that it is a permanent property of commodities, embodied in them. For me, on the contrary, only a pretence of value (potential) exists before exchange. Furthermore, the existence of value is an instantaneous reality, confined to the moment of exchange." (De Vroey, M., Value, Production and Exchange, in Steedman, I. [ed] 1981)
4. See Chapters Eleven and Twelve for an extensive critical examination of the various aspects of Marx's value theory.
5. The expression 'from the standpoint of the observer' which appears in both the *Grundrisse* and *Capital* on a number of occasions is a direct borrowing from Hegel as can be seen from the following words by Hegel:
"This content, or the will's determination on something specific, is in the first place immediate. Consequently the will is then free only *in* itself or *for* an external observer, or, to speak generally, it is the will in its concept. It is not until it has itself as its object that the will is for *itself* what it is in itself." (Ph.R. pp.24-5)

CHAPTER SIX

THE TWO FORMS OF SURPLUS-VALUE

The concept of surplus-value has a central role in Marx's theory of the capitalist mode of production. Yet the way Marx often characterizes surplus-value as simply surplus labour reduces this concept to a 'generic' one equally valid for all forms of social production based on the exploitation of labour. Towards the end of this chapter we hope to explore this question. But first we will try to establish that the concept of 'absolute surplus-value' in *Capital* far from representing a mere form of surplus-value alongside the other form, i.e. the relative surplus-value, or a first form historically preceding the latter or even a transitional form, rather represents primarily the very concept of surplus-value itself to the extent that it is only on its basis that relative surplus-value can be understood.

The Two Forms of Surplus-Value

Marx gives us two different, though interrelated concepts of surplus-value: absolute and relative surplus-value.

> I call that surplus-value which is produced by the lengthening of the working day, *absolute surplus-value*. In contrast to this I call that surplus-value which arises from the curtailment of the necessary labour-time, and from the corresponding alteration in the respective lengths of the two components of the working day, relative surplus-value. (C.I. p.432)

Thus, while the absolute form results from a prolongation of the working day, leading to an increase in the magnitude of labour performed beyond the necessary labour, i.e. surplus labour, the relative form is obtained by a shortening of the necessary labour-time. Both are forms of surplus-value and both represent surplus labour-time, i.e. labour performed in excess of necessary labour.

Why does Marx introduce these two forms? Can we say that the novelty of Marx's concept of surplus-value consists in this differentiation of the forms of surplus-value, in breaking the single concept of surplus-value, handed down to him from predecessors, into two elements?

The concept of surplus-value was nothing new in Marx's time. It was known not only to the classical economists but also to the Physiocrats and even the Mercantilists before them.[1] This concept as received by

Marx from classical political economy rested on two premises:

a) A part of the produced values constitutes a surplus.
b) This surplus is ultimately resolved into the excess labour performed by labourers in the production process, i.e. the labour in excess of what is necessary for the production of the commodity-value equivalent of the wages of workers.

The first premise can be found among the Mercantilists while the second is a direct result of the labour theory of value advocated by the classical economists.

Now the question of the novelty of the concept of surplus-value in Marx, a question that has continued to be a subject of many debates beginning immediately after the publication of the first volume of *Capital*, hinges on the question of whether or not Marx added anything new to the above premises.

Some have claimed that this novelty consists in Marx's *explicit* resolution of surplus-value into surplus labour. Others have sought the origin of surplus-value in the 'natural' productivity of labour.[2] The problem with these interpretations is that they are all at the level of the ideas shared by Marx and the classical economists. It is true that Marx often makes explicit what is implied by the discourse of political economy.[3] But Marx's conceptual innovations cannot be limited to this close 'sympathetic' or even 'symptomatic'[4] reading of the classics. Even if we accept this interpretation, the question arises as to the means, mechanisms and structure of this kind of reading, i.e. the question as to why Marx is reading or is able to read the classics in this manner.

In the following section we will show how Marx's critique of Ricardo's theory of surplus-value leads to the differentiation of surplus-value into the two forms mentioned above.

Marx's Critique of the Ricardian Theory of Surplus-Value

According to Marx, relative surplus-value was known to Ricardo. Ricardo succeeds in reducing the value of labour-power (wages) to the labour time necessary to produce the commodities on which the workers' wages are spent — a simple result of Ricardo's labour theory of value.

> ... Ricardo defines the average wages or the value of labour power correctly.
> For he says that it ... is determined ... by the *labour-time which it costs to produce*
> *it*; that is, by the *quantity of labour materialized* in the means of subsistence of

the labourer. (TSV.II. p.404)

Marx, however, finds this formulation inadequate: it must be shown that the labourer *reproduces* the value of his means of subsistence, i.e. a part of his working day is devoted to the production or reproduction of that value (TSV.II, pp.404-5). Ricardo, 'by not *directly* showing that one *part* of the labourer's *working day* is assigned to the reproduction of the value of his own labour-power ... introduces a difficulty and obscures the clear understanding of the relationship' (TSV.II. p.405).

According to Marx, Ricardo's formulation results in a two-fold confusion: firstly the origin of surplus-value is not grasped and secondly,

> ... the *total working day* is regarded as a fixed magnitude, the differences in the amount of surplus value are overlooked, and the productivity of capital, the *compulsion to perform surplus labour* — on the one hand absolute surplus-labour, and on the other its innate urge to shorten the necessary labour time — are not recognised and therefore the *historical* justification for capital is not set forth. (TSV.II. p.405)

The origin of surplus-value remains unclear in Ricardo since for him 'it is a fact, that the value of the product is greater than the value of the wages'. He never *questions* this '*fact*':

> The *magnitude of the total working day* is therefore wrongly assumed to be *fixed*, and directly entails wrong conclusions. The increase or decrease in surplus-value can therefore be explained *only* from the growing or diminishing productivity of social labour which produces the means of subsistence. That is to say, only relative surplus-value is understood. (TSV.II. p.406)

When the length of the working day is assumed to be fixed, surplus-value can arise only on the basis of the productivity of labour engaged in producing the means of subsistence, e.g. agricultural labour. This is where the 'natural productivity of labour' interpretation of surplus-value originates from. Marx recognizes the fact that labour productivity must reach a level in which the basic needs of labourers are met before surplus production can begin.

> Thus we may say that surplus-value rests on a natural basis, but only in the very general sense that there is no natural obstacle absolutely preventing one man from lifting from himself the burden of the labour necessary to maintain his own existence, and imposing it on another ... It would be absolutely mistaken to attach mystical notions to this spontaneously developed productivity of labour, as is sometimes done. It is only when men have worked their way out of their initial animal conditions, when therefore their labour has been to some

extent socialized, that a situation arises in which the surplus labour of one person becomes a condition of existence for another. (C.I. p.647)

It is obvious that if the labourer needed his whole day to produce his own means of subsistence (i.e. commodities equal to the value of his own means of subsistence), there could be no surplus-value, and therefore no capitalist production and no wage-labour. This can only exist when the productivity of social labour is sufficiently developed to make possible some sort of excess of the total working-day over the labour-time required for the reproduction of the wage — i.e. *surplus-labour*, whatever its magnitude. But it is equally obvious, that with a given labour-time (a given length of the working-day) the productivity of labour [may be very different], on the other hand, with a given productivity of labour, the labour-time, the length of the working-day, may be very different. Furthermore, it is clear that though the existence of *surplus-labour* presupposes that the productivity of labour has reached a certain level, the mere *possibility* of this surplus-labour (i.e. the existence of that necessary minimum productivity of labour) does not in itself make it a *reality*. For this to occur, the labourer must first be *compelled* to work in excess of the [necessary] time, and this compulsion is exerted by capital. This is missing in Ricardo's work, and therefore also the whole struggle over the regulation of the normal working-day. (TSV.II. p.406)

Ricardo by *implicitly* assuming the length of the working day to be *constant*, traces the origin of surplus-value to labour productivity. Ricardo, thus, grasps only the relative form of surplus-value. He does not understand absolute surplus-value and therefore the origin of surplus-value remains unknown to him.

Marx's critique of Ricardo's theory of surplus-value thus resolves into the following two points:

i) Ricardo grasps only the form of relative surplus-value.
ii) Ricardo does *not* grasp the origin of surplus-value because he does not recognize the form of absolute surplus-value.

We have a curious and apparently contradictory result here.

Ricardo grasps the relative form of surplus-value which is the specific form of surplus extraction under capitalism. Thus he grasps what is the most essential feature of the exploitation of labourers under capitalism but, at the same time, he fails to understand surplus-value, the driving force of capitalist production, through his lack of understanding of absolute surplus-value.

Marx's critique of Ricardo's theory of surplus-value has thus yielded two concepts of surplus-value — relative and absolute. It is this differentiation that constitutes the novelty of Marx's own theory. We will now look at these two concepts more closely.

177

If we were to interpret the form of absolute surplus-value only as a particular form of surplus-value alongside relative surplus-value (perhaps as a more primitive form preceding the relative form, a transitional form or a form subordinate to the relative form) the judgement passed by Marx on Ricardo, i.e. Ricardo's lack of understanding of the origin of surplus-value and therefore the essence of capitalist production, would look rather misplaced. Moreover, this judgement would seem to be paradoxical in view of the fact that Ricardo, according to Marx, grasps the specific form of capitalist exploitation, i.e. relative surplus-value.

According to Marx, Ricardo grasps what is the most essential and specific form of capitalist extraction of surplus labour while failing to understand the essence of capitalist relations (through his failure to recognize the form of absolute surplus-value).

The solution to this paradox must lie in the double determination of the concept of absolute surplus-value in Marx. Marx associates the two forms of surplus-value with the concepts of the formal and real subsumption of labour under capital:

> If the production of absolute surplus-value was the material expression of the formal subsumption of labour under capital, then the production of relative surplus-value may be viewed as its real subsumption.
>
> At any rate, if we consider the two forms of surplus-value, absolute and relative, separately, we shall see that absolute surplus-value always precedes relative. To these two forms of surplus-value there correspond two separate forms of the subsumption of labour under capital, or two distinct forms of capitalist production. And here too one form always precedes the other, although the second form, the more highly developed one, can provide the foundations for the introduction of the first in new branches of industry. (*Results of the Immediate Process of Production*, in C.I. p.1025)

In the above passage Marx is interpreting the two forms of surplus-value as two distinct methods for the extraction of surplus-value, each associated with distinct forms of capitalist production.

The first form obtains when capitalists take over a production process that was formerly run on a non-capitalist basis. The capitalist turns the enterprise into a profit-making organization: the entire output is put on the market. However, the capitalist does not change the technology of production. Thus only absolute surplus-value is obtained.

The second form obtains when the capital relation seizes production by its roots; it reorganizes the production process and thus introduces technological change. This change, which revolutionizes the technical basis of production leads to the extraction of relative surplus-value.

Thus in the first form, capital has a merely formal relation with the production process: this relation leaves the technology of production untouched and merely extends the length of the working day. In the second form the capital relation changes the entire basis of production: it reorganizes it with a view to profit-making.

Based on this interpretation the two forms of surplus-value correspond to two successive stages in the capitalist development. The absolute form is the original or the transitional form related to the stage of formal subsumption while the relative form is the fully developed form associated with the real subsumption of labour under capital. Thus the absolute form appears to be historically prior to the relative form ('one form always precedes the other') although, Marx adds, the relative form 'can provide the foundation for the introduction of the first in new branches of industry'. Thus absolute surplus-value functions as an historic premise and at most as a form subordinate to the highly developed form of relative surplus-value.

The passage under discussion does not represent the last word uttered by Marx on the theoretical status of the concept of absolute surplus-value. But even here we can detect the higher dimension of this concept developed by Marx in other places. In this passage there is a key word which forms the basis of Marx's analysis and qualifies his judgement in a crucial way. The word is 'separately'. Thus the above interpretation of the relation between the two forms of surplus-value is correct only 'if we consider the two forms . . . separately'.

The separation of the two forms of surplus-value, indeed, reduces them to separate and specific methods for the extraction of surplus-value. In this interpretation the concept of absolute surplus-value can only function as a limited and local concept.

We will see below that the concept of absolute surplus-value has a wider and more universal significance.

Absolute Surplus-Value as the Concept of Surplus-Value

The wider scope of the concept of absolute surplus-value in Marx is apparent in the following quotation, where Marx is discussing the general concept of the formal subsumption of labour and distinguishing it from its more specific local concept:

179

... the *formal subsumption of labour under capital* ... is the general form of every capitalist process of production; at the same time, however, it can be found as a *particular form* alongside the *specifically capitalist mode of production* in its developed form, because although the latter entails the former, the converse does not necessarily obtain [i.e. the formal subsumption can be found in the absence of the specifically capitalist mode of production]. (*Results* . . . , C.I. p.1019)

By way of inference we may say that absolute surplus-value is the general form of surplus-value under capitalism, although it can also function as a particular form alongside the specifically capitalist and developed form of relative surplus-value.

This point is put even more clearly in the following passage, where Marx says that the production of absolute surplus-value

... forms the general foundation of the capitalist system, and the starting-point for the production of relative surplus-value. The latter presupposes that the working day is already divided into two parts, necessary labour and surplus labour. In order to prolong the surplus labour, the necessary labour is shortened by methods for producing the equivalent of the wage of labour in a shorter time. (C.I. p.645)

This passage might easily lend itself to an 'historicist' reading: it may be argued that Marx is establishing the point that the production of absolute surplus-value is the historic origin and premise for the production of relative surplus-value. After all, he is referring to the former as the 'starting point' and he is saying that the latter 'presupposes' the former. Marx, however, before characterizing the production of absolute surplus-value as the starting point refers to it as 'the general foundation' and clearly distinguishes between these two aspects. One should not interpret the 'foundation' metaphor literally, since it can easily merge with the concept of the 'starting point'. Foundation refers to the essence — one which is not given and fixed but develops and deepens with the development of the capitalist mode of production. Furthermore, when Marx says that the production of relative surplus-value 'presupposes that the working day is already divided into two parts, necessary labour and surplus labour', this division of the working day constitutes, precisely, Marx's concept of surplus-value.

The general concept of absolute surplus-value thus represents the very concept of surplus labour time, the very concept of surplus-value in Marx. And as such it necessarily embraces both the specific form of absolute surplus-value and the more developed form of relative surplus-value.

180

Thus, the concept of absolute surplus-value, by focusing on surplus labour-time, reveals the essence of surplus-value as surplus labour. Once surplus-value is conceived as the difference between total labour time and necessary labour time it becomes obvious that any change in surplus-value must be the result of two types of variations:

i) a variation in total labour time with necessary labour fixed (i.e. absolute surplus-value in the narrow sense), and
ii) a variation in necessary labour time with the total labour time fixed (relative surplus-value).

In this manner, both the relative form and absolute form (in the narrow sense) are derived from the absolute form (in the general sense).

What is absent in Ricardo's understanding of surplus-value is the general concept of surplus-value as surplus labour (absolute surplus-value). This concept functions as the abstract universal concept of capitalist exploitation without which the more specific, the more developed and, indeed, the dominant, specifically capitalist form of surplus-value, i.e. the relative form, cannot be properly grasped.

We can, in fact, go so far to claim that Marx's concept of relative surplus-value is such a critical transformation of the Ricardian concept that it has an entirely new function in Marx's discourse. Ricardian theory is essentially static. By assuming the working day as a fixed magnitude he sees an inverse relation between wages and profits. This leads to Ricardo's vision of the demise of capitalist development in a closed economy. The law of diminishing returns in agriculture pushes wages up and thus reduces profits. Where Ricardo identifies a possible source of conflict of interest between workers and capitalists, Marx's more dynamic theory locates the very essence of capitalist development in technological change which removes the Ricardian basis for class conflict, while reproducing that conflict at a higher level.

With this interpretation of the concept of absolute surplus-value the latter is no longer restricted to playing the role of 'junior partner' in relation to relative surplus-value but is promoted to the highest echelon from which it can shed light on the function of the relative form.

The extraction of surplus-value is the object of the capitalist system, but extracting surplus labour naturally encounters certain limits (natural, socio-cultural, etc.) We thus arrive at the concept of relative surplus-value. Technological change is required to surmount these limitations. As a result real subsumption of labour replaces the formal subsumption.

181

In view of the foregoing discussion the concept of absolute surplus-value finds three interpretations:

1. Absolute surplus-value as the starting-point or the historic premise of capitalist production. As such it is related to the formal subsumption of labour under capital, which 'always precedes' the real subsumption. When capital takes over a labour-process, before any transformation in the technical basis of production, only the production of absolute surplus-value is possible.
2. Absolute surplus-value as a form that continues to exist after capitalism has become the dominant social form of production. This can take a variety of forms. If the capitalist mode is the dominant (but not the exclusive) form of production, the extension of the capitalist mode to non-capitalist branches of production normally begins with the extraction of absolute surplus-value. Certain enterprises or even sectors may continue this 'backward' method of producing surplus-value for a long time. During the industrial revolution large-scale industry depended heavily on this method. The production of absolute surplus-value may thus be viewed as a transitional form under capitalism.
3. Absolute surplus-value as the foundation of the capitalist production. As such it functions as the general concept of surplus-value and thus subsumes not only the other aspects (1 and 2 above) but also the form of relative surplus-value.

Is Surplus-Value a Generic Concept?

We have tried to demonstrate that Marx's dispute with Ricardo over the concept of surplus-value can only be understood if absolute surplus-value is interpreted in the general sense of that concept of surplus-value which is not reducible to its specific forms as the historic *prius*, the transitional form or the residual form subsisting under capitalism.

Ricardo grasps the specifically capitalist form of the extraction of surplus-value, i.e. relative surplus-value, but he fails to understand the basis of capitalist exploitation by assuming the length of the working day to be constant. Marx found this assumption untenable. Indeed the struggle of labour against capital since the industrial revolution centred around the length of the working day. The latter, far from staying constant, increased considerably during the industrial revolution and afterwards tended to decline as a result of rising trade union struggles in the second half of the nineteenth century. The decline in the working day, however, did not lead to a drying up of the sources of surplus-value. The specifically capitalist mode of production had by then taken over entire branches of production and thus the production of relative surplus-value was predominant. In such circumstances, a rise in real wages was conceivable *together* with constant or even rising profits. Thus the whole Ricardian doctrine of an inverse relation between wages and profits was put to a hard historic test.

The conception of surplus-value as relative surplus-value alone (based on the assumption of fixed working day) without the insight provided by the concept of absolute surplus-value deprives the capitalist mode of production of any autonomous effectivity in producing surplus-value. The size of surplus-value, then, becomes a matter of the strength of capitalists (or labourers) in dictating their terms concerning their 'share of the pie'.

For Marx, the problem is the *production* of surplus-value and not just its *distribution*. The latter depends on the former. For example Marx says the following when commenting on the interpretation of his theory of surplus-value as a 'deduction' or 'theft' from workers:

> On the contrary, I represent the capitalist as a necessary functionary of capitalist production, and indicate at length that he does not only 'deduct' or '*rob*' but enforces the *production of surplus-value* and thus first helps to create what is to be deducted: I further indicate in detail that even if in commodity exchange *only equivalents* are exchanged the capitalist — as soon as he has paid the labourer the real value of his labour-power quite legally, i.e., by the law corresponding to this mode of production, obtains *surplus-value*.[5]

Relative surplus-value as it functions in the Ricardian system is merely a category of distribution. Marx transforms it into a category of production: the production of relative surplus-value as the specifically capitalist mode of production (the real subsumption of labour under capital). When this method of production becomes the dominant form of social production it recedes into being a 'mere' method, a specific form of producing surplus-value.

> The specifically capitalist mode of production ceases in general to be a mere means of producing relative surplus-value as soon as it has conquered an entire branch of production; this tendency is still more powerful when it has conquered all the important branches of production. It then becomes the universal,

socially predominant form of the production process. It only continues to act as a special method of producing relative surplus-value in two respects: first, in so far as it seizes upon industries previously only formally subordinate to capital, that is, in so far as it continues to proselytize, and second, in so far as the industries already taken over continue to be revolutionized by changes in the methods of production. (C.I. p.646)

The conclusion we arrive at points to the complexities of the concept of relative surplus-value itself. Thus this concept itself now appears in two different modes:

The specifically capitalist mode of production appears as:

(1) a mere method of producing relative surplus-value, and
(2) the socially dominant form of the production process.

(1) embraces two cases:

i) When the capitalist mode has not conquered an entire branch of production but has only made sporadic inroads into it, i.e. when its general influence is limited to formal subsumption.

ii) When industries which have been taken over in the 'real subsumption' sense are still in the process of fermentation.

In both these cases the specifically capitalist mode functions merely as a method for the extraction of surplus-value.

(2), on the other hand, refers to circumstances in which the capitalist mode [case (1) above] has conquered all the key branches in the sense that it has completely revolutionized the labour processes in those industries. In this transition the specifically capitalist mode (1) has changed from a method of producing surplus-value into a dominant social form of production.

Suppose the above characterization of the general concept of absolute surplus-value and its distinction from its more specific concept in *Capital* is admitted. The point may still be raised as to the usefulness and objectivity of this distinction. It may be argued that if all surplus-value, in whatever form, is reduced by Marx to surplus labour, the latter is a characteristic of all forms of society in which unpaid labour is extracted from labourers. Does not this mean that Marx has, through the complex dialectical course of his investigations into the question of surplus-value, eventually arrived at a concept that designates what is common to all modes of production based on exploitation? And if so, has he not produced a concept which, instead of explaining the differences between the modes of exploitation in different forms of society, simply ignores

184

these differences by focusing on the common characteristics or the common 'essence'? Is not his concept of absolute surplus-value, reduced to its 'substance' i.e. surplus-labour, designed merely to portray the historical continuity of exploitation?

These questions become more serious in the light of Marx's own criticism of the classical economists for a similar reduction of different forms into a common essence. Marx reproaches classical political economy for a failure to analyse the form of value after having reduced various forms into their substance, i.e. labour.[6]

Has not Marx committed the same error in reducing surplus-value to surplus labour? This question cannot be fully explored at this point.[7] However, the following comments should help to problematize Marx's analysis of surplus-value in light of the above development.

There is a key concept in Marx's analysis of surplus-value whose equivalent is missing in the analysis of value put forward by classical political economy. This concept is relative surplus-value, a concept that is present in Ricardo in an 'unconscious' manner and which is made 'conscious' by Marx's reading of Ricardo. This concept helps Marx to make the transition from the specific and limited concept of absolute surplus-value (an historically prior form or transitional form of surplus labour extraction under capitalism) to the more general concept of surplus labour extraction. Absolute surplus-value, ideally, should throw light on the specific manner of exploitation under capitalism without being reduced to what is common between capitalism and pre-capitalist forms of exploitation. To do so it must refer to a *specific* form of surplus-labour that may be found on the fringes of pre-capitalist modes of production, but which fully develops only under capitalism.

Capitalism is the only historically known form of production which is completely organized on the basis of surplus production in such a way that the primary object of production is profit. Furthermore, capitalism is the only mode of production in which surplus labour is totally and systematically organized to produce *social wealth*, while in former exploitative modes *private accumulation* was the primary object.

The notion of relative surplus-value as conceptualized by Marx points precisely to this historical distinction. This concept, as we saw above, serves two functions in *Capital*. First, it acts as a specific form of surplus-value related to the specifically capitalist method of production. Secondly, upon becoming the generalized form of surplus-value relating to the *mode of production* under capitalism, it serves as its specific social form. Thus, when surplus production is the object of the organizers of

185

production given a fixed or even a declining working day, surplus labour can still be extracted by adopting appropriate technologies of production (designed to reduce the necessary labour-time either by increasing the intensity of labour or by increasing the productivity of the 'wage-goods industries'). Thus the *production* of surplus-value, the *enforcing* of surplus labour becomes a real possibility. Lacking these methods of producing relative surplus-value, surplus labour manifests itself mainly as surplus product resulting from 'natural' increases in the productivity of labour. This was the basis of pre-capitalist forms of exploitation. What was taken in these social forms of production from labourers can surely be called their surplus labour. But this surplus, in a sense, was there to be taken: it was not in any way occasioned by the particular nature of the production process, as is the case under capitalism. It was not 'produced' by the organizers of production but simply 'appropriated'.

The differentiation between the two forms of surplus-value helps Marx to situate the capitalist mode of production as an historical *and* as the most developed mode of exploitation. The concept of absolute surplus-value in its general sense cannot designate surplus labour pure and simple, since this would amount to a 'generic' concept that reduces the foundation of the capitalist system to a notion designating the common characteristics of all modes of production based on the exploitation of labour.

Absolute surplus-value thus should denote the specific character of exploitation under capitalism. As such it should embrace all forms of surplus-value existing under capitalism (including relative surplus-value) while providing insight into pre-capitalist forms of the extraction of surplus labour.

We conclude that the concept of absolute surplus-value cannot fully embrace those pre-capitalist forms of exploitation not oriented to circulation, although it does cover the forms of exploitation that arise on the basis of the 'pre-capitalist' forms of capital, such as, merchant's and interest-bearing capital. These forms necessarily impose an external, economic compulsion (as opposed to a non-economic compulsion) on labour-power and result in the lengthening of labour-time.

The Three Aspects of Absolute Surplus-Value and their Unity

The concept of absolute surplus-value is now seen to possess three aspects:

SV.1: The concept of surplus-value extraction by pre-capitalist forms of capital.

SV.2: The concept of surplus-value extraction representing a subordinate form under capitalism. As such, this form of surplus-value is a transitional form functioning under capitalism. It represents the form of surplus-value in those branches of production where capital is introduced for the first time.

SV.3: The concept of surplus-value as the general form of the capitalist extraction of surplus labour, embracing SV.2 as well as the more developed 'specifically capitalist' form of surplus-value, i.e. the relative form.

The unity of these aspects of absolute surplus-value can be explained in the following way.

The existence of pre-capitalist forms of capital implied the existence of absolute surplus-value extraction. However, this form of exploitation was alien to contemporary forms of production: it resulted in their ruin rather than their development.

Under capitalism, this form of exploitation becomes the life blood of the whole system. A primitive relation, destructive of the old forms of production is turned into the living principle of a new mode of production. In this process SV.1 is transformed into SV.3 through the operation of the principle represented in the concept of relative surplus-value.

In the course of the transformation of SV.1 into SV.3, the former is not completely eliminated but transformed into SV.2 where it functions as a transitional form under capitalism.

Notes to Chapter Six

1. See Engels's Preface to *Capital II*, where he states: "The *existence* of the part of the value produced that we now call surplus-value was established long before Marx . . ." (C.II. p.98).

2. An example of the first view is Engels (see his Preface to *Capital II* [C.II, pp.98-9]). Here Engels argues that in order to have a theory of surplus-value a theory of value is essential. Thus he implicitly proposes that Marx derives the concept of surplus-value from his labour theory of value.

As an example of the second view see Dobb, M., Marx's *Capital* and its place in economic thought, in Howard & King (1976), pp.131-9. Here Dobb characterizes Marx's theory of surplus-value "as a development of the 'deduction theory' of profit to be found in Adam Smith" (ibid. p.131). He does not agree with the proposition that "profit as surplus value is somehow derived from the labour theory of value" (ibid. p.133) but states: "If there was some premise from which the notion of surplus value was derived as a conclusion, this was the definition of 'producer' and of 'productive' in terms of human activity." (ibid. p.134).

187

3. See Althusser & Balibar (1970), Part I, where Althusser identifies this as Marx's 'first kind of reading' of the classical economics.
4. See Althusser & Balibar (1970), Part I for an extensive discussion of 'symptomatic' reading which, according to Althusser, constitutes a 'second kind of reading' in Marx.
5. Marx (1975), p.186.
6. On this point see Chapter Three above.
7. See Chapters Eleven and Twelve below for an extensive treatment of Marx's theory of value.

CHAPTER SEVEN

SIMPLE REPRODUCTION AND EXTENDED REPRODUCTION

Marx introduces two concepts of reproduction in *Capital*. He distinguishes between, on the one hand, simple reproduction and, on the other, extended reproduction (or reproduction on an enlarged scale). One possible interpretation of this conceptual distinction is that it is designed simply to distinguish between two successive historical stages of production. Extended reproduction is thus a characteristic of the capitalist mode of production in which a part of surplus-value is not personally consumed by capitalists but is 'ploughed back' into production in order to expand the scale of the labour process. Compared to the capitalist system, pre-capitalist forms of production may be characterized as involving a 'stationary' economy with no expansion in the scale of production, i.e. involving 'simple' reproduction.

This 'historicist' interpretation, which tends to create a fixed opposition between simple and extended reproduction, cannot be easily reconciled with historical facts. This is how Rosa Luxemburg criticizes Lenin for holding such a view:

> ... [Lenin] is responsible for the statement that enlarged reproduction begins only with capitalism. It quite escapes him that under conditions of simple reproduction, which he takes to be the rule for all pre-capitalist modes of production, we should probably never have advanced beyond the stage of the palaeolithic scraper. (Luxemburg 1951, p.317, fn.)

Furthermore, this interpretation, criticized by Luxemburg, is based on a narrow and one-sided interpretation of simple reproduction. In fact Marx uses the concept of simple reproduction in two different ways, as we shall see presently.[1]

The Two Concepts of Simple Reproduction

The concept 'simple reproduction' finds two distinct interpretations. On the one hand it denotes a condition of the economy in which the means of production and the labour-power consumed during the production process are *exactly* replaced on the scale of the previous period:

> No society can go on producing, in other words no society can reproduce, unless

it constantly reconverts a part of its products into means of production, or elements of fresh production. All other circumstances remaining the same, the society can reproduce or maintain its wealth on the existing scale only by replacing the means of production which have been used up — i.e. the instruments of labour, the raw material and auxiliary substances — with an equal quantity of new articles. These must be separated from the mass of the yearly product, and incorporated once again into the production process. (C.I. p.711)

Here Marx is giving us the definition of 'simple' reproduction in the first, 'simple' and quantitative sense. The above-mentioned interpretation, thus, can be seen as relying exclusively on this quantitative definition of simple reproduction.

However, another sense of simple reproduction is suggested by Marx in the chapter on Simple Reproduction in *Capital I* from which the above quotation is taken:

A division between the product of labour and labour itself, between the objective conditions of labour and subjective labour-power, was therefore the real foundation and the starting-point of the process of capitalist production.

But what at first was merely a starting-point becomes, *by means of nothing but the continuity of the process, by simple reproduction*, the characteristic result of capitalist production, a result which is constantly renewed and perpetuated. On the one hand, the production process incessantly converts material wealth into capital, into the capitalist's means of enjoyment and his means of valorization. On the other hand, the worker always leaves the process in the same state as he entered it — a personal source of wealth, but deprived of any means of making that wealth a reality for himself. (C.I. p.716, emphasis added)

This conception of simple reproduction is clearly independent of the scale of reproduction, i.e. on whether the process of production is renewed on the previous scale or on a higher one. In either case the separation or division between labour-power and the means of production, which is the premise of capitalist production, is reproduced. Marx states explicitly that this separation is reproduced 'by means of nothing but the continuity of the process, by simple reproduction'. We have thus a conception of reproduction which embraces both cases of 'simple' (in the first sense suggested above) and expanded reproduction. As such, simple reproduction represents the very concept of reproduction — a concept which is introduced by Marx at the very beginning of the chapter on Simple Reproduction in *Capital I* (even before the first sense of simple reproduction is developed):

Whatever the social form of the production process, it has to be continuous, it must periodically repeat the same phases. A society can no more cease to

190

produce than it can cease to consume. When viewed, therefore, as a connected whole, and in the constant flux of its incessant renewal, every social process of production is at the same time a process of reproduction.

The conditions of production are at the same time the conditions of reproduction. (C.I. p.711)

Thus Marx begins his analysis of simple reproduction with its more general concept and only later introduces the more limited sense of simple reproduction.

Thus if one were to conceive of simple and extended reproduction in fixed opposition to each other, as two principles relating to two different historical modes of production (the historicist interpretation), Marx's second, qualitative concept of simple reproduction would contradict this view for the following reasons. In the second sense simple reproduction refers to the renewal, the continuity of the production process: simple reproduction characterizes *social* production, i.e. production not as an individual act but as a social process. And this is why Marx says that 'the conditions of production are at the same time the conditions of reproduction'. Thus this concept applies equally to pre-capitalist and to capitalist modes of production. Furthermore, as we shall see below, if we interpret 'simple' reproduction as production 'on the same scale' it contradicts one of the basic laws of capitalism.

However, besides the historicist interpretation, a structuralist and a rationalist view of simple reproduction are also possible. These latter two have been succinctly stated by Balibar as among various interpretations of simple reproduction. Balibar first mentions that simple reproduction may be viewed as 'an *exposition procedure*', as 'a *simplification*'. We are already familiar with this view of 'simple' concepts in Marx, i.e. the rationalist approach. He then presents the view that simple reproduction may be conceived as 'the study of a *particular case*'. This is a rather crude structuralist view according to which some sectors of the capitalist economy may not engage in accumulation. A more sophisticated structuralist view emerges if one considers simple reproduction as 'the study of *a part*, an always necessary part, of extended reproduction'.[2]

So far we have identified three views of simple reproduction — as an historically first condition of production, as a part subordinate to capitalist accumulation and as a simple model of capitalist extended reproduction. Although all these views have some partial truth and all have their roots in Marx's various statements on this question, they are all (with the possible exception of the rationalist one) based on a fixed opposition between accumulation and simple reproduction. All these views, furthermore, invariably interpret simple reproduction in the quantitative

191

sense. When we consider the second, qualitative sense of reproduction we realize that simple reproduction not only is not in opposition to extended reproduction, but is in fact its basis. It is the accumulation of capital that deepens and enriches this concept of reproduction.

Simple reproduction in the limited and quantitative sense is not adequate to the basic law of capitalist production, namely, reproduction on an extended scale. In other words, this sense of simple reproduction contradicts the basic law of capitalist reproduction, which involves accumulation. Marx is aware of this contradiction and in *Capital II* he addresses this question explicitly:

> Simple reproduction on the same scale seems to be an abstraction, both in the sense that the absence of any accumulation or reproduction on an expanded scale is an assumption foreign to the capitalist basis, and in the sense that the conditions in which production takes place do not remain absolutely the same in different years (which is what is assumed here). The supposition is that a social capital of a given value supplies the same mass of commodity values and satisfies the same quantity of needs in both the current year and the previous year, even if the forms of the commodities may change in the reproduction process. But since, when accumulation takes place, simple reproduction still remains a part of this, and is a real factor in accumulation, this can also be considered by itself. Moreover, the value of the annual product may decrease, even though the volume of use-values remains the same; the value may remain the same, even though the volume of use-values declines; the value and volume of use-values reproduced may decrease simultaneously. What emerges from all this is that reproduction either takes place under more favourable circumstances than previously, or under more difficult ones, and the latter may result in an incomplete — defective — reproduction. All this can affect only the quantitative aspect of the various elements of reproduction, and not the role they play in the total process as capital reproducing itself or as reproduced revenue. (C.II. pp.470-1)

In the above passage the two concepts of simple reproduction are clearly distinguished. It is said that 'simple reproduction on the same scale [simple reproduction in the limited sense] seems to be an abstraction . . .' It is an abstraction if we interpret this concept in the limited, quantitative sense. Marx also emphasizes the fact that simple reproduction in this sense is 'foreign to the capitalist basis' and that, moreover, 'the conditions in which production takes place do not remain absolutely the same in different years'. This last point puts into doubt the legitimacy of using the concept of simple reproduction in the first sense to conceptualize the conditions of reproduction in pre-capitalist societies. We are then surreptitiously led to the second concept: 'But since when accumulation takes place, simple reproduction still remains a part of this, and it is a real factor in accumulation, this can also be considered by itself. In this passage the quantitative sense of simple reproduction is distinguished from its qualitative sense.

Let us first explore the idea that simple reproduction is a part of and a factor in accumulation. It is only the quantitative sense of simple reproduction that can be used as such a basis. Consider first the case of reproduction on the same scale. For reproduction on the same scale to take place it is *pre-supposed* that the *same kind* of products will be produced in the *same quantities* as before. Now let us consider extended reproduction. When the scale of production is expanded the *same kind* of products are produced in *larger quantities*. To ensure further reproduction, the proportion of different products must remain *constant*. It is this constancy of the proportion between different products that ensures reproduction. Although the scale is expanding, the result of production is a renewal of the *relation* (the proportion) between different factors of production.

Accumulation must take place on a certain basis and it must be an accumulation of 'something'. The concept of accumulation or reproduction on an extended basis does not by itself account for the basis and the content of accumulation. It is simple reproduction as a part and a factor of accumulation that provides the basis for enlarged reproduction by showing that for any accumulation to take place, the relation between different factors of production, the proportion between products that replace products consumed productively and personally (the means of production and wage-goods) remains constant. This is the essence of simple reproduction as the basis of capitalist reproduction.

The argument may now be put forward that extended reproduction, involving the use of surplus-value for productive rather than personal consumption always leads to a disequilibrium, a disturbance of pre-existing relations and ratios of production between different departments of social production, namely between departments I and II. Therefore, it may be argued, simple reproduction in the sense of the renewal of the pre-existing balances between departments of social production would be violated by extended reproduction.

It is true that the capitalist process of accumulation historically has involved major structural shifts in the economy, often precipitated by technological change. In this sense extended reproduction itself has a qualitative aspect. Accumulation often takes place when either new products are invented or when new processes of production replace older technologies. It is here that simple reproduction in the quantitative sense as a factor in accumulation breaks down. Can we say the same thing about the qualitative sense of simple reproduction?

If we consider simple reproduction as the very essence of the reproduction of social relations of production, as the 'other' of the production process itself, then the accumulation of capital not only does not contradict simple reproduction but is in fact in its service. Let us be more specific. It is clear that accumulation under pre-capitalist modes of production often takes the form of conquest (of unused land or other settled communities). Often the relationship between the conqueror and the conquered is of tributary kind, i.e. the former extracts surplus products in the form of a tribute and does not reorganize the production process of the conquered. Thus accumulation has a passive and external relationship to the mode of production. With capitalist production, however, older sectors of production, when brought under capitalist control are reorganized on capitalist lines; when new products are invented their mass production normally acquires a capitalist form. Thus capitalist accumulation is internal to the capitalist mode of production. Furthermore, accumulation is a necessary law of capitalist production, compared to pre-capitalist modes where it may be contingent upon external factors. Thus what distinguishes capitalist production from pre-capitalist forms of production is not that accumulation occurs in the former but not in the latter. The difference lies rather in the fact that accumulation is a *necessary and internal* aspect of capitalism while it is only *contingent and external* for pre-capitalist modes of production.

Simple reproduction as an S.3 concept presupposes a high degree of interdependence and cohesion between units comprising an economic system. The industrial age ushered in by capitalism has created greater economic interdependence compared to the past and therefore a greater need for continuity of production and thus security in procuring the essential elements of the production process.

The capitalist process of accumulation involves the progressive reorganization of older non-capitalist sectors as well as the creation of new fields of activity for capitalist production. Thus constant renewal, the 'simple' reproduction of relations of production relies upon accumulation, and the latter is deepened and enriched by the former.

Conclusion

We have shown that conceiving simple reproduction in fixed opposition to extended reproduction is only possible if simple reproduction is interpreted in a narrow quantitative sense. On the other hand, when one considers the qualitative concept of simple reproduction it not only does not contradict capitalist (or any other) accumulation but in fact expresses the essence of this accumulation. In this sense simple reproduction is an S.3 concept (R.3), a concept defined not in opposition to the particular form of capitalist reproduction (accumulation) but in active relation to it. The other concepts of simple reproduction, i.e. as a pre-capitalist form (R.1) or as a part or factor (R.2) of accumulation are quantitative concepts that are subordinate to R.3.

The difference between the quantitative and the qualitative aspects of simple reproduction is crucial to understanding the two concepts of simple reproduction in Marx. The quantitative aspect is subordinate to the qualitative one. Simple reproduction, far from referring to reproduction on the same scale represents the very concept of reproduction. Thus reproduction is always 'simple reproduction': it is always the renewal of the same set of relationships between the elements of production regardless of the scale of material production.

In the capitalist mode of production R.3 is an essential law of social production.

Notes to Chapter Seven

1. In debates about economic development in recent years the same narrow view of simple reproduction has often been expressed. For details see the Conclusion.
2. Althusser & Balibar, 1970, pp.259-60. Balibar's discussion of reproduction is in many ways very close to the interpretation in this chapter, although both his purpose and approach differ from ours.

CHAPTER EIGHT

CO-OPERATION AND SIMPLE CO-OPERATION

A greater socialization of production under capitalism compared with pre-capitalist forms of production has often been associated with an enlargement of the scale of operations within single production units. That capitalist enterprises would grow in size not only through an expansion of the scale of operations but also by acquiring increasingly diverse lines of production was accepted by Marx's followers as an article of faith by the late nineteenth and early twentieth centuries.[1] Marx in fact had predicted the tendencies towards the concentration and centralization of capital.[2] For the theorists of the Second International these processes had reached the highest point possible under capitalist conditions by the early twentieth century.[3] The monopolization of industry became the cornerstone of the theories of imperialism advocated at the time. This tradition has continued up to the present time and has produced various theories of 'monopoly capital'.[4] Furthermore, these views on the tendencies of capitalist development led to certain practices in the construction of socialism in the Soviet Union — first in the form of 'war communism' during 1917-1922 and second in the form of central planning after 1929.[5]

In this chapter, through examining Marx's concept of co-operation, we will address the question of the connection between capitalist development and large scale production. In the next chapter we will pursue similar problems by examining Marx's views on the division of labour.

In his elaboration of the concept of co-operation in *Capital* Marx tends to use the word 'simple' to characterize what he sometimes calls 'the simple shape' of co-operation (or just 'simple' co-operation) whenever he is referring to co-operation in its restricted, local aspect (S.2 concept: CO.2) or at most co-operation as an historically first form (S.1 concept: CO.1).

However, as we will show in this chapter, a more general concept of co-operation (CO.3) is present in Marx's discourse although it is not referred to as simple co-operation but as co-operation.

The Simple Shape of Co-operation

Co-operation remains the fundamental form of the capitalist mode of production,

196

although in its simple shape it continues to appear as one particular form alongside the more developed ones. (C.I. p.454)

Here Marx is distinguishing between two forms of co-operation:

1. Co-operation as the fundamental form of capitalist production, and
2. co-operation 'as one particular form alongside the more developed ones'.

The latter form is characterized as the 'simple shape' or simple form of co-operation. It is also implied that 'simple' co-operation is a less developed and more primitive form of co-operation functioning 'alongside the more developed ones'.

Let us see what Marx means by simple co-operation as a particular, less-developed form:

Simple co-operation has always been, and continues to be, the predominant form in those branches of production in which capital operates on a large scale, but the division of labour and machinery play only an insignificant part. (C.I. p.454)

Thus the absence of extensive use of the division of labour and machinery and the presence of large-scale capitalist production help to determine the concept of 'simple' co-operation or the 'simple shape' of co-operation as a particular, less-developed form of capitalist production (CO.2). It follows that any large-scale capitalist production without extensive division of labour and use of machinery has the 'simple shape' of co-operation as its basis. However, large-scale production is not a characteristic exclusive to capitalist production as it may exist and, historically, has existed in the absence of the capitalist mode of production. In fact, there is an inherent and intimate connection between simple co-operation and large-scale production, regardless of the social form of production:

In its simple shape ... co-operation is a necessary concomitant of all production on large-scale, but it does not in itself represent a fixed form characteristic of a particular epoch in the development of the capitalist mode of production. At the most it appears to do so, and then only approximately, in the handicraft-like beginnings of manufacture and in that kind of large-scale agriculture which corresponds to the period of manufacture, and is distinguished from peasant agriculture mainly by the number of workers simultaneously employed and the mass of means of production concentrated for their use. (C.I. pp.453-4)

Here we learn that i) co-operation in its 'simple shape' always accompanies large-scale production; ii) this form is not a characteristic of a particular stage of capitalist development, i.e. it is always a particular form alongside other forms in all stages; iii) the distinguishing mark of this form is the large 'number' of workers and the 'mass' of concentrated means of production.

Indeed, this quantitative feature is a characteristic of the *beginning* of capitalist production, a beginning marked by the concentration of a large number of workers working side by side under 'one roof'. Marx begins his chapter on co-operation (Chapter 13 of *Capital I*) with such a description:

> Capitalist production only really begins, as we have already seen, when each individual capital simultaneously employs a comparatively large number of workers, and when, as a result, the labour-process is carried on, on an extensive scale, and yields relatively large quantities of products. A large number of workers working together, at the same time, in one place (or, if you like, in the same field of labour) in order to produce the same sort of commodity under the command of the same capitalist, constitutes the starting-point of capitalist production. This is both true historically and conceptually. With regard to the mode of production itself, manufacture can hardly be distinguished, in its early stages, from the handicraft trades of the guilds, except by the greater number of workers simultaneously employed by the same individual capital. It is merely an enlargement of the workshop of the master craftsmen of the guilds. At first, then, the difference is purely quantitative. (C.I. p.439)

But this quantitative difference implies a qualitative difference: when numerous labourers work side by side, whether or not they are performing similar tasks or complementary ones, the result is always a collective one exceeding the mechanical sum of individual efforts involved. Thus through simple co-operation social labour as opposed to individual labour manifests itself as a power far exceeding what could be achieved by individuals working in isolation from each other.

The reasons for this superiority of social labour as manifested through simple co-operation are discussed in detail by Marx in Chapter 13 of *Capital I*, and are enumerated in the following passage where he sums up his arguments:

> The combined working day produces a greater quantity of use-values than an equal sum of isolated working days, and consequently diminishes the labour-time necessary for the production of a given useful effect. Whether the combined working day, in a given case, acquires this increased productivity because it heightens the mechanical force of labour, or extends its sphere of

action over a greater space, or contracts the field of production relatively to the scale of production, or at the critical moment sets large masses of labour to work, or excites rivalry between individuals and raises their animal spirits, or impresses on the similar operations carried on by a number of men the stamp of continuity and many-sidedness, or performs different operations simultaneously, or economizes the means of production by use in common, or lends to individual labour the character of average social labour — whichever of these is the cause of the increase, the special productive power of the combined working day is, under all circumstances, the social productive power of labour, or the productive power of social labour. This power arises from co-operation itself. When the worker co-operates in a planned way with others, he strips off the fetters of his individuality, and develops the capabilities of his species. (C.I. p.447)

We may conclude that the simple or elementary form of co-operation is characterized by a purely quantitative (mechanical) agglomeration of labourers performing similar or complementary tasks, the result of which is an increase in the productive power of labour. As such it has a pre-capitalist existence (CO.1) and forms the beginning of capitalism (a transitional form) both in the historical sense of the absolute beginning and in the sense of the specific form of penetration of the capitalist mode of production in the pre-capitalist forms co-existing with the dominant capitalist mode of production, and thus retained as a subordinate form or moment (CO.2).

Marx is often keen to distinguish these various sides of the concept of 'simple' co-operation from co-operation in general. For example he refers to 'the colossal effects of simple co-operation . . . in the gigantic structures erected by Asiatics, Egyptians, Etruscans, etc.' (C.I. p.451). Obviously the reference is to the existence of the 'simple shape' of co-operation under pre-capitalist conditions. At the same time Marx warns against the confusion of pre-capitalist and capitalist forms of co-operation. This warning becomes all the more important in view of the fact that since co-operation forms the beginning of the capitalist mode of production ('both historically and conceptually'), capitalism and co-operation may be virtually mixed up and identified with each other:

> The sporadic application of co-operation on a large scale in ancient times, in the middle ages, and in modern colonies, rests on direct relations of domination and servitude, in most cases on slavery. As against this, the capitalist form presupposes from the outset the free wage-labourer who sells his labour-power to capital. Historically, however, this form is developed in opposition to peasant agriculture and independent handicrafts, whether in guilds or not. From the standpoint of the peasant and the artisan, capitalist co-operation does not

199

appear as a particular historical form of co-operation; instead, co-operation itself appears as a historical form peculiar to, and specifically distinguishing, the capitalist process of production. (C.I. pp.452-3)

Finally,

> If then, on the one hand, the capitalist mode of production is a historically necessary condition for the transformation of the labour process into a social process, so, on the other hand, this social form of the labour process is a method employed by capital for the more profitable exploitation of labour, by increasing its productive power. (C.I. p.453)

The main points of the foregoing passages may be summarized as follows:
1. In the pre-capitalist conditions of production, 'simple' co-operation ('co-operation on a large scale') is used 'sporadically', i.e. it is by no means the fundamental form of production.
2. In pre-capitalist modes, simple co-operation rests on the 'direct relation of domination' (slavery, serfdom), while under capitalism simple co-operation is based on free wage-labour.
3. Since capitalist simple co-operation historically develops in opposition to small-scale production, it is only from the latter's point of view that this form of co-operation appears *not as a particular form used by capital but as a form specific to capitalism.*
4. In all forms of production, capitalist or not, co-operation is a 'social form of the labour process'. This point has the wide-ranging implication that there are 'social' forms that may exist in many or all modes of production and therefore, because of their 'socialness', may be inherited and utilized by new modes of production.

Thus simple co-operation has a pre-capitalist existence as a 'social form', although it is alien to peasant agriculture and independent handicraft — forms which may have been dominant in pre-capitalist conditions. This social form is employed by capital, and is a necessary historic condition for 'the transformation of the labour process into a social process'. Thus CO.1 (the pre-capitalist social form of simple co-operation) is transformed into CO.2, the method employed by capital at its birth to transform the labour process into a social process, a method which also continues to be used by capital to transform spheres of production into a capitalist process in the same country, or production in other countries subjugated to the rule of capital. Finally, simple co-operation is not a defining characteristic specific to capitalism.

It might appear that Marx has basically contradicted himself by also claiming that co-operation is the fundamental form of capitalist production. This is only true if we identify simple co-operation with a more general form to which we now turn.

The General Form of Co-operation

We have already referred to the presence of a more general concept of co-operation (CO.3) in *Capital*, which forms the foundation of capitalist production. But this concept is not reducible to the 'simple shape' or the elementary form of co-operation either in the sense of the pre-capitalist forms of co-operation, or in the sense of those forms of co-operation that constitute the historical beginning of capitalism or serve as stepping stones for the transformation of pre-capitalist forms of production into capitalist production (CO.2). It is obvious that the general form of co-operation (CO.3) is not reducible to either CO.1 or CO.2, but subsumes the latter as its historically prior simple form (CO.1) or as a moment of itself. Marx does not use the word simple to characterize this sense of co-operation but merely refers to it as 'co-operation'.

Let us now see how Marx defines co-operation in general, regardless of the social form:

> When numerous workers work together side by side in accordance with a plan, whether in the same process, or in different but connected processes, this form of labour is called co-operation. (C.1. p.443)

Here, Marx is advancing a definition of co-operation in general, as distinct from 'simple' co-operation, that is scarcely different from the definition given for simple co-operation. Probably the key to any distinction between the two determinations is the expression 'different but connected processes'. But what is the criterion for distinguishing 'different but connected processes'? We will see in the next chapter on division of labour that this distinction is provided by the concept of commodity production.

We can reconcile Marx's characterizations of 'simple' co-operation as follows: on the one hand it is an historically prior form and a transitional form subsisting under capitalism. On the other hand, it is linked to his general definition of co-operation as the fundamental form of capitalist production: capitalist production generalizes large-scale production (a circumstance which had existed historically but never became predominant prior to capitalism) to all branches of production. In the process of this generalization it loses its dependence on the mere quantitative agglomeration of labourers and labour processes. The par-

201

allel development of both machine-based production and of the market expands the frontiers of 'simple' co-operation: the co-operation of numerous labourers in a single labour process expands to co-operation at the level of the nation-state and internationally. This sense of co-operation leads directly to the formulation of the concept of co-operation as the fundamental, predominant form of capitalist production (CO.3).

Let us recall that Marx defined the 'simple shape' of co-operation by reference to the absence of the extensive use of machinery and the division of labour. The general concept of co-operation (CO.3) overcomes this limitation and encompasses both the 'simple shape', which depends on the mere quantitative and mechanical sum of the labour of numerous workers, and the more complex forms which depend on the use of machinery and the division of labour.

This general concept of co-operation pre-supposes the development of manufacture and machine-based production. This latter development, in effect, intensifies the effects obtained from the 'simple shape' of co-operation — effects which result in an increase in the productive power of labour exceeding the mechanical sum of the individual labours applied. Since the object is not the simple concentration of workers (which runs into definite physical limits) but an increase in productivity, i.e. if it can be achieved by the substitution of machines for workers, so much the better from the viewpoint of the capitalist.

Thus the general concept of co-operation as the foundation of capitalism does not rest on the restrictive basis of the 'simple shape' of co-operation (although the latter forms the beginning of capital), but on the basis of the generalized co-operation of labourers and the means of production.

The Unity of the Three Concepts of Co-operation

What Marx calls the 'simple shape' or elementary form of co-operation is based on the quantitative and mechanical bringing together of numerous labourers or labour processes for the purpose of producing a common product or result. This merely mechanical aggregation in itself leads to an increase in the productivity of labour and heralds the birth of 'social labour'. This form of co-operation has a pre-capitalist historical existence (CO.1). But it also appears in the beginning of capitalism and, furthermore, serves as the transitional form, when capital has established its dominance, for those branches of production which are still dominated by pre-capitalist forms (CO.2).

202

We have shown that Marx defines co-operation in general terms which include the 'simple' form as a special case. The 'bow' that connects the 'simple shape' (CO.1 and CO.2) with the general concept of co-operation (CO.3) is the concept of social labour. Thus the socialization of labour assumes ever more complex forms under capitalism, which are not reducible to the simple aggregation of labourers (the simple shape of co-operation).

The key to the socialization of labour lies in the development of machine-based industry. This development transforms co-operation from its simple shape, which is *contingent* on a mechanical agglomeration of labourers, into a *necessary* relation among workers based on the dictates of machinery:

> In simple co-operation, and even on the more specialized form based on the division of labour, the extrusion of the *isolated* worker by the *associated* worker still appears to be more or less *accidental*. Machinery . . . operates only by means of *associated labour*, or labour in common. Hence the co-operative character of the labour process is in this case a technical *necessity* dictated by the very nature of the instrument itself. (C.I. p.508, emphasis added)

What can we conclude from the preceding discussion with regard to the relation between capitalism and large-scale production?

For Marx large-scale production marks the beginning of capitalism both objectively and conceptually. The beginning of capitalism in Britain was characterized by a process of increasing the scale of production through the conversion of the 'putting-out' system into a system of workshops which gradually developed into manufactories by division of labour within workshops. Industrial revolution enabled the industrial capitalists to transform the manufacture system into large-scale machine-based production. But can we conclude that large-scale production is also conceptually necessary for any other capitalist beginning? If so, we have established an inherent connection between capitalism and large-scale production and, in this light, the dualistic development experienced by many developing countries today and the Preobrazhensky-Trotsky-Stalin approach to industrialization in the Soviet Union[6] would seem inevitable. But, on the other hand, if we consider the particular conditions under which industrialization took place in Britain, it becomes clear that the increase in the physical scale of production was the result of a number of concrete circumstances, e.g. the Enclosures and the underdeveloped infrastructure. For instance, the putting-out system became an inefficient method of capitalist production when the communication costs associated with this system due to the undeveloped state of the infrastructure became too high; furthermore, the Enclosures had already severed the connection of the great mass of peasantry with the land and thus had created a vast urban labour force.

Thus large-scale production may not be a necessary condition for the beginning of capitalism (and economic development in general) in all times and all places but rather a particular form of capitalist development. So far we have only considered the physical aspect of the scale of production. It is clear that from the social point of view capitalist production is by nature large-scale. This means that the number of different lines of production as well as the general level of output is massive compared to all pre-capitalist economies. Largeness interpreted in this way may or may not necessarily involve largeness of every single production line. This depends on many factors, including technology, infrastructure and the market. For instance, the increasing productivity of labour in manufacturing as a result of modern technology in recent decades has not only resulted in a smaller industrial labour force, but also in a smaller share of manufacturing output in GDP compared with other sectors (notably the service industry).[7]

Recent trends in the internationalization of capital, furthermore, have created a world-wide system of division of labour and subcontracting that has been assimilated to a modern putting-out system.[8] This modern putting-out system has been made possible by rapid progress in contemporary means of communication, just as the old putting-out system disappeared partially due to the lack of necessary means of communication. Market expansion may at first be dealt with by an expansion in the scale of production, but may later lead to an increase in the number of units of production producing the product. In particular although the socialization of production involves social 'largeness', this development does not necessarily correspond to large-scale production in all branches and units of production.

If we go back to the forms of co-operation discussed above, we can see that CO.3 is social production on large scale, while CO.1 refers to specific forms of large-scale production in pre-capitalist and early capitalist conditions (usually limited to one or very few sectors of the economy) and CO.2 points to *individual* branches of production. Thus, only a conflation of these different meanings of co-operation can result in identifying increasing scales of production in individual branches with the increasing socialization of labour.

1. On this see Auerbach (1984) and Auerbach, Desai & Shamsavari (1988).
2. See Marx, C.I, Chap. 25, particularly pp.775-80 & p.804.
3. See references in Note (1) above; also see the Conclusion.
4. The literature in this field is quite extensive; therefore we will only mention some of the most important ones.

Major early works include Hilferding, R., 1981, *Finance Capital* (originally published in German in 1910); Luxemburg, R., 1951, *The Accumulation of Capital* (originally published in German, 1913); Lenin, V.I., *Imperialism, the Highest Stage of Capitalism*, originally published in Russian in 1917 (see Lenin, 1975, vol. one); Bukharin, N., 1972 (a); *Imperialism and World Economy* (originally published in Russian, 1917) and 1972 (b) *Imperialism and the Accumulation of Capital*. Later works (post-World War II) include Baran, P. & Sweezy, P., 1968, *Monopoly Capital*.

For a review of Marxist theories of imperialism see Brewer (1980). For a recent critical review of the theories of monopoly capital see Auerbach & Scott (1988).
5. For an introductory analysis of early Soviet economic history see Nove (1969), Chaps. 1-8.
6. There is some disagreement as to the nature of Trotsky's approach to industrialization. On Preobrazhensky's views see his *The New Economics* (Preobrazhensky 1965). For a review of the views of these three figures see Bideleux (1985), Chaps. 6 & 7.
7. On the development of the service economy see Fuchs (1968), Stenback (1979) and Gershuny & Miles (1983).
8. See World Bank (1987).

CHAPTER NINE

THE DIVISION OF LABOUR IN MANUFACTURE AND THE SOCIAL DIVISION OF LABOUR

Adam Smith advanced a unitary concept of the division of labour, which represents a conflation of two systems of division of labour, i.e. that which we find within the workshop and that which exists in society at large. For Smith, the difference between the two types of division of labour is a matter of 'degree' and therefore depends on the vantage-point of 'the spectator'.

Thus he argues that the effects of the division of labour 'will be more easily understood' if we consider its operation in particular manufactures. 'It is commonly supposed' Smith argues, that this system is 'carried furthest in some very trifling ones'. In other words, it is commonly supposed that the division of labour is developed to the highest degree in certain enterprises or branches of production, each of which contribute to a small degree to the total output of the economy, or in Smith's words, supplies 'the small wants of but a small number of people'. He then goes on to say that

> In those great manufactures, on the contrary, which are destined to supply the great wants of the great body of the people every different branch of the work employs so great a number of workmen that it is impossible to collect them all into the same workhouse ... Though in such manufactures, therefore, the work may really be divided into a much greater number of parts than in those of a more trifling nature, the division is not nearly so obvious, and has accordingly been much less observed. (Smith 1970, p.109)

Thus, for Smith, the difference between the division of labour within individual workshops or manufactures and the division of labour in society is reduced to a question of observability: the latter division of labour is of the same grade and kind as the first. The only difference between them is a difference in scale, such that while the former, which is carried out in a single workhouse and under one roof can be observed by a 'spectator', the latter, which occurs on a more extensive social scale cannot be so observed simply because the collection of all the different activities and enterprises composing an entire economy in a single 'workhouse' is simply impossible.

It is precisely at this point that Marx's intervention begins. What for

Smith constitutes a quantitative difference, a difference in the scope of observability by a human subject, for Marx signifies a difference in kind, a qualitative distinction. What constitutes a single concept of the division of labour for Smith is split into two distinct concepts in Marx, i.e. the division of labour in manufacture and the division of labour in society, or the social division of labour.

Let us now see what Marx himself has to say about this distinction.

The Distinction Between the Two Concepts of the Division of Labour

In the following passage Marx addresses himself to the question directly, with Smith's characterization of the difference between the two kinds of the division of labour very much in his mind:

> ... in spite of the numerous analogies and links connecting them, the division of labour in the interior of a society, and that in the interior of a workshop, differ not only in degree, but also in kind. The analogy appears most indisputable where there is an invisible bond uniting the various branches of trade. For instance the cattle breeder produces hides, the tanner makes hides into leather and the shoemaker makes the leather into boots. Here the product of each man is merely a step towards the final form, which is the combined product of their specialized labours . . . . Now it is quite possible to imagine, with Adam Smith, that the difference between the above social division of labour and the division in manufacture is merely subjective, exists merely for the observer who in case of manufacture can see at a glance all the numerous operations being per- formed on one spot, while in the instance given above, the spreading-out of the work over great areas and great number of people employed in each branch of labour obscure the connection. But what is it that forms the bond between the independent labours of the cattle breeder, the tanner and the shoemaker? It is the fact that their respective products are commodities. What, on the other hand characterizes the division of labour in manufacture? The fact that the specialized worker produces no commodities. (C.I. pp.474-5)

Thus the major difference between the two kinds of division of labour consists in the fact that the (capitalist) social division of labour is mediated by commodities, while in the case of the division in manufac- ture it is not so mediated.

Marx's development of the concept of division of labour reflects the distinction he makes between concrete and abstract labour — a distinc- tion which Marx claims as one of the two or three most novel points in *Capital*.[1] This distinction is sometimes characterized by Marx as one between directly social labour and labour mediated by commodities.

Marx traces the origin of social division of labour to two different, although related circumstances:

1) When communities come into contact with each other a form of social division of labour is originated through the exchange of surplus products. 'In this case, the social division of labour arises from the exchange between spheres of production which are originally distinct from and independent of one another' (C.I. p.472).

2) When self-sufficient communities with an already developed system of what Marx calls the physiological division of labour enter into a process of internal differentiation, normally through the impact of 'the exchange of commodities with foreign communities', a social division of labour within the community results. Marx comments that in the first case 'what was previously independent has been made dependent' while in the second case 'what was previously dependent has been made independent' (C.I. p.472).

The Relationship of the two Concepts of the Division of Labour

Marx definitely agrees with Smith on the relationship between the division of labour in manufacture and the division in society:

> Since the production and the circulation of commodities are the general prerequisites of the capitalist mode of production, division of labour in manufacture requires that a division of labour within society should have already attained a certain degree of development. Inversely, the division of labour in manufacture reacts back upon that in society, developing and multiplying it further. (C.I. p.473)

It is clear that although the division of labour in manufacture 'reacts back upon that in society', it is the latter that dominates the former and subsumes it as a subordinate moment of itself.

This result seems obvious in view of the fact that the social division of labour under capitalism is defined by Marx as commodity production. Thus it would seem that the technical division of labour in manufacture being subsumed under commodity production depends, as a matter of course, on the (capitalist) social division of labour. In other words, since the social division of labour is capitalist, the division of labour in manufacture merely bends itself to this capitalist form of social division.

This interpretation is, however, contradicted by Marx's characterization of the division of labour in manufacture as specifically capitalist:

> While the division of labour in society at large, whether mediated through the

208

exchange of commodities or not, can exist in the most diverse economic formations of society, the division of labour in the workshop, as practised by manufacture, is an entirely specific creation of the capitalist mode of production. (C.I. p.480)

This formulation by Marx has two important consequences:

1) The concept of the social division of labour is disengaged from capitalist commodity production and is generalized to include not only non-capitalist commodity production but also non-commodity producing modes of production.
2) The division of labour in manufacture is described as a specifically capitalist phenomenon.

How are we to account for the status of the technical division of labour under capitalism as specifically capitalist, while it is entirely subsumed under the capitalist form of the social division of labour (commodity production)?

The Significance of the Division of Labour in Manufacture

Although Adam Smith conflated the two forms of the social division of labour on the one hand and the technical division of labour on the other, his eyes were fixed on the technical division of labour, as is evident from his celebrated account of the division of labour in a pin-making factory. Indeed, the technical division of labour is the 'engine', the motive force of the capitalist division of labour.

Marx traces the origin of the social division of labour under capitalism to the division of labour as it arises between independent communities through external trade. This development then leads to an internal differentiation within communities leading to an internal social division of labour based on the external division of labour (between communities).

This internal development, however, is still external so long as it is based on an external division of labour. True internalization is achieved when the social division of labour finds an internal basis. This internal basis is provided, under capitalism, by the division of labour in manufacture, because this division creates ever more opportunities for the greater social division of labour.

Without the division of labour in manufacture, capitalism lacks an internal technical basis. Without such a basis, modern industrial capital would be hardly distinguishable from merchant's capital, a relationship that had coexisted with many pre-capitalist modes of production without constituting a proper mode of production by itself. Indeed the beginning of the capitalist mode of production is only quantitatively different from pre-capitalist forms of capital relation.

In one of the passages in the Chapter on Co-operation in *Capital I*, quoted in Chapter Eight above, Marx comments that manufacture at the dawn of capitalist development 'can hardly be distinguished, in its earliest stages, from the handicraft trades of the guilds, except by the greater number of workers simultaneously employed by the same individual capital. It is merely an enlargement of the workshop of the master craftsmen of the guilds'. He adds that 'at first, then the difference is purely quantitative'.

Thus what effectively transforms the early stage of capitalist development (which consisted of the subsumption of earlier forms of production under the principle of commodity production and profit-seeking on a grand scale) to a full-fledged mode of production is the principle of the technical division of labour under capitalism (the division of labour in manufacture).

Therefore the division of labour in manufacture is the essence of the capitalist social division of labour (generalized commodity production). But as such an essence it is superceded by the social division of labour and is subsumed by the latter as a moment of itself. And it is this movement that makes for difficulties in the understanding of the technical division of labour as specifically capitalist.

These difficulties arise from two circumstances:

a) As Marx has remarked on several occasions the principle governing the technical division of labour under capitalism is the absence of commodity exchange (e.g. between workers engaged in different stages of production in a factory). This seems contradictory to the fundamental principle of commodity production under capitalism.
b) Technology seems to be independent of the social organization of production. Therefore any technical division of labour, capitalist or non-capitalist, should be evaluated in a 'means-ends' manner.

These problems, however, arise only on the basis of an *analytical* distinction between the two forms of the division of labour. In fact this analytical approach seems to be a widespread interpretation. According to this view while factories represent islands of 'planning', market and commodity

210

exchange represent 'chaos'.[2] This position is obviously contradictory to Marx's characterization of the technical division of labour as 'specifically capitalist'. If we invoke the D-model developed in Chapter Two above, these problems are resolved.

We may claim that while in the early stages of capitalist development changes in the methods of production were dominated by the social division of labour (i.e. they simply reacted to the requirements of the expanding market for manufactured goods) in more mature stages, when capitalism found an internal technical basis,[3] technological development became a dominant factor. Thus technology, which was a passive element earlier, is transformed into an active moment. But it should be clear that technology continues to develop in active relationship with the development of markets. Capitalism could advance only on the basis of the division of labour in manufacture. The urge for surplus-value on an increasing scale could not but react on the technical basis, resulting in a greater productivity of labour made possible by the division of labour in the workshop. Furthermore, this technical division of labour provides a 'rational' basis for the ever-increasing and ever-widening possibility for the social division of labour under capitalism (commodity production). It transforms the narrow subdivisions of technical units of production (e.g. factories) into new industries which participate in the social division of labour by producing and marketing products that were formerly 'raw materials' circulating only within the technical unit and thus adds to the number and range of commodities available on the market.

The Three Forms of the Social Division of Labour

The first (and pre-capitalist) form of social division of labour postulated by Marx is often characterized by him as the 'physiological' division of labour based on age and sex differences:

> The division of labour within society develops from one starting-point; the corresponding restriction of individuals to particular vocations or callings develops from another starting-point, which is diametrically opposed to the first. This second starting-point is also that of the division of labour within manufacture. Within a family and after further development, within a tribe, there springs up naturally a division of labour caused by differences of sex and age, and therefore based on a purely physiological foundation. (C.I. p.471)

In the above passage Marx is first of all distinguishing between the origin of the division of labour in manufacture and the social division of labour as it arises naturally, based on differences in sex and age, among families

211

and tribes in the early stages of social development. Marx is also defining the first, primitive form of the social division of labour, which is based on the 'natural' grounds of sex and age differences, as the 'physiological' division of labour. Presumably, this is the form of social division of labour found among primitive communities. For example when Marx states that "labour is socially divided in the primitive Indian community . . .' (C.I., p.132) he is referring to an elementary or 'simple' form of the social division of labour that appears at the dawn of social-human history.

This form roughly corresponds to an S.1 concept and therefore it can be called the Social Division of Labour 1 (SDL.1).

There is a second form of the social division of labour (SDL.2), the form arising from trade between independent communities. This is a transitional form leading to greater social division of labour inside communities related to each other through external trade on the one hand, and preparing the way for the launching of capitalism, on the other. This historical transitional form, pre-dating the dominance of the capitalist mode of production, continues to serve as a transitional form even after capital has become dominant, mainly as a form of penetration by capital into non-capitalist modes of production before their full transformation into the capitalist mode of production.

The third form of the social division of labour (SDL.3) is obviously the form found under capitalism, that which is based on generalized commodity production. As we have shown in the previous section, this form of the social division of labour is based on the technical division of labour in manufacture, which is specific to capitalism, and thus cannot be reduced to either SDL.2 or SDL.1. On the contrary it is only on the basis of SDL.3 that we can fully comprehend the social significance of the earlier or subsumed forms.

1. See, for instance, Marx's letter to Engels dated Aug. 24, 1867 (LC. p.111).
2. As we have shown in detail elsewhere this view was quite predominant among Marxist economists of the Second International: see Auerbach, Desai & Shamsavari (1988). See also Chapter Twelve and the Conclusion below.
3. According to Marx, the industrial revolution leading to machine-based industry provided such a technical basis for capitalism.

CHAPTER TEN

THE GENERAL FORM OF THE CIRCUIT OF INDUSTRIAL CAPITAL

The role of money and finance in capitalist and socialist development has only recently been given serious examination in the literature.[1] In Marxist literature in general there is a one-sided emphasis on the production side of capitalism as opposed to commercial, monetary and financial aspects. This is not surprising, as it was Marx himself who believed that production for its own sake was the aim of the capitalist system and the development of productive forces was the historic mission and justification for the capitalist mode of production. This production-ist bias in the analysis of capitalism is also present in approaches related to the analysis of the construction of a socialist society, as is evident from the prevalent view that socialism will be an economy without markets or money.[2]

Although, as we shall see in Part III and in the Conclusion, certain statements by Marx can be blamed for this productionist bias, these statements stand in sharp contrast to Marx's detailed analysis of the role of money under capitalism.[3] Throughout Part II, particularly in Chapter Five, we have attempted to combat this bias. In this final chapter of Part II we hope to demonstrate that Marx's analysis of the circuits of industrial capital leaves no doubt about the importance he attached to the circuit of money capital.

The Three Circuits of Industrial Capital

Marx analyses the total circuit of industrial capital into three circuits. These three circuits are 1) the circuit of money capital, 2) the circuit of productive capital and 3) the circuit of commodity capital. These three circuits are represented symbolically by the following three formulae:

1) $M - C \ldots P \ldots C' - M'$
2) $P \ldots C' - M' - C \ldots P$
3) $C' - M' - C \ldots P \ldots C'$

All of the three circuits, when combined together form the total circuit of industrial capital, i.e. the latter is a union of the three circuits. But there is one circuit that Marx reserves for a special mention, the circuit of money capital. Let us see why this circuit is accorded such a privileged position — something denied to the other circuits or forms of the circuit of industrial capital.

Marx characterizes the circuit of money capital in the following way:

> The circuit of money capital remains the permanent general expression of industrial capital, in so far as it always includes the valorization of the value advanced. (C.II. p.140)
>
> The general form of the circuit of industrial capital is the circuit of money capital. (C.II. pp.142-3)

Thus the significance of the circuit of money capital derives from the fact that the latter represents the general form or expression of the entire circuit of industrial capital. As a result, the circuit of money capital acquires a double significance:

a) As a circuit fully subsumed under the total circuit of industrial capital alongside the two other circuits of commodity and productive capital (CT. M-2)

b) As the general form of the circuit of industrial capital (CT.M-3)

But besides these two distinct aspects of the concept of the circuit of money, there is another aspect of this concept that should be added to the above list:

c) The circuit of money capital as one of the historically prior forms of capital, i.e. merchant's capital (CT. M-1)

The latter point comes up very clearly in Marx's discussion of 'the general formula of capital' in *Capital I*:

> Buying in order to sell, or, more accurately, buying in order to sell dearer, M-C-M, seems admittedly to be a form peculiar to one kind of capital alone, merchants' capital. But industrial capital too is money which has been changed into commodities, and reconverted into more money by the sale of these commodities. Events which take place outside the sphere of circulation, in the interval between buying and selling, do not affect the form of this movement. (C.I. p.256)
>
> M-C-M' is in fact therefore the general formula for capital, in the form in which it appears directly in the sphere of circulation. (C.I. p.257)

214

It may seem that the characterization of the circuit of money capital as the general form of the circuit of industrial capital amounts to the reduction of the general form of the most developed form of capital, i.e.industrial capital, to its 'lowest common denominator', namely the pre-capitalist form of merchant's capital. Marx is well aware of this complication, but still maintains his position.

Before justifying Marx's position let us look at the reservations and qualifications that Marx expresses in relation to the form of money capital:

> The circuit of money capital is thus the most one-sided, hence most striking and characteristic form of appearance of the circuit of industrial capital, in which its aim and driving motive — the valorization of value, money-making and accumulation — appears in a form that leaps to the eye (buying in order to sell dearer). (C.II. p.140)
> The formula $M - C \ldots P \ldots C' - M'$, with the result $M' = M+m$, contains in its form a certain deception; it bears an illusory character that derives from the existence of the advanced and valorized value in its equivalent form, in money. What is emphasized is not the valorization of the value, but the *money form* of this process . . . (C.II. p.141)

Marx is characterizing the circuit of money capital not only as the general form but also as a one-sided, characteristic and illusory form of the circuit of industrial capital. While Marx justifies the generality of the form of money capital on the basis of its inclusion of the valorization of the value on one page (p.140), he derives the illusory character of this circuit (or form) from the absence of the same fact on the very next page: 'What is emphasized is not the valorization of value, but the *money form* of this process' (C.II. p.141).

Thus the circuit of money capital may represent the most developed form of capital or an illusory form depending on whether attention is focused on the valorization of value or on 'the money form of the process'. The latter tendency corresponds to a strand of mercantilist thought that Marx calls 'the monetary system'.

Mercantilist, Physiocratic and Classical Views of the Circulation of Capital

> The so-called Monetary System is simply the expression of the superficial form $M - C - M'$, a movement that proceeds exclusively in the circulation sphere . . . . (C.II. p.141)

The form of the circuit implicit in mercantilist thought, especially in the first stage of this trend of economic thought (the Monetary System), was the form M-C-M' as it 'proceeds exclusively in the circulation sphere'. Thus the circuit is none other than the circuit of merchant's capital.

The Mercantilist doctrine was in vogue in the age of the growing weight of mercantile capital in Europe prior to the birth of industrial capital. The Mercantilists were absorbed by problems of monetary circulation and foreign trade and therefore their attention was primarily focused on the sphere of circulation. Since they considered the circuit M-C-M' only as it operates within the circulation process, what stands out in this form of the circuit 'is the money form of this process'.

Thus the form of the circuit on which the Monetary System rests is neither the circuit of money capital as one of the constituent circuits of the entire circuit of industrial capital (CT.M-2) nor the general form of the latter (CT.M-3), but simply the form of the circuit of merchant's capital (CT.M-1).

Assessed against this historical background it is not surprising that Marx calls this form one-sided and illusory. The one-sided and illusory character of the circuit of money capital, which Marx calls the general form of the circuit of industrial capital, arises not from its determination as an S.3 concept (CT.M-3) *per se* but its possible degeneration into (CT.M-1), because of a formal identity of the two. This reduction takes place if the circuit of money capital is divorced from the other two circuits and is regarded as a sole, self-contained whole:

> The illusory character of M - C ... P ... C' - M' and the corresponding illusory significance it is given, is there as soon as this form is regarded as the sole form, not as one that flows and is constantly repeated: i.e. as soon as it is taken not just as one of the forms of circuit, but rather as its exclusive form. In itself, however, it refers to other forms. (C.II. pp.141-2)

Since the Mercantilists conceived of capital only in the form of mercantile capital, the form of the circuit used by them was the circuit of mercantile capital. Therefore its application in the analysis of industrial or agricultural capital by economists who came after them could only result in illusion and deception. As we will see presently both the Physiocrats and classical economists use different forms to analyse the circuit of capital.

According to Marx, the Physiocrats chose the circuit of commodity capital while classical economists opted for the circuit of productive capital. We may see in this historical development of economic thought some form of progression, i.e. from sphere of circulation to sphere of production. We may then rush to the conclusion that while the Physiocrats took a step ahead of the Mercantilists, the classical economists in their turn made progress over the Physiocrats by choosing production as their model. Such a conclusion, although very tempting in view of the prevalence of a 'productionist' bias in most Marxist economic writing, is in fact untenable as Marx's own analysis clearly shows.

> C' . . . C' is the basis of Quesnay's *Tableau Économique*, and it shows great discernment on his part that he selected this form in opposition to M . . . M' (the form fixed on and isolated by the Mercantile System), *and not* P . . . P. (C.II. p.179 — emphasis added)

Thus Marx praises Quesnay for choosing the form of the circuit of commodity capital and *not* the form of the circuit of productive capital (i.e. the form chosen by the classical economists) in opposition to the Mercantilists. Let us look at the reasons for the superiority of the Physiocrats' analysis over that of classical economists in this respect.

The choice of P . . . P by the classical economists suffers from the following drawback:

> The general form of the movement P . . . P' is the form of reproduction, and does not indicate, as does M . . . M', that valorization is the purpose of the process. For this reason, classical economists found it all the more easy to ignore the specifically capitalist form of the production process, and to present production as such as the purpose of the process . . . . (C.II. p.172)

Thus if the form of the circuit of productive capital is taken as the exclusive form of the circuit of industrial capital (as is the case with classical political economy) the specificity of capitalism as a form of social production is abstracted from and the latter is presented as the general, typical natural form of production and reproduction. With this approach capitalist production is reduced to production 'in general'.

On first examination this result may seem curious in view of the following circumstance.

In his analysis of the Physiocratic system in *Theories of Surplus Value*, Marx gives credit to the Physiocrats for being the first contingent of economists (prior to classical economists) who analysed the capitalist mode of production independently of circulation. Since the Physiocrats concentrated their attention on agricultural production — a sphere in which the process of circulation proceeds primarily between man and nature and not between men — they could analyse production in abstraction from circulation.

> Since it is the great and specific contribution of the Physiocrats that they derive value and surplus-value not from circulation but from production, they necessarily begin, in contrast to the Monetary and Mercantile system, with that branch of production which can be thought of in complete separation from and independently of circulation, of exchange; and which presupposes exchange not between man and man but only between man and nature. (TSV.I. p.49)

On the other hand, as we have seen above, in *Capital II*, Marx praises the Physiocrats for choosing the circuit of commodity capital and not that of productive capital in their analysis of capital, in contrast to Mercantilism.

Marx is using two different concepts of circulation in the two different contexts mentioned above. When Marx says that the Physiocrats derive value and surplus-value from production and not from circulation, circulation in this context refers only to the transformation of the product (commodity) into money: C - M. Since in agricultural production the product does not need to go through this phase in order to resume reproduction, the process of reproduction can be studied in abstraction from this type of circulation. On the other hand, when Marx praises the Physiocrats for choosing the circuit of commodity capital, the commodity circulation implied here corresponds to the entire process of reproduction and not simply to the 'simple' circulation of commodities.

The peculiarity of agriculture consists in the fact that agricultural output has often the 'use-form' or the physical shape exactly required of the inputs in agricultural production (seed for sowing, food for feeding labourers). Therefore, the output does not necessarily have to be sold to be turned into fresh elements of production. Thus the circuit of 'industrial' capital in agriculture can be studied in abstraction from 'circulation' (i.e. the circuit of money capital).

> Since in C' . . . C' the total product (the total value) is the point of departure, it is evident here that, leaving aside foreign trade, reproduction on an expanded scale, with productivity otherwise remaining the same, can take place only if the material elements of the additional productive capital are already contained in the part of the surplus product to be capitalized. That is to say, in so far as the production of one year serves as the precondition for that of the next, or, in so far as production can occur together with simple reproduction process within a year, surplus product is immediately produced in the form that enables it to function as additional capital. (C.II. p.179)

218

In agricultural production the surplus product (surplus grain) *by nature* contains 'the material elements of the additional productive capital' needed for production on an expanded scale. In this sphere of material production the 'surplus product is immediately produced in the form that enables it to function as additional capital.'

We can see now how the 'fortunate' choice of agricultural production by the Physiocrats as the field of the operation of capital led them to choose the circuit of commodity capital. In what follows we will show what Marx considers to be the superiority of this circuit over not only the circuit of productive capital but also (curiously enough) over the circuit of money capital.

The circuit of commodity capital (form III of the total circuit of industrial capital) is distinguished from the other two by the fact that it is only in this circuit that self-expanded capital-value, i.e. the original capital value plus surplus-value, appears as the starting-point of its self-expansion:

> In the form C' . . . C', the consumption of the entire commodity product is presupposed as the condition for the normal course of the circuit of capital itself . . . . Thus consumption in its entirety — both individual and productive consumption — enters into the circuit of C' as a precondition. (C.II. p.173)

Another interesting feature of this form compared to other forms of the circuit of industrial capital is the following.

All circuits share this in common — they all begin their movement in the same form as they conclude it: the initial form is always the form in which capital-value is advanced (in form III augmented by surplus-value) and the concluding form is a transformation of a preceding functional form (e.g. M' in I is a change of form of C', final P in III is a changed form of M, C' in III is a changed form of P, although here the transformation does not merely concern a change of functional form but also a change of the magnitude of value). Furthermore, this transformation is not merely a formal change of place in circulation but a real transformation of the use-form and the value of the commodity constituents of the productive capital in the production process (C.II. pp.174-5).

> The form of the first extreme M, P and C' is given for each circuit, I, II, or III; the returning form at the closing extreme is produced and hence determined by the series of metamorphoses of the circuit itself. (C.II. p.175)

For example, I presupposes that M is in the hands of the buyer and exists outside of the circuit; II presupposes the existence of L (labour-power) and MP (means of production) outside the circuit. But, in general, I does not presuppose the existence of money-capital nor does II presuppose the existence of another circuit of productive capital. Thus in I, M may be the first money-capital and II, P the first productive capital.

In III, however, i.e.

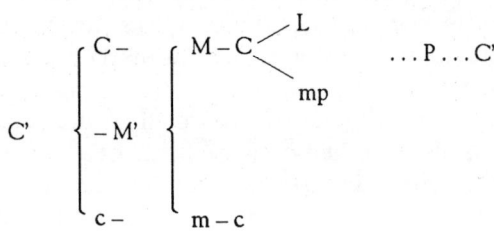

C is twice presupposed outside the circuit. Firstly in the circuit C' – M' – C⟨L/mp⟩
This C, in so far as it consists of means of production, is a commodity in the hands of its seller; it is itself commodity capital, in so far as it is the product of a capitalist production process; and even when this is not the case, it appears as commodity capital in the hands of the merchant. (C.II. p.175)

It is only in this form III, within the circuit itself, that C appears as a premise of C. This because the starting-point is capital in commodity form. (C.II. p.176)

In I and II it is only presumed at the end that M' and P exist in the hands of others (these terminal points are the direct results of circulation). III, on the other hand, presupposes the existence of C (L and mp) as commodities of others.

But precisely because the circuit C' . . . C' presupposes in its description the existence of another industrial capital in the form C (= L + mp) . . . , it itself demands to be considered not only as the *general* form of the circuit, i.e. as a social form in which every individual industrial capital can be considered . . . , hence not only as a form of motion common to all individual industrial capitals, but at the same time as the form of motion of the sum of individual capitals, i.e. of the total social capital of the capitalist class, a movement in which the movement of any individual industrial capital simply appears as a partial one, intertwined with the others and conditioned by them. (C.II. pp.176-7)

C' . . . C' is the only circuit in which the capital value originally advanced forms only a part of the extreme that opens the movement, and in which the movement in this way proclaims itself from the start as a total movement of industrial capital; a movement both of the part of the product that replaces the productive capital and of the part that forms surplus product and is on average partly spent as revenue, and partly has to serve as an element of accumulation. (C.II. p.177)

The significance of the circuit of commodity capital consists in that it begins from the result, the end of capitalist production, i.e. surplus value. C', which opens this circuit, already contains surplus-value and thus it presupposes the end and the motive force of capitalist production. Thus in this circuit the 'beginning' contains the 'end'. It is for this reason that the circuit 'itself demands to be considered not only as the *general* form of the circuit . . . but at the same time as the form of motion of the sum of individual capitals . . .' Since the circuit from the beginning presupposes the capital relation, it presupposes the existence of other circuits of commodity capital and thus it cannot be assumed to be or analysed as an individual and isolated circuit.

The Significance of the Circuit of Money Capital

Now that we have seen why Marx defends the position of the Physiocrats against those of the Mercantilists and the classical political economy, let us look at the reasons for Marx's choice of the circuit of money capital as the general form of the circuit of industrial capital.

Marx clearly does not consider the circuit of productive capital as the general form because this circuit (which was chosen by the classical economist) can easily degenerate from being one special circuit of industrial capital into a fundamental relation of production and reproduction true for all times and places. As to the circuit of commodity capital, this circuit, in spite of its superior 'social form' compared to both the circuits of productive and money capital, suffers from the following shortcomings:

First, since it begins with the result of the valorization process (C', which contains both the advanced capital value and the surplus-value), it does not show the *process* of valorization.

Secondly, in the circuit of commodity capital

the commodities on the market form the permanent premise of the process of production and reproduction. Hence if attention is fixed exclusively on this figure, all the elements of the production process seem to proceed from commodity circulation and to exist only as commodities. This one-sided conception overlooks the elements of the production process that are independent of the commodity element. (C.II. p.179)

We can see that the general form must not only show the valorization

221

process but it should also consider this process in relation to the production process.

Now the circuit of money capital is the only circuit that explicitly shows the valorization process. As such it acquires a generality describing all forms of capital in time and space. We have seen earlier that Marx called M-C-M' the general formula of capital, equally valid for pre-capitalist forms of capital (merchant's capital) and industrial capital. Marx also says:

> M . . . M' can be the first circuit of a capital, it can be its last; it can be taken as the form of the total social capital . . . (C.II. p.140)

Thus it is a form showing the common features of all individual capitals as well as representing their sum total. Whether new capital is advanced in the form of money and then withdrawn, or it is transferred to another business, or it is put back into the same business does not make any difference as far as the general form is concerned.

The problem with the above conception of the circuit of money capital is that the circuit degenerates from a form describing the total circuit of industrial capital (an S.3 concept based on the most developed form of capital) into either a form subsumed under the circuit of industrial capital or into a pre-capitalist form (e.g. merchant's capital). If we were to hold on to this conception, the whole point of not only Marx's critique of the Mercantilist System but also his critique of the Physiocrats and classical economists would be lost.

There must be a specific function that money capital performs under developed (industrial) capitalism, which merchant's capital does not perform.

> As a form comprised in all circuits, money capital performs this circuit precisely for that part of the capital that creates surplus-value, the variable capital. The normal form of advance for wages is payment in money . . . . Hence the worker must constantly come face to face with the capitalist as money capitalist, and with his capital as money capital. Here there can be no question, as in the purchase of means of production and the sale of productive commodities, of a direct or indirect balancing of accounts . . . . (C.II. pp.140-1)

The same thing is true of the part of surplus-value spent by the capitalist for his personal consumption.

> Thus both M, as the variable capital value advanced, and m, as its increment, are necessarily retained in money form, to be spent as such. (C.II. p.141)

222

Now we have the key to Marx's characterization of the circuit of money capital as the general form of the circuit of industrial capital. What distinguishes this circuit from the other circuits is that it shows the valorization process essential to *all* forms of capital. (This characteristic unites all forms of capital, e.g. merchant's capital and modern industrial capital.) Secondly; this circuit is essential for the fundamental relation underlying industrial capital, namely wage-labour, in so far as in the relationship between the labourers and the capitalists, the former relate to the latter as money capitalists (this characteristic definitely distinguishes industrial capital from all pre-capitalist forms of capital, e.g. merchant's capital or capitalism based on slavery).

We conclude this chapter by summarizing the main points developed above.

Summary

1. The circuit of money capital, in its very general form, i.e. M-C-M', is the general formula of capital representing the valorization process essential for any capitalist relation. This is also the form in which capital appears in ('simple') circulation. This form is the starting point for the Mercantilist school, which analyses capitalism as it appears in circulation. As such, it directly corresponds to a pre-capitalist form of capital, namely merchant's capital. This establishes the circuit of money capital as an S.1 concept (CI.M.1)

2. The circuit of money capital is one of the forms comprising the entire circuit of industrial capital. As such it is fully subsumed by the latter. This distinction of form allows the existence of a sub-class of 'money capitalists' operating *under* industrial capital. Their *raison d'être* under capitalism is rooted in the functional differentiation between the three forms of the circuit of industrial capital. Thus the circuit of money capital in this form or function is entirely dependent upon the total circuit of industrial capital. Thus the circuit of money capital also has an S.2 form (CI.M.2)

3. The circuit of money capital as the general form of the total circuit of industrial capital is not reducible to either CT.M.1 or CT.M.2 for the following reasons. This form of circuit as analysed by Marx presupposes the other forms, i.e. it is not a form isolated from the others. Thus it is based on the highest development of the capitalist relations of production, that is to say capitalism when it penetrates production and is not

223

simply an appendage of the productive apparatus of society (industrial capital). This signifies that the circuit of money capital further appears as an S.3 concept (Cl.M.3).

We may conclude that the significance Marx attaches to Cl.M.3 shows that money and finance, far from being simple reflections of the 'real', productive side of the capitalist economy describe the general movement of the most characteristic form of production under capitalism, i.e. industrial capital.

Notes to Chapter Ten

1. In the literature on economic development the first significant contribution was Gurley & Shaw (1967). In this work the authors establish that financial development is a causal factor in economic development. Later works include Shaw (1973), McKinnon (1973). Also see Drake (1980), Gillis, et. al., 1988, chap. 13. On the role of finance in socialist transition see Griffith-Jones (1981).
2. See the Conclusion.
3. Marx attached a great deal of significance to the role of money in the capitalist economy. See Shamsavari (1986) for a detailed discussion of Marx's views on money, where it is argued that Marx's views are well developed when compared with the classical, Keynsian and neo-Keynsian views on money.

PART III

MARX'S THEORY OF VALUE: A CRITIQUE

CHAPTER ELEVEN

THE DIALECTICS OF VALUE AND VALUE-FORM

I have postponed the discussion of Marx's concept of value, which is fundamental to Marx's *Capital*, for two reasons:

a) Marx made a deliberate attempt at 'dialectical presentation' in the treatment of value in the first chapter of *Capital I*. Therefore his presentation of the value question is an ideal ground for 'testing' the validity of the dialectical structure of Marx's concepts as presented in the previous chapters of this work.
b) In spite of Marx's important breakthroughs on the question of value, especially in his value-form analysis, I believe his formal presentation of the value question suffers from serious difficulties whose nature can be explained by a failure to apply the dialectical method thoroughly and consistently.

In what follows I will first show that Marx's analysis of the form of value fits into the dialectical structure that has emerged from my examination of Marx's concepts in earlier chapters of this work. We will see that this is so in spite of terminological difficulties and historicist traces in Marx's presentation. These difficulties are present especially in the final version of chapter 1 of *Capital I*.[1] Referring to the first version of this chapter,[2] where the dialectical presentation is clearer and less encumbered with difficulties, I will demonstrate the essence of Marx's dialectical method. I will then move on to a discussion of the reasons why Marx attached such importance to the analysis of the value-form through an examination of those works of Marx which represent earlier versions of *Capital*, such as the *Grundrisse* and the *Critique*. We will reserve the study

227

of the nature of difficulties in Marx's analysis of value in *Capital* for the next chapter.

The Dialectics of the Value-Form

Marx, in the early stages of his analysis of the commodity, prior to the elaboration of his value-form concept, refers to the exchange value of commodities as nothing 'other than the mode of expression, the "form of appearance", of a content distinguishable from it'; and as 'the necessary mode of expression, or form of appearance, of value' (C.I. pp. 127-8). Thus, for Marx, exchange value represents the *necessary* phenomenal form of value. It is in the third section of the chapter on the commodity that Marx sets out to establish this *necessity* through the development of the various determinations of the value-form, starting from the simplest expression and ending with the complete value-form, i.e. the money form, or *the* form of value. In the beginning of his discussion Marx refers to the purely social existence of value:

> However, let us remember that commodities possess an objective character as values only in so far as they are all expressions of an identical social substance, human labour, that their objective character as values is therefore purely social. From this it follows that it can only appear in the social relation between commodity and commodity. (C.I. pp.138-9)

Thus the necessity of the phenomenal form of value, i.e. exchange-value, which expresses 'the social relation between commodity and commodity', is rooted in the specific social nature of labour constituting the substance of value, namely 'abstract labour'. At this point Marx goes on to trace the development of the money-form — the value-form common to all commodities (a form 'which contrasts in the most striking manner with the motley natural forms of their use values' [C.I. p.139]) beginning with the 'simplest' and the most elementary value relation of one commodity with another.

> The simplest value-relation is evidently that of one commodity to another commodity of a different kind . . . Hence the relation between the values of two commodities supplies us with the simplest expression of the value of a single commodity. (C.I. p.139)

This 'simplest expression of the value of a single commodity' serves as the departure point for Marx's analysis of value-form. Before following Marx further, let us see why Marx calls this relation simple and whether this simple relation fits any of the three concepts of simple developed in the present work.

Marx calls this form or expression 'The Simple, Isolated, or Acciden-tal Form of Value', a description that appears as the title of the section devoted to this particular form. From this characterization it would naturally follow that Marx is using an S.1 concept as his beginning: the words 'isolated' and 'accidental' clearly show this. Thus Marx's charac-terization of this simple value-relation (between two commodities) as 'isolated' and 'accidental' shows that the value-relation that his analysis begins with represents an elementary or accidental relation, a relation that can occur randomly at any place and any time. Marx's subsequent discussion provides us with further proof that this is exactly what he had in mind. The 'simple' he begins with is an historically first form or an elemental relation that can be found whenever two 'persons' exchange commodities:

> . . . the simple form of value of the commodity is at the same time the simple form of value of the product of labour, and also that the development of the commodity form coincides with the development of the value form. (C.I. p.154)

Thus the historical development of the commodity form (from barter to money exchange) runs parallel to the logical development of the value form as analysed by Marx. This raises a serious question. Throughout the previous chapters we have been at pains to prove that Marx's beginning, while being simple, is not reducible to S.1, that it is definitely S.3, i.e. the beginning is not with an isolated, historically first relation but a relation that presupposes the highest development. The question now is why Marx begins his analysis, especially in a context where he attempts an explicitly dialectical presentation, with an S.1 concept. Before dealing with this question we must examine the structure of this 'simple' form of value.

Marx expresses the simple form by the following equation

$$x \text{ commodity } A = y \text{ commodity } B;$$

and he adds, by way of explanation: x commodity A is worth y commodity B.

In the above expression the two commodities A and B play two different roles. A, whose value is being expressed is in 'the relative form' while B which expresses the value of A is in 'the equivalent form'. In this relation, A and B form polar opposites, i.e. neither of them could be in the relative and the equivalent form at the same time although they could change roles or places.

Marx proceeds to analyse both forms in detail. His analysis of the equivalent form is of particular interest to us here. This analysis shows that the equivalent form is already a prototype of the money form, which arises at the end of the development as the 'universal equivalent':

i) Unlike the commodity whose value is being expressed (A), which acquires a form (of value) separate from and independent of its physical form (i.e. in the shape of the commodity which expresses its value, namely the commodity in equivalent form, [B]), the latter commodity does not possess an independent value-form itself (C.I. p.147).

ii) 'The equivalent form of a commodity . . . is the form in which it is directly exchangeable with another commodity.'

Marx then identifies three peculiarities of the equivalent form:

1) 'use-value becomes the form of appearance of its opposite, value' (C.I. p.148). Thus in the simple value relation the *use-value* of B (the commodity in the equivalent form) measures the *value* of A (the commodity in the relative form).

2) 'concrete labour becomes the form of manifestation of its opposite, abstract human labour'. (C.I. p.150)

3) 'private labour takes the form of its opposite, namely labour in its directly social form'. (C.I. p.150)

As we have mentioned above, the equivalent form, in a number of important ways, anticipates the qualities of the money-form, which is the perfected form of the equivalent. For example money, like the equivalent form of the simple value-relation, is 'directly exchangeable with other commodities', it does not possess an independent value-form, because *use-value* (e.g. gold) 'becomes the form of appearance of its opposite, value'. Furthermore it is only in the case of money that we can see in clear outline the manifestation of concrete-private labour as its opposite abstract — social labour. It is precisely these similarities that prompt Marx to say that 'the whole mystery of the money form of value lies hidden in this simple form'. This is not surprising in view of the fact that Marx structures the simple relation in such a way that it contains the money form, although in a 'hidden' way. In other words, Marx's simple relation presupposes a more advanced development. It is based on the end-product of the development of the commodity form, namely the money form. To go back to the question raised above, I would

230

conclude that although Marx calls his beginning simple, isolated, accidental (and thus an S.1 concept), his actual beginning is constructed on the basis of the most developed form of value, i.e. the money form (and this is an S.3 type concept).

Note that the expressions Marx uses to describe the simple form, i.e. isolated and accidental, bring to mind Marx's exposition of the beginnings of the exchange of products in human history. Exchange begins when different communities, isolated from one another, come into contact by chance. The exchange of products is at first accidental and sporadic (C.I. p.182). At first products are exchanged directly with each other without a medium of exchange. Can we claim that in this direct exchange of products, especially when these acts of barter are isolated and accidental, the simple value-relation materializes? Not so, according to Marx:

> The direct exchange of products has the form of the simple expression in one respect, but not as yet in another. That form was x commodity A = y commodity B. The articles A and B in this case are not as yet commodities, but become so only through the act of exchange. (C.I. p.181)

Marx's words above clearly imply that in the simple expression of value the existence of regular exchange and value relations, including the money form, is presupposed. Marx is saying that the direct barter of products possesses the simple form of value only partially, since these products are not yet *commodities* and 'become so only through the act of exchange'. Marx makes the same point in the *Critique*:

> Direct barter, the spontaneous form of exchange, signifies the beginning of the transformation of use-values into commodities rather than the transformation of commodities into money. Exchange-value does not acquire an independent form, but is still directly tied to use-value. (CR. p.50)

Thus the direct exchange of use-values does not fully possess the simple form of value. The point, however, is that it is these kinds of exchanges that would qualify as isolated and accidental.

The problem can be approached from yet another angle. If the exchange relation is restricted to two use-values only in a single act of exchange, the need for an objective, social value expression does not arise at all. The relation between two goods in exchange under such conditions need not go beyond the utilities of these goods for the respective partners to the exchange. Here, only an agreement based on subjective evaluation is required for exchange to take place (this is indeed how the subjectivist approach to economics has interpreted the exchange relation). No independent, objective value relation needs to arise here.

It is only when exchanges become regular and extend beyond the narrow horizon of sporadic, isolated one-to-one acts of barter that the need for an objective value relation arises. For any two goods to be in an objective value relationship, either at least one other independent, competitive supplier of one or the other good must emerge or there should exist a third good in exchange supplied by a third independent supplier. With the existence of a choice of partners or choice of goods for any holder of use-values, an objective basis for evaluation arises: the use-values can acquire a value expression in terms of other use-values that are independent of subjective evaluations. There is then no way in which a value-form, simple or not, can be derived solely on the basis of the relation between two use-values alone in a single act of exchange.

If my claim, i.e. that Marx's simple value relation is structured on the basis of the perfected value-form, i.e. the money form, and that it is not an S.1 but an S.3 concept, is assumed to be true, the rest of the development from this form to the money form is straightforward. Let us now look at this process.

> We perceive straight away the insufficiency of the simple form of value: it is an embryonic form which must go through a series of metamorphoses before it can ripen into the price-form. (C.I. p.154)

If my interpretation of the simple expression or form of value is correct, the process of the 'ripening' into the money form involves a progressive revelation of aspects or sides of the value-form that are already presumed in the simple form. This process indeed involves progressive concretization of the original simple form but not in the empiricist sense of 'external addition' or 'successive approximation'. It is a purely internal development.

The transition from the simple form to the money form is made through 'the total or expanded form' (b) and 'the general form' (c). These are intermediate stages in which the one-sidedness of the simple form, if taken as an isolated form, is revealed. This involves contradictions which are inherent in the simple form itself.

The total form is obtained when other commodities besides the two considered in the simple form are brought into a value relation with one another. But this form proves to be inadequate because it represents a chaotic and endless series of value expressions that lack coherence and

232

unity. For example in this expanded form there are many commodities which are in the 'equivalent form', but this circumstance contradicts the nature of the equivalent form (e.g. being directly exchangeable with all other commodities):

> Since the natural form of each particular kind of commodity is one particular equivalent form amongst innumerable other equivalent forms, the only equivalent forms which exist are limited ones, and each of them excludes all the others. Similarly the specific, concrete, useful kind of labour contained in each particular commodity equivalent is only a particular kind of labour and therefore not an exhaustive form of appearance of human labour in general. It is true that the completed or total form of appearance of human labour is constituted by the totality of its particular forms of appearance. But in that case it has no single, unified form of appearance. (C.I. pp.156-7)

Let us recall that one of the peculiarities of the equivalent form in the simple expression was that private labour took the form of its opposite, social labour. Now in the total or expanded form we are faced with many commodities which are in the equivalent form and therefore each one represents social labour in its own way. But social labour by its nature cannot admit of more than one representation. Thus it is the nature of the equivalent form that comes into conflict with the total or expanded form. These contradictions lead Marx to the 'general form' of value, in which all commodities have a single, common commodity to express their values (a single, common equivalent form):

> The commodities now present their values to us, (1) in a single form, because in a single commodity; (2) in a unified form, because in the same commodity each time. Their form of value is simple and common to them all, hence general. (C.I. p.157)

Now the transition from this form to the money form is simply a matter of fixing a single, common equivalent form in one particular commodity sanctioned by law or custom.

Thus what we arrive at, at the end of the development of the simple form of value, is an equivalent form which is '*simple* and common to all, hence *general*', fixed by convention or law. The nature of the equivalent form remained unchanged throughout the whole process, in all the intermediary stages or 'metamorphoses'.

I believe that Marx's procedure itself provides the best confirmation of my interpretation of his simple beginning. Although, superficially, each form, each stage in the development of the money form can be assimilated to some historical stage in the development of exchange and money (e.g. the assimilation of the simple form to the beginnings of external exchange in the form of barter, or the resemblance of periods in history in which more than one form of commodity money circulated side by side to the total-expanded form, etc.), it is clear that Marx's analysis is purely logical. His procedure starts with a highly abstract value-relation involving only two commodities. As I have demonstrated above, this relation cannot be identified with an elemental exchange relation, be it the *isolated* historic beginnings of exchange or the *accidental* exchanges taking place even under capitalism. The simple form of value presupposes the entire richness of development of the value-form as it occurs in the most developed commodity economy, i.e. the capitalist system. Therefore Marx begins with an S.3 type concept of the value-form. In this form the end-result is reflected like the world in a drop of water. Further development is a purely logical progression, in which different aspects of the value-form that are implicit and 'hidden' are made more explicit by progressive negation of the simple form as such, i.e. as simple and immediate. At the end of the process we arrive at the concrete Notion, i.e. the money form.

The difference between the concrete Notion and the simple beginning consists in that the beginning is only *potentially* the end result. It is the simple summary, *précis* or synopsis of the entire development, while the concrete Notion embraces the totality of the development, i.e. it is the process and not simply the result. In case the above description may sound too 'abstract' or even 'mystified', I will attempt to look at the problem from a different angle. It is clear that in a commodity economy there are numerous acts of exchange that take place on a regular basis. Each individual act of exchange may seem like a self-contained whole from the point of view of the participants in such an act, but in fact it is intertwined with many other acts of exchange. Each act of exchange, being a link in a totality comprising numerous exchange relations, has reference to a whole. But the fact remains that in spite of this social nature of exchange, exchange always involves two 'parties' or 'persons' and *two* use-values. Thus we are faced with a social reality that involves numerous persons and use-values but whose actual medium of materialization is a two-person, two-good relationship. *This is the essence of the simple form of value. This is why Marx begins with such a relationship, not as an isolated, accidental relation but as a necessary one.*

I will conclude this discussion by referring to Marx's analysis of the simple form of value in the first German edition of *Capital I*, in which Marx's treatment lends additional support to my interpretation above.

In this earlier version, Marx uses the words 'first' and 'simple' to describe the form; he calls it the 'first or simple form of relative value'. The words 'accidental' and 'isolated', which were later (in the second German edition) used to characterize this form further, do not appear in this first version. Furthermore, Marx right from the beginning intimates the 'complexity' of this simple form, i.e. that it contains different aspects albeit in a 'veiled' fashion and that these various facets exist in an underdeveloped form and thus are in need of further development.

> This form is rather difficult to analyse, because it is *simple*, the different specifications which are contained in it are veiled, undeveloped, abstract and consequently only able to be distinguished and focused upon through the rather intense application of our power of abstraction. (Marx 1976[b], p.18)
> . . . if one considers the value relation of both commodities in their qualitative aspect, then one discovers in that simple expression of value the mystery of value form, and hence, *in nuce* of money. (Marx 1976[b], p.22)

A 'simple' that is difficult to analyse and one which is in need of an 'intense application' of the power of abstraction to be fully developed can in no way be mistaken for an S.1 concept, a concept of an accidental, isolated and/or primordial relation. I have intentionally concentrated upon Marx's value-form analysis since, apart from its explicitly dialectical form of presentation, I believe it holds the key to understanding the dialectical nature of Marx's analysis of value and more specifically to an appreciation of its profound originality compared with the analysis of classical political economy.

Unfortunately, the presentation of the value analysis in the final version of Marx's chapter on commodities in *Capital I* (second German edition onwards) is marred by serious conceptual difficulties which prevent the dialectical structure of his theory from shining through in clear outline. Due to these difficulties I will refer mostly to the first version (the first German edition) of Marx's chapter in the following discussion.

Marx concludes his first chapter with the following words, which provide us with a clear summary of his analysis of the commodity and his differences with the classical economists.

> The commodity is *immediate unity of use-value and exchange-value*, thus of two opposed entities. Thus it is an immediate *contradiction*. This contradiction must enter upon a development just as soon as it is no longer considered as hitherto in an analytic manner (at one time from the viewpoint of use-value and at another from the viewpoint of exchange-value) but is really related to other commodities as a totality. The *real* relating of commodities to one another, however, is their *process of exchange*. (Marx 1976[b], p.40)

In referring to the 'analytic manner' Marx clearly has the method of classical political economy in mind. In this method the commodity is simply 'analysed' into a 'use-value' and an 'exchange-value'. The classical analysis, in absence of further development, establishes the commodity as an immediate, contradictory unity of these two aspects. Marx's dialectical break with the analytical approach occurs precisely when the commodity 'is really related to other commodities as a totality'. This theoretical act of relating the commodity to other commodities is indeed what Marx has accomplished in his value-form analysis — an analysis which is missing in the discourse of political economy.

Classical economy, indeed, conceived the commodity as the unity of use-value and exchange-value. But these two aspects of the commodity remain isolated and separated from each other. This separation is manifested in the most striking manner when classical economists relate one commodity to another. In their mode of relating, one of the two aspects of the commodity, namely, its use-value, falls by the wayside and vanishes without leaving the slightest trace. The relation between commodities is conceived merely in terms of their relative exchange values, i.e. quantitatively. The novelty of Marx's approach consists in the fact that in developing the contradiction between the two aspects of the commodity in the process of relating commodities to each other, both aspects are reproduced. Thus the commodity as an immediate contradictory unity of use-value and exchange-value, in which the relation between the two aspects is merely contingent and abstract, is transformed in the totality of the exchange process into the necessary and concrete division of the world of commodities between a particular commodity singled out as money and all other commodities. Money, as the universal equivalent represents an inseparable relation between use-value and exchange-value. Money is a use-value that functions as pure exchange-value: it is a commodity whose use-form or natural shape is the very embodiment of the value of other commodities.

This suspension, sublation or conservation-transformation of use-value which is at the heart of Marx's dialectical method is put in the most elegant fashion in the following passage from the first version of the chapter on commodities:

> We stand here at the jumping-off point of all difficulties which hinder the understanding of *value-form*. It is relatively easy to distinguish the value of the commodity from its use-value, or the labour which forms the use-value from the same labour in so far as it is merely reckoned as the expenditure of human

236

labour power in the commodity-value. If one considers commodity or labour in the one form, then one fails to consider it in the other, and vice versa. These abstract opposites fall apart on their own, and hence are easy to keep separate. It is different with the *value-form* which exists only in the relationship of commodity to commodity. The use-value or commodity-body is here playing a new role. It is turning into the form of appearance of the commodity-*value*, thus of its own opposite. Similarly, the *concrete*, useful labour contained in the use-value turns into its own opposite, to the mere form of realization of *abstract* human labour. Instead of falling apart, the opposing determinations of the commodity are reflected against one another. However incomprehensible this seems at first sight, it reveals itself upon further consideration to be necessary. The commodity is right from the start a *dual* thing, use-value *and* value, product of useful labour *and* abstract coagulate of labour. In order to manifest itself as what it is, it must therefore *double* its form. It possesses right from nature the form of a use-value. That is its natural form. It only earns a value form for itself for the first time in circulation with other commodities. But its value-form has then to be itself an objective form. The only *objective* forms of commodities are their use forms, their natural forms.

Now since the natural form of a commodity (e.g., linen) is the exact opposite of its value-form, it has to turn *another* natural form — *the natural form of another commodity* — into its commodity form. A thing that it cannot do immediately for itself it can do immediately for another commodity, and therefore by a detour for itself. It cannot express its value in its own body or in its own use-value, but it can relate itself to another use-value or commodity-body as an immediately existent value. It can relate itself not to the concrete labour contained in itself, but doubtless to that contained in another species of commodity as a mere form of realization of abstract human labour. For that, it only needs to equate the other commodity to itself as an *Equivalent*. The use-value of a commodity only exists at all for another commodity in so far as it serves in this fashion for the form of appearance of its value. If one considers only the *quantitative* relationship in the simple, relative value-expression: x commodity A = y commodity B, then one finds also only the laws developed above concerning the motion of relative value, which all rest upon the fact that the amount of value of commodities is determined by the labour-time required for their production. But if one considers the value relation of both commodities in their *qualitative* aspect, then one discovers in that simple expression of value the mystery of value form, and hence, *in nuce* of money. (Marx 1976[b], pp.21-2)

Marx is clearly stating that the *analysis* of the commodity into its two aspects of use-value and exchange-value is easily *understood*. Nor does the distinction between the labour which forms the commodity's use-value from the labour that constitutes its exchange value present unsurmountable difficulties. In both distinctions the opposites, i.e. the two aspects of one commodity, stand in 'abstract opposition'. These opposites 'fall apart on their own, hence are easy to keep separate'. It is only when one considers the value-form that the difficulties of *understanding*[3] crop up. The difference lies in the fact that value-form exists only in

237

relationships between commodities. In these relations the abstract opposition between use-value and exchange-value is transformed into the concrete division of the world of commodities into commodities on the one hand and money on the other. Thus, 'instead of falling apart', the opposing determinations of the commodity now are no longer in a contingent relationship to each other: they are in a necessary relationship. Their separation has been overcome. The use-value does not disappear when we come to exchange-value but plays 'a new role': it turns into the 'form of appearance of the commodity-value, thus of its opposite'. This analysis represents the essence of Marx's dialectical method.

The Significance of Marx's Analysis of the Value-Form

We have so far highlighted the dialectical nature of Marx's analysis of the value-form. This exercise would have been purely formalistic if it were not for the fact that Marx considered the analysis of the form of value as one of the crucial advances he had made over classical political economy. As we saw in Chapter Three, Marx criticized the classical economists for their neglect of the value-form. In order to demonstrate the tremendous advance made by Marx over the analysis of value by classical political economy I will now turn to an examination of the significance of Marx's value-form analysis for his critique of political economy. In what follows I will first trace Marx's value-form analysis to its origins in his criticisms of the notion of 'labour money' and his critique of Ricardo's view of money. I will then show that Marx's preoccupation with value-form is the pivot around which his various criticisms of the classical school and especially of Ricardo turn.

In both the *Grundrisse* and the *Critique* Marx criticizes the notion of 'labour money', an idea popular among 'Ricardian socialists' such as Gray. For these socialists the notion was a natural conclusion from Ricardo's theory of value. If labour is the source and cause of exchange-value and the quantity of labour expanded its measure, then there is no need for a special commodity to be used as a medium of exchange: the quantity of labour can be used as a measure of value, a function that is performed by money under capitalist conditions, and a 'time-chit' bank can issue tokens to each labourer equivalent in value to the labour spent on his commodity. The worker then can purchase the commodities he needs by using these tokens or labour money. Perhaps it was this 'ingenious' idea that made Marx aware of the difficulties of Ricardo's formulation of the labour theory of value. As we will see later, his critique

238

of the notion of labour money is closely related to his critique of Ricardo's conception of money in particular and his theory of value in general.

Marx's main point in his critique of labour money is the necessity for the functioning of a money object that is separate and distinct from labour time under conditions of capitalist commodity production. The premise underlying the labour money scheme is the identity of the private labour of commodity producers and of social labour. However, it is precisely the contradiction between the two, inherent in commodity production, that necessitates the transformation of the result of private labour into a money object that represents the crystallization of social labour:

> The very necessity of first transforming individual products or activities into exchange-value, into money, so that they obtain and demonstrate their social power in this objective form, proves two things: (1) that individuals now produce only for society and in society; (2) that production is not directly social, is not 'offspring of association', which distributes labour *internally* .... There can be therefore nothing more erroneous and absurd than to postulate the control by associated individuals of their total production on the basis of exchange-value, of money, as was done above in the case of the time-chit bank. (G. pp.158-9, emphasis added)

Thus the demand for labour money presupposes that labour 'is directly social' — a requirement which is obviously not met by commodity production. Under commodity production, labour is not distributed 'internally', the activities of individual workers are not co-ordinated and evaluated according to a 'plan' resulting in their functioning as social labour from the outset. On the contrary it is only through the process of exchanging commodities that individual-private labour acquires a social form. This social form must have the same objective qualities as the commodities themselves. Since not activities but products are exchanged, and activity has all but disappeared into the product, the social form of that activity cannot but be a product itself. This product is money.

> Money is the physical medium into which exchange values are dipped, and in which they obtain the form corresponding to their general character .... The necessity of a money other than labour time arises precisely because the quantity of labour time *must not* be expressed in its immediate, particular product, but in a mediated, general product; in its particular product, as a product equal to and convertible into all other products of an equal labour time; of the labour time not in a particular commodity but in all commodities at once, and hence in a particular commodity which represents all the others. *Labour*

239

time cannot directly be money (a demand which is the same, in other words, as demanding that every commodity should simply be its own money), precisely because in fact labour time always exists only in the form of particular commodities (as an object): being a general object, it can exist only symbolically and hence only as a particular commodity that plays the role of money. Labour time does not exist in the form of a general object of exchange which is independent of and separate (in isolation) from the particular natural characteristics of commodities. *But it would have to exist in that form if it were directly to fulfil the demands placed on money.* (G. pp.167-8, emphasis added)

The notion of labour money, as I have pointed out earlier, is a natural deduction from the formulation of the law of value by Smith and Ricardo. Marx, while implying such a connection goes on to criticize the idea in the following way:

Money is labour time in the form of a general object, or the objectification of general labour time, labour time as a *general commodity*. Thus it may seem a very simple matter that labour time should be able to serve directly as money . . . because it regulates exchange values and indeed is not only the inherent measure of exchange values but their substance as well . . . . However, this appearance of simplicity is deceptive. The truth is that the exchange-value relation — of commodities as naturally equal and equivalent objectifications of labour time — comprises contradictions which find their objective expression in a *money which is distinct from* labour time. (G. pp.168-9)

A. Smith's thesis, that the worker has to produce a 'general commodity' alongside his particular commodity [meaning he must produce social use-values, i.e. exchange-values] . . . — This statement means . . . nothing more than that *the worker's particular labour time cannot be directly exchanged for every other particular labour time*, but rather that this, its general exchangeability, has first to be mediated, that it has first to take on an objective form, a form different from itself, in order to attain this general exchangeability. (G. p.171, emphasis added)

The basic elements of Marx's critique are:

1) The inherently private nature of commodity production and the necessity of the social relation also inherent in this form of production lead to contradictions which find their objective expression in money.
2) Under commodity production the social form of labour results from the exchangeability of the product of private labour with money. It is only through the process of the social exchange of products that commodities obtain their social form.

This latter point is most explicitly stated by Marx in the *Critique*:

240

> Commodities are the direct products of isolated independent individual kinds of labour, and through their alienation in the course of individual exchange they must prove that they are general social labour, in other words, on the basis of commodity production labour becomes social labour as a result of the universal alienation of individual kinds of labour. (CR. pp.84-5)

The absolute exchangeability of commodities with money, the necessity of the representation of the individual labour contained in commodities in the form of money is the essential ingredient of Marx's conception of social labour under commodity production.

The points raised by Marx in his critique of the notion of labour money closely parallel his critique of Ricardo's theory of money. Ricardo, in harmony with the whole classical school, regarded money as a mere contrivance, a convenience without which the process of exchange of commodities would be laborious, lengthy and cumbersome. One of Marx's most original contributions to the theory of value is his brilliant refutation of this view. For Marx the necessity of money both as a measure of value and as a means of exchange arises from contradictions inherent in commodity exchange.

Let us now see why Marx believes that Ricardo 'does not understand money'.

> All commodities can be reduced to labour as their common element. What Ricardo does not investigate is the *specific* form in which labour manifests itself as the common element of commodities. That is why he does not understand money. That is why in his work the transformation of commodities into money appears as something merely formal, which does not penetrate deeply into the very essence of capitalist production. (TSV.III, p.138)

Ricardo identifies the concrete labour of the commodity producer as the cause of value. The representation of this labour in the form of money is thus merely formal, i.e. in this representation and in fact in the actual transformation of commodities into money nothing happens to the qualitative and quantitative determination of the labour contained in commodities. For Ricardo, like Gray, value is identical with the labour expended and thus its representation in money is formal (Ricardo) or unnecessary (Gray).

Marx relates Ricardo's lack of understanding of money to the absence of an analysis of the 'specific form' in which labour functions as the common essence of value. Let us see what Marx means by this specific form and why he thinks Ricardo disregarded it.

The representation of the commodity as money implies not only that the different magnitudes of commodity values are measured by expressing the values in the use-value of one exclusive commodity, but at the same time that they are all expressed in a form in which they exist as embodiment of *social labour* and are therefore exchangeable for every other commodity, that they are translatable at will into any use-value desired. Their representation as money — in price — therefore appears first only as something nominal, a representation which is realized only through actual sale. *Ricardo's* mistake is that he is concerned only with the *magnitude of value*. Consequently his attention is concentrated on the *relative quantities of labour* which the different commodities represent, or which the commodities embody. But the labour embodied in them must be represented as *social* labour, as alienated individual labour. In the price this representation is nominal; it becomes reality only in the sale. This transformation of the labour of private individuals contained in the commodities into *uniform social labour*, consequently into labour which can be expressed in all use-values and can be exchanged for them, this *qualitative* aspect of the matter which is contained in the representation of exchange-value as money, is not elaborated by Ricardo. This circumstance — the necessity of *presenting* the labour contained in commodities as *uniform social labour*, i.e. as money — is overlooked by Ricardo. (TSV.III. p.130-1)

In the above passage Marx makes an important distinction between the quantitative and the qualitative aspects of value. The quantitative aspect relates to the relative proportions in which commodities are exchanged for each other. Ricardo's false view of money and, ultimately, of the value relation is traced to his preoccupation with the quantitative aspects of value. Value as a quantity, i.e. viewed quantitatively, may be measured by any commodity, by money, or indeed directly by labour time itself. Thus the representation of the value of commodities in money is purely *contingent* and *formal*. There is nothing *necessary* or *essential* about this representation.

The qualitative side, on the other hand, involves the *necessity* of the representation of the labour contained in commodities as money (their prices) and their transformation into money in the exchange process.

Marx makes the same point over and over again on numerous occasions in the *Grundrisse*, *Theories of Surplus Value* and the *Critique*. Here are some more examples:

But whenever a commodity is sold, transformed into money, its exchange-value acquires an independent existence, separate from its use-value. The commodity now exists only as a certain quantity of social labour-time, and it proves that it is such by being *directly* exchangeable for any other commodity whatsoever and convertible (in proportion to its magnitude) into any use-value whatsoever. This point must not be overlooked in relation to money any more than the formal transformation undergone by the labour a commodity contains

242

as an element of value. But the examination of money — of that absolute exchangeability which a commodity possesses as money, of its absolute effectiveness as *exchange-value* which has nothing to do with the magnitude of value — shows that it is not *quantitatively but qualitatively determined* and that as a result of the process through which the commodity itself passes, its *exchange-value* becomes independent, and is really represented as a separate aspect alongside its use-value as it is already nominally in its price. (TSV.III. pp.136-7)

As a commodity, a commodity can only express its value in other commodities, since general labour-time does not exist for it as a commodity. (TSV.III. p.142)

We see how Marx's criticism of Ricardo's view of money and value closely approximates his critique of the notion of labour-money. These two views, criticized by Marx, share a common problematic, which consists in regarding labour expended on the production of commodities as an invariant 'essence' — an essence that does not admit of any form-determination. The form thus appears as purely contingent and formal, as something merely *external* to the essence. Marx's objection to this viewpoint is that the essence cannot remain indifferent to form but has to be sublated and appear as a moment of a higher unity of form and essence.

The consequence of Marx's argument is that in a system of commodity production the labour expended on producing commodities is not directly involved in the exchange process. The exchange of commodities is not an exchange of activities but of their results, in which these activities form a fleeting moment. 'As a commodity, a commodity can only express its value in other commodities'. The necessity of the expression of value in money arises precisely because a commodity cannot express its value in a non-commodity, e.g. labour, 'general labour-time does not exist as a commodity', 'labour-time cannot directly be money'. After a product has entered the process of exchange there is a parting of the ways between the quantity of labour expended on the product and the quantity of social labour, i.e. money, it can command. Thus the commodity must go it alone, must prove its social acceptability by conversion into money.

The above discussion of Marx's criticisms of the notion of labour money, Ricardo's theory of value and his view of money clearly show the considerations underlying Marx's value-form analysis in *Capital* and the reasons why he attached such an importance to this question.

Earlier in this chapter I have shown that Marx's dialectical method is most explicit in his analysis of the value-form. I will show now that this analysis is also the central aspect of Marx's critique of political economy and demonstrate the identity of Marx's critique with his dialectics.

243

Marx's criticism of the Ricardian system comprises many points, including Ricardo's absorption in the quantitative aspect of the value question, his view of money, his lack of understanding of absolute surplus-value, his search for an invariable standard of value, his formulation of the law of value in a manner that admits of exceptions to the general law, etc. I believe that all these criticisms have a common basis, i.e. all the deficiencies that Marx detects in the Ricardian system can be reduced to a common source, i.e. Ricardo's analytical method, as Marx claims on numerous occasions (see Chapter Three above). This method involves an isolation of certain elements from a presumed reality and the relating of these elements to one another in a way that maintains their separation and does not admit of the 'passing-over' of one element into another. As a result, these isolated and separated elements 'fall apart' rather than hang together.

As we have seen earlier in this chapter, according to Marx, the defects of the analytical approach to the value-relation are revealed in the most striking manner only when the value-form is considered. Here, the elements isolated by political economy, namely the use-value and the exchange-value of commodities, can no longer be maintained in their separation since the value-form involves the representation of exchange-value through a use-value.

This neglect of the value-form by the political economists, a consequence of their analytical method, explains most of the points of disagreement between Marx and the classical economists mentioned above:

1. The preoccupation of Ricardo with the quantitative aspect of the value relation is a consequence of his neglect of the qualitative value relation, i.e. the value-form. Quantitative analysis is based on abstraction from all quality, which in relation to value relates primarily to the use-value of commodities.
2. Ricardo's view of money is also a direct result of the neglect of the value-form, since money is the perfected form of value.
3. Ricardo's conception of surplus-value which leads to Marx's formulation of the relative form of surplus-value is based on the quantitative relation between wages and profits, assuming a fixed labour-day. Thus that form of surplus-value, i.e. absolute surplus-value, which holds the key to an understanding of the essence of surplus-value escapes Ricardo (See Chapter Six above). We may say that here it is the *surplus-value-form* which has been ignored.
4. As we saw in Chapter Three above one of Marx's critical comments

on Ricardo's treatment of value was that he first formulated the law of value in a general fashion but he later admitted exceptions to the law based on empirical phenomena directly contradicting the general law. Here again since value-form analysis is absent in Ricardo the forms of value must appear as exceptions to the law of value. These forms contradict Ricardo's quantitative conception of value and thus appear as exceptions to the law of value.

Notes to Chapter Eleven

1. Chapter 1 of *Capital I* was extensively revised by Marx in the second German edition (see Marx's Preface to this edition in C.I. p.94). Marx also revised certain passages concerned with value for the first French edition. Furthermore, Engels also inserted a passage or two in this chapter in the fourth edition (the third and fourth editions appeared after Marx's death) to clarify some difficult points. The final version of Chapter 1 referred to in the text is the one that appeared in the fourth German edition.

2. The English translation of this first version of Chapter 1 used here appears in Marx (1976 [b]).

3. Marx here is using the word 'understanding' in the same way that Hegel employs this concept (see Chapter Four).

CHAPTER TWELVE

THE DIALECTICS OF PRICE AND MONEY

As I have remarked at the beginning of Chapter Eleven, Marx's treatment of value in *Capital I*, while representing a significant achievement involves a number of difficulties which prevent his theory of value from achieving full dialectical maturity. I have already dealt with the positive aspect of his theoretical breakthrough (his analysis of the value-form). I will devote the present chapter to the problems and difficulties which mar Marx's elaboration of his value theory.

It is a well-known and well-documented fact that Marx had his greatest difficulties in preparing *Capital I* for print in his chapter on commodities and value.[1] Ricardo, too, is known to have experienced his greatest difficulties in preparing the *Principles* in his first chapter on value.[2] Perhaps this is not a coincidence. It may very well be that it was the nature of the object they were dealing with that plagued both of them. At this point, however, I am concerned not with the cause of these difficulties but rather with their nature.

The problems with Marx's presentation of value have been recognized in the literature and have, indeed, formed the basis for a number of debates among Marx's interpreters. Although I will not attempt a review of these debates, in the course of the following discussion some of the issues raised in the literature will naturally arise as points of reference.

The central problem with Marx's presentation of his theory of value in Chapter One of *Capital I*, as I see it, concerns the curious isolation of the value-form analysis both from the question of the essence and the measure of value (which precedes the analysis of value-form) and from the fetishism of commodities (which follows the section on value-form). In this chapter, I will deal first with the implications of value-form for the analysis of the essence and measure of value and then with the question of the fetishism of commodities.

The Essence and Measure of Value

Marx's value-form analysis is an important ingredient in his critique of the theory of value of the classical economists. As such it cannot remain separate from or indifferent to the essence of value as postulated by the classical economists. It is true that Marx makes an important conceptual

246

innovation in transforming this essence from concrete labour into abstract labour. Marx was very well aware of the significance of this transformation and in fact counted this as one of the two or three novel aspects of *Capital*.[3] However, this transformation remains, at least formally, separate and isolated from the value-form analysis in *Capital I*. This separation is reflected in the structure of the first chapter of the latter in that Marx's analysis of the essence and the measure of value precedes his analysis of the form of value. In the sections dealing with the essence and measure of value Marx declares that the essence of value is labour and its measure is labour-time. He then adds that what remains to be investigated is the form of value. He then moves on straight away to section 3 where he analyses the form of value.

Marx's formal procedure of first discussing the essence and the measure of value and then proceeding to the form of value raises a number of questions. Does Marx's procedure imply that these questions, i.e. essence, measure and form are independent of each other and thus can be dealt with in isolation from each other? Does not Marx's analysis of the form of value (which he considers lacking in the discourse of political economy) have profound implications for the analysis of the essence of value?

Let us look at one of the symptoms of this separation of the value-form from the essence of value. In developing the concept of abstract labour as the essence of value Marx uses a peculiar mode of reasoning which is completely at variance with his dialectical method — a mode independent of his value-form analysis.

This is how Marx deduces the concept of abstract labour in *Capital I*:

> If then we disregard the use-value of commodities, only one property remains, that of being products of labour. But even the product of labour has already been transformed in our hands. If we make abstraction from its use-value, we abstract also from the material constituents and forms which make it a use-value .... With the disappearance of the useful character of the products of labour, the useful character of the kinds of labour embodied in them also disappears; this in turn entails the disappearance of the different concrete forms of labour. They can no longer be distinguished, but are all together reduced to the same kind of labour, human labour in the abstract. (C.I. p.128)

This mode of reasoning by 'reduction' of a manifold into what is common to, what unites a variety of objects yields a 'rational abstraction' in Marx's own words but does not help to determine the specific mode of the expenditure of labour in different forms of production. In the language of Hegelian logic this procedure yields the lowest conception of Notion.

247

We have called these concepts 'generic' and have shown how they are either empty or else refer to a lower form of development. But besides this deficiency of logic inherent in the mode of reasoning used by Marx, there is another flaw in Marx's argument that is not admissible even if we accept his mode of reasoning, i.e. the fact that in the kind of abstraction Marx is performing it is not true that the only common element between commodities is that they are products of labour. Furthermore, Marx's argument is tautological since he has already defined the commodity as a product of labour; his further reasoning simply re-establishes what was presupposed from the beginning.

Given these difficulties it is not surprising that Marx ends up with a 'physiological' definition of his most important concept, i.e. abstract labour:

> If we leave aside the determinate quality of productive activity, and therefore the useful character of the labour, what remains is its quality of being an expenditure of human labour-power. Tailoring and weaving, although they are qualitatively different productive activities, are both a productive expenditure of human brains, muscles, nerves, hands, etc., and in this sense both human labour. They are merely two different forms of the expenditure of human labour-power. Of course human labour-power must itself have attained a certain level of development before it can be expended in this or that form. But the value of a commodity represents human labour pure and simple, the expenditure of human labour in general. (C.I. pp.134-5)

In spite of his reference to a certain stage of development where human labour can be expended in a variety of forms, it is clear that Marx is interpreting abstract labour in a narrow, physiological sense. This interpretation is also supported by Marx's famous letter to Kugelmann, in which he grounds his concept of abstract labour in the social distribution of labour indispensable in any form of social production, a distribution which only finds specific forms of manifestation in different modes of production.[4]

This tendency to find a common basis for value-determination (specific to commodity production, especially in its capitalist form) and the social organization of production in all modes of production in the distribution of human labour has been variously called by more recent interpreters of Marx: his 'classical residue', referring to the lingering influence of the classical labour theory of value, or Marx's 'naturalism' referring to Marx's tendency to ground the essence of value-determination in the distribution of labour among various branches of production, a distribution which is common to all modes of production.[5]

248

This tendency in Marx, however it is labelled, has profound roots in the intellectual climate of eighteenth and nineteenth century Europe under whose influence Marx's thoughts crystallized. The natural law philosophy of the eighteenth century as manifested in the works of the French *Philosophes* and the Physiocrats as well as British philosophers such as John Locke had profound influence on the classical economists. Marx could not easily have distanced himself from these influences. Furthermore, as I have argued elsewhere,[6] classical political economy set such high standards of rigour that, coupled with the British lead in industry, technology and sciences in the nineteenth century, it established an intellectual tradition which was hard to ignore for continental thinkers.

Whatever the causes for the contradictions in Marx's writings they have serious consequences for a coherent theory of value. I believe that what is missing in Marx's theory of value, in spite of his explicit intent at a dialectical presentation, is precisely the Hegelian leap from Essence to Notion. From this perspective Marx's abstract labour, far from being reduced to the common element of all forms of production should have advanced to become a moment of the Notion of value under the capitalist mode of production. To make this meaning clear — a meaning which is by no means at variance with Marx's explicit intentions as evidenced by his critical comments on the method of political economy — I will offer the following words of explanation.

What were Marx's main quarrels with the political economists on the question of value? We have already discussed one of these quarrels, namely the question of the value-form, without however reaching a conclusive result as to the difference between the essence in classical economy and the essence in Marx. Let us look at more specific issues in classical economy that Marx objected to:

1) Adam Smith, after formulating the law of the determination of value by labour, relegates this law to a prehistoric stage when land and 'stock' are not accumulated. Thus, for him, the labour law of value applies only to a society of hunters and fishermen. After the accumulation of stock the operation of the law of value entails the constitution theory of prices involving the addition of wages, profits and rent.
2) Ricardo, who formulated the labour theory of value more consistently than Smith, did not relegate its operation to a prehistoric stage. For Ricardo the labour law of value was the *main* determinant of value under capitalism. However, he admitted of exceptions to this law, e.g. when the ratio of fixed to circulating capital differs between different lines of

activity (an anticipation of Marx's transformation problem).

The problem in both cases above appears to be a fundamental dichotomy: the general law of value as formulated in both cases comes into contradiction with empirical facts (wage-labour in the case of Smith and the inequality of the ratio of fixed to circulating capital in different branches of production in the case of Ricardo). This contradiction can be resolved in two ways, in an empiricist fashion or theoretically (critically). The empiricist approach would either abandon the law completely and construct empirical models to suit 'facts' or transform the law into a model, side by side with auxiliary models. This seems to be Smith's solution. Ricardo, on the other hand, while in favour of a theoretical solution (for which Marx praises him) ends up by sticking to his labour theory of value and maintaining the dichotomy in the form of a co-existence between the rule (his law of labour-value) and exceptions to the rule (a procedure criticized by Marx).

Marx is in favour of a critical resolution of the theory-reality contradiction. Such a resolution, it appears to me, would involve an internalization of the conflict into the Notion of value in such a way that both essence (the theoretical) and the appearance ('reality') become moments of the Notion.

The question is whether Marx succeeds in producing such a Notion of value. There is no doubt that Marx's formulation of the value question in *Capital* and his critical comments on the procedure of political economy all point in this direction. However, I believe that Marx stops short of taking the final critical step towards a solution.

As I have shown above, although Marx's value-form analysis clearly points in the direction of a critical theory of value it does not advance far enough to transform the essence of value in classical theory. Marx's concept of abstract labour did not prove adequate in this respect, as it was grounded in a natural, physiological basis. On the other hand Marx's value-form analysis which, ideally, should have advanced to rid the concept of abstract labour of its 'natural residues', leads to Marx's theory of fetishism, which is again a return to the classical problematic of inter-subjective personal relations.

Some may argue that Marx in fact has resolved these dichotomies in *Capital III* by transforming values into prices of production. We shall attempt to show below that this is not the case.

The inadequacy of Marx's concept of abstract labour as the essence of value becomes particularly obvious when the transition is made from the labour-values of volume one of *Capital* to the production prices of volume three. In this latter volume Marx introduces two assumptions: 1) the necessity of a general rate of profit and 2) unequal organic composition of capital between different branches of social production. With these two assumptions exchange ratios cannot correspond to labour-values. Therefore Marx introduces his system of production prices which deviate systematically from labour-values.

The nature of Marx's procedure in transforming values into prices, i.e. his solution to the so-called 'transformation problem' has been a subject of many controversies for nearly a century now.[7] My concern here, however, is rather with Marx's logic in maintaining these two systems of value determination. In Chapter One above I outlined three basic approaches to Marx's method, namely the historicist, the structuralist and the rationalist positions. In all three schools Marx's scheme of labour-value-production price find convenient interpretations.

The historicist school relegates labour-values to the prehistory of capitalism and attributes production prices to mature capitalism.

The structuralist school would conceive of labour-values as a simple subordinate structure and production prices as relating to the complex reality of capitalism.

The rationalist school interprets labour-value as a simple 'model' which goes through a process of complication as more 'realistic' assumptions are introduced finally leading to the more complex model involving production prices.

I have criticized all these three schools in Chapter One in a general way and I have shown why none of these approaches capture the essence of Marx's method. The fact that Marx's double system of labour-values and production prices fits so 'neatly' into the methodological perspectives of these three approaches is an indirect witness to what I have indicated as a deficiency in Marx's theory of value. I attribute it to a failure by Marx to make the Hegelian leap from Essence to Notion.

The maintenance of the two separate systems of value which we witness in Marx is alien to Marx's critical and dialectical method. What is missing is a Notion of value which would absorb both systems and reduce them to interconnected moments of that Notion.

251

It may be argued that Marx in fact has produced the Notion of value by transforming labour-values into prices of production. The latter effectively replaces the former as the theory of value under mature capitalism. That this is not so is obvious from the very fact that Marx does not call production prices by the name *value*. In fact production prices are conceived of as being *derived from values*. They are *systematic deviations* from values which, for Marx, remain identified with (abstract) labour. Thus Marx in fact maintains his labour-value system side by side with his production-price scheme.

It may also be suggested that Marx's development of the production-price scheme was designed to 'correct' Ricardo's theory of value. Ricardo, we recall, had a 'strict' labour theory of value, but he admitted exceptions to the law of value based on differences between different industries regarding the ratio of fixed to circulating capital. Marx devised a different concept, the concept of the organic composition of capital, to explain Ricardo's exceptional cases. Marx criticized Ricardo for not formulating the law of value at such a general level so as to take care of these exceptions as forms of manifestation of the general law. Thus, the argument goes, Marx's scheme of production-prices derived from labour-values is devised to meet Marx's criticism of Ricardo. The problem with the above argument is that, in fact, Marx does not succeed in formulating the law of value at such a general level, one that would not admit of any exceptions and modifications and would incorporate such exceptions as forms of manifestation of the general law. In effect, the prices of production remain as modifications of the general law of value in Marx.

The Fetishism of Commodities

Marx's analysis of this question forms the final section of Chapter One. We see here that Marx, instead of extending his value-form analysis to formulate a general theory of value and money, merely regresses to an essentialism that is very much like the one we discussed above in relation to his analysis of the essence and measure of value.

Marx had already established (in the first two sections of Chapter One of *Capital* I) that the commodity is a social product and that its value is a social category having no relation whatsoever with the physical, natural form or the use-value of the product of labour. This fixed opposition between value and use-value, between the social form and the natural form of the products of labour is further developed in the section on fetishism.

Here Marx is trying to show that commodities have an enigmatic character in that they are use-values (natural objects) which are easily accessible to human senses, i.e. they are transparent, while at the same time they are also values which are not so accessible to human senses. Hence we have the fetishism of commodities, which arises from the specific social form of the product of labour in a system of production where products assume the form of commodities. The opacity of the commodity arises from the fact that the relationships between labour of commodity producers are expressed not directly as such but as relations between products and objects.

> The mystical character of the commodity does not therefore arise from its use-value. Just as little does it proceed from the nature of the determinants of value. For in the first place, however varied the useful kinds of labour, or productive activities, it is a physiological fact that they are functions of the human organism, and that each function, whatever may be its nature or its form, is essentially the expenditure of human brains, nerves, muscles and sense organs. Secondly, with regard to the foundation of the quantitative determination of value, namely the duration of that expenditure or the quantity of labour, this is quite palpably different from its quality. In all situations, the labour-time it costs to produce the means of subsistence must necessarily concern mankind, although not to the same degree at different stages of development. And finally, as soon as men start to work for each other in any way, their labour also assumes a social form.
>
> Whence, then, arises the enigmatic character of the product of labour, as soon as it assumes the form of a commodity? Clearly, it arises from this form itself. (C.I. p.164)

According to Marx it is the *indirect* way in which labour is allocated and the product of labour distributed that accounts for the fetishism of commodities. Under capitalism labour and the product of labour are social but not *directly social* as in all other forms of production preceding and succeeding capitalism. Now we know that the social form of the product of labour in the capitalist mode of production is the commodity form or the value form. The question is, however, what is the social form of the product of labour in non-capitalist economies? Marx never manages to produce a single social form of human products that would apply to a non-capitalist economy. In fact on numerous occasions he asserts that in such economies the social form of the product of labour is its *natural form*. Thus the social form under capitalism is *particularized to a point that it stands capitalism completely apart from non-capitalist economies as an exceptional mode of production*. Let us be more specific.

As we have argued in the Introduction in relation to Cohen's

253

interpretation of Marx's theory of history there are two kinds or levels of abstraction of the social form of an economy:

1. If we abstract from a specific social form, for instance, capitalism we still have the social form in general that applies to all forms of production. In other words abstraction from a social form of production does not yield natural relations of people with each other and with the physical environment.
2. On the other hand if we abstract from the social form altogether we end up with non-social relations.

To clarify this point I will use an example. Consider a specific variety of mammals, e.g. whales. We can abstract from the specific whale-form, which will give us the abstract mammal. But if we wish to abstract from all the characteristics specific to mammals we then end up with the abstract animal.

In Marx's analysis the opposition between value and use-value, social form and natural form is so rigidly maintained that it effectively implies that all non-capitalist economies are natural economies (as opposed to social economies) based on use-values. This obviously is in complete opposition to the general thrust of Marx's theory of history, which conceives of all modes of production as social forms. It also is in sharp contrast with Marx's value-form analysis, which involves a dialectical relationship between use-value and exchange-value. These misleading formulations by Marx have profoundly influenced many of his followers and interpreters, leading to reductionist views of capitalism and socialism.

As we have seen in Chapter Eleven, Marx on numerous occasions criticizes this dualism, this dichotomy between value and use-value and attempts to overcome it in his value-form analysis, which we have identified as the most original and most fruitful of his contributions. In the present chapter we have shown how this value-form analysis remains isolated in Chapter One of *Capital I* both in relation to the substance and measure of value and to the question of fetishism. Now one may speculate what direction Marx's theory of value would have taken if the value-form analysis had been extended to other aspects of value. We have already dealt with this question in a general way. As a conclusion to the present chapter, I will now focus on a specific point which may help to provide an answer to this question.

254

Conclusion

Throughout this chapter I focused on what has been known as the 'qualitative' aspect of Marx's theory of value. While in the qualitative aspect the concept of abstract labour is the primary theoretical construct, on the quantitative side the concept of 'socially necessary labour time' functions as the basic concept. This is how the concept is introduced by Marx in the first volume of *Capital*:

> It might seem that if the value of a commodity is determined by the quantity of labour expended to produce it, it would be the more valuable the more unskilful and lazy the worker who produced it, because he would need more time to complete the article. However, the labour that forms the substance of value is equal human labour, the expenditure of identical human labour-power. The total labour-power of society ... counts here as one homogeneous mass of human labour-power although composed of innumerable individual units of labour-power. Each of these units is the same as any other, to the extent that it has the character of a socially average unit of labour-power and acts as such, i.e. only needs, in order to produce a commodity, the labour time which is necessary on an average, or in other words is socially necessary. Socially necessary labour-time is the labour-time required to produce any use-value under the conditions of production normal for a given society and with the average degree of skill and intensity of labour prevalent in that society. (C.I. p.129)

This basically *technological* view of the *socially* necessary labour time is interpreted differently by Marx in the third volume. This is how socially necessary labour is defined in the latter volume:

> Even though the labour of the direct producers of foodstuffs, taken by itself, breaks down into necessary and surplus labour, in relation to society it thus represents the necessary labour required simply for the production of foodstuffs. The same thing is the case, incidentally, with any division of labour within society as a whole, as distinct from the division of labour within the individual workshop. It is the labour necessary for the production of particular articles — for the satisfaction of a particular social need for particular articles. If this division is in due proportion, products of various types will be sold at their values (at a further stage of development, at their prices of production), or at least at prices which are modifications of these values or production prices as determined by general laws. This is in fact the law of value as it makes itself felt, not in relation to the individual commodities or articles, but rather to the total products at a given time of particular spheres of social production, autonomized by the division of labour; so that not only is no more labour-time devoted to each individual commodity than necessary, but out of the total social labour-time only the proportionate quantity needed is devoted to the various types of commodity. Use-value still remains a condition. But if in the case of the

255

individual commodity this use-value depends on its satisfying in and of itself a social need, in the case of the mass of social product it depends on its adequacy to the quantitatively specific social need for each particular kind of product and therefore on the proportional division of the labour between these various spheres of production in accordance with these social needs, which are quantitatively circumscribed. (C.III. pp.773-4)

Here Marx is advancing a general concept of 'socially necessary labour-time'. Social necessity of labour time is no longer restricted to a given arbitrary sphere of social production but is grounded in the totality of all spheres in relation to each other. What is socially necessary labour-time from the viewpoint of an individual branch of production may not necessarily correspond to the socially necessary amount of labour in relation to the rest of the economy. Thus a modification may occur based on the necessity of the social equilibrium between all branches of production.

The significant aspect of Marx's generalization consists in the fact that Marx retains his earlier definition of socially necessary labour-time. His main point of reference is *use-value*. Under the first definition which relates to a given, individual branch of production producing a *homogeneous* use-value, the social necessity of labour is determined by the ability of that use-value in 'satisfying in and of itself a social need'. Thus each unit of a homogeneous mass of products has the same utility (use-value) as any other and, therefore, the labour time spent on each individual unit should count as *socially* equal no matter how different the amounts of labour expended *individually* (by each individual worker and/or by each enterprise comprising the given industry) may be.

When more than one branch of production is brought into the picture, it is no longer the ability of each branch to satisfy a social need which is the focus of attention. Social demand dictates a certain equilibrium between these different branches. Social use-value is no longer limited to one homogeneous mass of products but is based on a totality of heterogeneous masses of products. This use-value 'in the case of the mass of social product . . . depends on its adequacy to the quantitatively specific social need for each particular kind of product'.

Marx is clearly stretching the concept of use-value in order to generalize his concept of socially necessary labour-time from one which is adequate for one single industry to one appropriate for a multitude of interrelated branches of social production.

Marx's comments on the more general concept of socially necessary labour-time remains isolated in the third volume. However, the fact that

256

Marx makes these comments shows that he was clearly aware of the problems involved in the mode of presentation of value and its related concepts in the first volume. These problems and Marx's solution to them may be interpreted in an empiricist way. Thus it may be argued that Marx in the third volume is abandoning the 'one-departmental model' of the first volume in favour of a multi-departmental model. In this interpretation Marx's generalization of the concept of socially necessary labour-time simply parallels his move from labour-values to production prices.

I believe this analogy is false. Marx does not give us a more general concept of value, and therefore of abstract labour, in moving from labour-values to production prices. The latter are modifications of the former and thus do not represent 'genuine' values. And this is where the problem lies. The concept of value and abstract labour should have gone through a process of generalization similar to the generalization of the concept of socially necessary labour-time discussed above.

The above example shows that the concepts of use-value and exchange value as well as the associated concepts of abstract labour, socially necessary labour, etc. are not used in an analytical manner. They are not fixed concepts but concepts which are interdependent and which develop, in this interconnection, Marx's theory of value. Thus the questions as to what value is and how it is measured do not have fixed and ready made answers.

If Marx were capable of such degree of flexibility, then one can imagine that he could have stretched his own value-related concepts to a point where the Notion of value could have emerged. In order to develop value theory along Hegelian (and Marxian) lines one must overcome the fixed opposition between value and use-value. Why is this important? One can claim that all theories of value from the classical to Marxian to marginalist and neo-classical as well as neo-Ricardian (with the possible exception of Marx's value-form analysis and the Austrian approach) have all been based on this opposition. In all these approaches the spheres of production/consumption remain isolated from the sphere of circulation and the latter represents a passive moment that reflects labour costs (classical) or utilities (marginalist) or both (neo-classical). In none of these models is there an autonomous sphere of circulation where values are formed in such a way that they do not simply reflect production or utility functions but in effect influence the parameters as well as the functional forms of those functions.

In the classical theory, value reflects production. The sphere of production with its labour-quantity coefficients is assumed as given. The production data determine exchange ratios in the market. The question as to the possible role of markets in the determination of these production coefficients does not arise. Ricardo, for instance, in his early 'corn model' attempted to determine the 'social' rate of profit independently of the market valuation of the products.[9] He abandoned this model later. In his *Principles* he first tries to establish exchange ratios on the basis of the quantities of labour embodied in commodities. However, almost immediately after this determination, he assumes a certain distribution of income (a given rate of profit) and tries to show how this circumstance modifies exchange ratios according to the durability of the fixed capital, the time of circulation, etc.[10] Later in his life Ricardo was preoccupied with a search for an invariable standard of value, one which would not vary with changes in, for instance, income distribution.[11] This represented a path in exactly the opposite direction from his early 'corn model'. All of these examples demonstrate the problems involved in formulating a law of value when the spheres of production, consumption, circulation and distribution are conceived in abstract opposition to each other. Even when Ricardo attempts to show the influence of income distribution on exchange ratios, he is reluctant to abandon his pure labour theory of value. On the contrary he kept on insisting that in spite of all exceptions to this theory, the labour-embodied principle was the major determinant of values.

In marginalist economics values reflect utilities, i.e. the valuation in the market is a reflection of the sphere of consumption. Utility functions of individuals are based on individual preferences and depend solely on the consumption levels of given goods. Incomes, wealth or prices do not enter utility functions. In fact where such influences may be present they result in exceptions to the law of demand, e.g. certain luxury goods which may be desired due to their high prices (and thus their prestige value).

In neo-classical economics, consumption and production both influence market valuation. Income distribution is a passive result of this valuation. Here again there is no sphere of autonomous circulation and exchange. Rather the latter are passive reflections of the utility functions and production functions of the individuals and firms respectively.

To sum up: value theory has occupied the centre stage in the analyses of capitalism. In this sense the classical economists, Marx, the marginalists and neo-classical economists stand on common ground. This, of course, reflects the paramount importance of value relations under capitalism. To criticize value theory is not to downgrade the significance of the value concept, but to point out that in almost all approaches to value all the spheres of the economy except for circulation are assumed to be given. Value is taken from the sphere of circulation and then is related to factors outside that sphere: the very sphere in which values are formed, i.e. circulation, is ignored. This is accompanied by a systematic neglect of the causal role of money and finance. This is not surprising as money seems to be the only object which is not directly either a consumer good or a physical input in production. It thus has an autonomous existence only in the sphere of circulation. Since values are primarily circulation phenomena, their determination must be linked to the conditions (forces, means, relations, etc.) of the market; in contemporary 'analytical Marxism' many of these factors which would be central to such an analysis would be dismissed as 'superstructural'. And since money is a basic 'means' of circulation it should be at the centre rather than the periphery of value theory. Thus without a monetary theory a value theory is like a production theory without a theory of the means or the technology of production or a consumption theory without a concept of utility or use-value.

Notes to Chapter Twelve

1. See Note 1 to Chapter Eleven.
2. Ricardo's *Principles* went through three editions in his lifetime. The nature of the revisions he made in Chapter 1, *On Value*, in the second and the third editions have been subject of controversy. The extent of these revisions is evaluated by the editors of his Collected Works in the following terms: 'The alterations were certainly extensive; little more than half of the final version (edition 3) of the chapter *On Value* being found in the same form in edition 1' (Ricardo, 1951, p.xxxviii).
3. See, for instance, Marx's letter to Engels dated Aug. 24, 1867 (LC. p.111).
4. In a letter to Kugelmann, dated July 11, 1868, Marx states: 'Every child knows that any nation which stopped work — I will not say for one year — but just for a couple of weeks, would die. And every child knows that the volume of products corresponding to the various needs calls for various and quantitatively determined amounts of total social labour. It is self-evident that this *necessity* of the *division* of social labour in certain proportions is not at all negated by the *specific form* of social production, but can only alter its *mode of appearance* . . . the *form* in which this proportional division of labour assets itself in a social situation and in which the connection of social labour asserts itself as a *private exchange* of the individual products of labour, is precisely the exchange-value of those products'. (LC. p.148)
5. Itoh (1980), Chap. 2 uses the term 'classical residue' and Lippi (1979) speaks of Marx's 'naturalism'.
6. See Shamsavari (1986).
7. For an extensive and critical analysis of the transformation problem based on the perspectives developed in the present book see Shamsavari (1987).
8. For a detailed examination of these three positions and others see Shamsavari (1987).
9. Since in the simple 'corn model' of agricultural production inputs and outputs have the same physical form, Ricardo thought he could form the social rate of profit by simply dividing the

agricultural surplus over the expenditure. Of course this was also based on his belief that agricultural profit regulates the rate of profit in other branches of production. See the Introduction to (Ricardo 1951).

10. See Ricardo's Chapter 1 (Ricardo, 1951). See also Shamsavari (1987).

11. See the Introduction to (Ricardo, 1951). Marx criticized Ricardo's notion of an invariable standard of value: see for instance TSV.III. p.137.

CONCLUSION

The Japanese economy in the 1920s combined elements of both relatively advanced capitalism and feudal institutions (particularly in the agrarian sector) including the Emperor system. This circumstance led to debates among Japanese Marxists concerning the nature of Japanese capitalism. What these theorists were struggling with was the application of a model of a pure capitalist economy to an economy that had feudal 'remnants' or 'survivals'.[1] The pure model was presumably based on the theory of the capitalist mode of production to be found in Marx's *Capital*, which in turn seemed to emerge from the British experience of capitalist development.[2] This attempt was clearly rooted in a certain interpretation of Marx's concepts, an analytical approach which conceptualizes different modes of production in such a fixed opposition to each other that, for instance, the surviving feudal institutions under capitalism appear as anomalies or 'remnants'.

The problems faced by Japanese Marxists were not at all new. About half a century earlier the Narodniks in Russia were also debating the appropriateness of Marx's model to conditions in their country — a debate in which Marx himself eventually became involved.[3] At the time (1870s) Russia was one of the least industrialized countries in Europe and was certainly much less capitalistically developed than Japan was in the 1920s, it having a fair share of feudal survivals in spite of the abolition of serfdom in the 1860s. The debate continued in one form or another for a long time and was one of the factors generating the future conflicts within the Russian social democratic movement. Lenin's advocacy of a 'democratic stage' before the socialist revolution (in which proletariat and peasantry would have a key influence on state policy) as an alternative to 'normal' capitalist development was an attempt to create a pure capitalist mode of production — completely free of feudal survivals, such as undemocratic institutions and national conflicts. In such a state the contradiction between labour and capital would appear in its pure form free from other contradictions such as national antagonisms and would allow the opposition of labour to capital to develop under conditions most favourable for the cause of labour.[4] Thus for Lenin like many other Marxists, the pure capitalist model was taken very seriously. It was only on the eve of the October Revolution that Lenin abandoned his stage theory and successfully attempted to 'skip stages'. Four years later Lenin's stage theory resurfaced again in the form of his New Economic

261

Policy (NEP).[5]

What seemed to Japanese Marxists in the 1920s to be the 'exceptional' path of capitalist development in Japan was not exceptional at all; even the path of capitalist development in Britain, which is often upheld as a 'classic' case, has not been free of feudal survivals.[6]

In her research on the debates among Japanese Marxists concerning the nature of Japanese capitalism Germain Hoston makes the following comments which aim at generalizing the main thrust of these debates beyond the Japanese context:

> Yet in outlining the development of capitalism in Japan, participants in the debate were not merely engaged in a mechanistic application of Marxian categories of analysis to interpret Japan's past and present. The relationship between history and theory is intimate in Marxism; and in pursuing their concerns historically, Japanese Marxists also emerged as theorists of political and economic change. Over the last several decades, Western Marxists like Maurice Dobb and Paul Sweezy have been engaged in a controversy on the character of the development of capitalism in Western Europe. In confronting the issue of whether an external force, world trade (Sweezy), or some factor inherent in the feudal system (Dobb) was the principal factor that precipitated England's evolution of industrial capitalism, these have addressed important gaps remaining in Marx's original theory. The participants in the debates on Japanese capitalism undertook this endeavour twenty years before Western Marxists did, and in their study of a non-Western case, spoke to the question of *the relationship between the universal and the particular that is fundamental to any conception of political development, whether Marxist or non-Marxist.* (Hoston 1986, p.99; emphasis added)

The emphasized words above are a good way of describing the essence of the present work, especially if one were to change the words 'political development' to social development in general and if the relationship between the particular and the universal is extended to include other oppositions of analytical thought such as essence and appearance, content and form, etc. And the best way of expanding on this succinct formulation is to examine some of the controversies of recent times, of which the Dobb-Sweezy debate (mentioned by Hoston above) is an example. We will also examine the Dependency-Modes of Production debate, aspects of Third World development policies and the debate about the role of markets under socialism.

All these debates are closely connected with each other. We have already seen how Hoston emphasizes the similarities between the debate on the nature of Japanese capitalism and the Dobb-Sweezy debate. The latter in turn is closely associated with the controversy on the Dependency school of development as one of the major protagonists in the debate, Immanuel Wallerstein, has clearly pointed out:

> There is, after all, a substantive issue in this debate [Frank — Laclau]. It is in fact the same substantive issue that underlay the debate between Maurice Dobb and Paul Sweezy in the early 1950s about the 'transition from feudalism to capitalism' that occurred in the early modern Europe. (Wallerstein 1979, pp.8-9)

The 'substantive issue' referred to by Wallerstein will be revealed shortly below.

The Transition from Feudalism to Capitalism

The Dobb-Sweezy debate was sparked off by the publication in 1946 of Maurice Dobb's *Studies in the Development of Capitalism*.[7] In this work the author had challenged the traditionally accepted view of the decline of the European feudalism, i.e. that it was caused by the increase in external trade. On the contrary, Dobb argued, external trade often led to the intensification of the feudal mode of exploitation, e.g. in Eastern Europe, the so-called Second Serfdom. Dobb claimed that the decline of feudalism may be best explained by an analysis of the internal factors of the feudal mode of production. He argued that the internal dynamics of the class struggle in this mode, leading to a crisis of production through the exhaustion of the labour force eventually brought about the demise of the system.

In 1950 Paul Sweezy wrote a paper criticizing Dobb's theory, which led to further exchanges between the two adversaries as well as several contributions by others.[8] Sweezy argued that in fact what Dobb took as factors internal to the feudal mode of production such as the increased need for revenue on the part of feudal lords (leading to greater exploitation of the serfs) were due to the rise of external trade. Thus the increase in long-distance trade created conditions that in many ways exhibited the superiority (e.g. greater efficiency) of the exchange economy over the natural economy of feudal mode, a circumstance that eventually led to the decline of this system of production.

The arguments on both sides were detailed and complex. My purpose here is not to reopen the case and propose an alternative explanation for the decline of feudalism but to show the methodological underpinnings of these arguments in the light of the interpretation of Marx's method offered in this book.

The major methodological point in this debate is the fixed opposition between production and circulation (exchange, trade). But first, let us see how Sweezy attempts to identify a methodological basis for the debate:

> Historical factors which are external with respect to one set of social relations are internal with respect to a more comprehensive set of social relations. And so it was in the case of Western European feudalism. The expansion of trade, with the concomitant growth of towns and markets, was external to the feudal mode of production, but it was internal as far as the whole European-Mediterranean economy was concerned. (Hilton 1978, p.105)

Let us recall that Wallerstein, comparing Dobb-Sweezy debate with the Dependency/Modes of Production debate (e.g. Frank-Laclau), identified a common 'substantive issue'. It turns out that this common issue follows directly from Sweezy's point above:

> The substantive issue, in my view, concerns the appropriate unit of analysis for the purpose of comparison. (Wallerstein 1979, p.16)

Thus for both Sweezy and Wallerstein the methodological basis of the debate is the appropriate unit of analysis. In other words it is the differences in the scale of observation and analysis that leads to opposing conclusions on the causes of feudal decline. But as insightful and useful as this point is, it really does not go into the root of the problem, which is the fixed opposition between production and circulation, a qualitative point rather than a quantitative one of scale or unit of observation.

If one conceives of capitalism as a system which has circulation as the foundation, as an S.3 concept, as an active moment (which is the correct interpretation, as we have argued in this book) then the question of the origin or the impetus of change from feudalism to capitalism (whether internal or external to the feudal mode) is largely irrelevant. It is only when exchange is treated as an S.1 or S.2 concept, as a passive moment of production, that we may face the problem of the externality versus the internality of trade and exchange to a given mode of production.

Dobb's point was that capitalism had somehow to arise from the internal contradictions of the feudal mode of production, in which exchange was limited and played a subordinate role. Expanding the unit of analysis would not theoretically invalidate Dobb's point since his argument is about production and not trade. For him trade is an S.1/S.2 concept, a passive moment, under both feudalism *and* capitalism. On the other hand, in examining the Sweezy and Wallerstein approach the question may be asked as to how and why external trade developed in a particular point in time (the sixteenth century) and undermined only West European feudalism and not other pre-capitalist areas in the world, which were also participants in this external exchange. In addition it is not clear in Sweezy-Wallerstein approach whether this mode of transition from feudalism to capitalism is a universal one or is true only for the transition in Western Europe.

Sweezy and Wallerstein also operate with an S.1/S.2 concept of trade. If trade is treated as the active element of capitalist development, as an S.3 concept, as 'inside' as well as 'outside' of the capitalist mode of production, then the expansion of trade whether internally or externally motivated becomes an essential prerequisite.

In the transition from feudalism to capitalism, if we follow Dobb, there is a change in the social relations of production (from serfdom to free wage-labour) and if we believe Sweezy there is also a change from an economy based on use-value to one based on exchange-value. What both authors ignore is that in this transition there is a structural change in the economy in which the share of agricultural sector declines and that of traditional industry and modern manufacturing rises. The fact that industry produces largely traded (both internally and externally) goods implies that trade must play a predominant role in the capitalist system. This structural transformation changes the nature of production as well as the relationship between circulation and production. Once this point is grasped then the increased productivity of agriculture (a point emphasized by Dobb) and institutional factors such as property rights (emphasized by later writers)[9] are seen to be essential pre-conditions for the rise of capitalism. But these pre-conditions may also develop in response to an increase in internal trade based on increased industrial production and an increase in internal or external trade. A whole set of institutional changes may be required for the rise of capitalism, as the experience of less developed countries shows us today. These developments imply a process of internal change and evolution which may or may not lead to a crisis of production (Dobb's basic point) but will prepare a pre-capitalist formation for the development of capitalism. But one must not insist on the formation of all these pre-conditions before one can identify an economy as capitalist or as developed since many of these so-called pre-conditions may simply be the *results* of capitalist development.

The main reason for confusion in the transition debate is that most authors engaging in the debate use generic concepts of production, circulation, labour, use-value, exchange-value, etc. These concepts are so general that they are either useless or, at best, they define only a particular form and not a truly universal one. As a result of their analytical approach, the concepts that they use are in fixed opposition to each other. Furthermore, cause and effect, premises and results are assumed to follow each other chronologically in a linear fashion. Again it is the search for a pure model of capitalism that is at the root of confusion — one that becomes even deeper as we examine debates on economic development.

From Dependency to the Modes of Production Debate

The so-called modes of production approach began with Ernesto Laclau's critique of the dependency school of development.[10] The latter had emerged as a reaction to the sociology and economics of development in the late 1940s and 1950s, which was represented by the modernization and stage theories.[11] These theories tended to dismiss the problem of backwardness in these countries as a special case. They conceived of underdevelopment as a pre-modern stage of historical development and argued that given certain conditions the higher stage of a developed economy will emerge. The dependency school changed this comfortable view of development by claiming that the underdevelopment of certain areas in the world is the mirror image of the development in other areas. Thus development and underdevelopment, far from being apparently unrelated phenomena dislocated in time and space, are both part of a world-wide unitary process going back to the sixteenth century.

The original works of the dependency school dealt a sharp blow to the basically analytical approach of the modernization and stage theories. They introduced an historical and international dimension to the problem. Thus as opposed to the analytical method of their opponents the works of dependency theorists had a dialectical flavour. However the dependency school, particularly in the works of A. G. Frank, gets involved in logical contradictions. For instance, Frank takes the incorporation of Latin America since the sixteenth century into trade relations with emerging Western capitalist nations as evidence that Latin America is not pre-capitalist but part of capitalist system. At the same time he denies that countries in this region are capitalist (developed) in the proper sense of the term because they are dependent on Western capitalism. Thus we have either a minimal generic definition of capitalism that would make every economy engaged in trade with major capitalist economies capitalist, or else two definitions: a pure type of capitalism that has all the prerequisites such as wage-labour, accumulation of capital, etc. and an impure one in which capitalist forms exist but are encumbered by feudal survivals.

We are not here concerned with the details of various dependency approaches to development but rather with the essence of the modes-of-production response to the dependency paradigm. As mentioned above, one of the early critics of dependency was Laclau, who argued that capitalism is a mode of production based on free wage-labour and cannot be defined as one based on trade for profit, which is what the 'capitalist' relations in Latin America amounted to: in particular these relations were based not on free forms of labour but on unfree forms such as slavery and serfdom.

We have already criticized in detail the notion that free wage-labour (and even more, a freely mobile labour force) is an absolute pre-condition of capitalist development, especially in early stages of development.[12] On the contrary, it is a *result* rather than a pre-condition of capitalist development. If by free wage-labour we mean primarily a labour force that has essentially been separated from its means of *reproduction* (and not just means of production, which is a weaker requirement) then it is the breakdown of the subsistence economy of agricultural workers that yields such a labour force. This breakdown is often the result of either the capitalist organization of agriculture (which took place in Britain in the seventeenth century: the enclosures) or the monetization of the economy (due, for instance, to some degree of state-led industrialization in urban areas or an expansion of foreign trade) which brings both the landlord and the worker into the orbit of capitalist relations. Free wage-labour defined not only as a labour force which is cut off from its means of reproduction but is also freely mobile between different sectors of the economy is only tangentially present in the advanced forms of capitalism and even then, according to Marx, in a 'negative' and imperfect way. In fact Marx believed that only under socialism is labour truly free and mobile. To make such an important feature of socialism into the pre-condition of capitalism is overdoing the case.

Laclau's critique is based on defining capitalism in terms of pure categories in a model that is ultimately rooted in an artificial fixed opposition between production and exchange.

What we observe both in Frank and Wallerstein is a 'minimal' definition of capitalism while Laclau and particularly Robert Brenner offer a 'maximal' definition. Let us contrast these two views of capitalism by quoting some typical passages from Wallerstein and Brenner:

> If capitalism is a mode of production, production for profit in a market, then we ought, I should have thought, to look to whether or not such production was occurring. It turns out in fact that it was, and in a very substantial form. Most of this production, however, was not industrial production. What was happening in Europe from the sixteenth to the eighteenth centuries is that over a large geographical area going from Poland to the north-east westwards and southwards throughout Europe and including large parts of the Western Hemisphere as well, there grew up a world-economy with a single division of labour within which there was a world market, for which men produced largely agricultural products for sale and profit. I would think the simplest thing to do is to call this agricultural capitalism. (Wallerstein 1979, p.16)

The definition offered here is so general (generic) that, as we have pointed out in Chapter Two, it is either empty or else refers to a particular form. To define capitalism as a system of production for profit in general is so broad that it can refer to any society in which markets exist and profits are made through trade. Here, even expanding the unit of analysis does not save the day. In particular if one does not specify what kind of production was involved it will not be adequate to the reality of capitalism even in the sixteenth century. For instance the evolution of capitalism is unthinkable without developments in industry and the manufacturing sector. What Wallerstein describes as an agricultural capitalism (a particular form) would not have come about without trade in non-agricultural goods, some of which at least was produced by industry.

Capitalism cannot be defined simply in terms of the properties that one may detect in its early forms without benefit of the knowledge of the fuller forms of development that come at higher stages. In other words, in terms of the terminology developed in this book, Wallerstein's view of capitalism is an S.1 concept and not an S.3 one. Wallerstein has produced a generality that is really a particular and not a true universal, since the latter can only be defined in active relation to concrete and particular forms of development. The opponents of dependency attempt to produce such a concept but commit an error in the opposite direction: capitalism becomes such a particularized and rigidly defined system that is hardly applicable to any capitalist economy as we know it today and thus is not a universal.

Let us see if in fact the opponents of the dependency and world-system approaches produce a more adequate concept of capitalism. Brenner, responding to Wallerstein's definition of capitalism as a system of production for profit via exchange — one in which, furthermore, scales of production expand and innovations take place, makes the following remarks:

> Now, there is no doubt that capitalism is a system in which production for a profit via exchange predominates. But does the opposite hold true? Does the appearance of widespread production 'for profit in the market' signal the existence of capitalism, and more particularly a system in which, as a characteristic feature, 'production is constantly expanded and men constantly innovate new ways of producing'. Certainly not, because production for exchange is perfectly compatible with a system in which it is either unnecessary or impossible, or both, to reinvest in expanded, improved production in order to 'profit'. Indeed, we shall argue that this is the norm in pre-capitalist societies. For in such societies the social relations of production in large part confine the realization of surplus labour to the methods of extending absolute surplus labour. The increase of relative surplus labour cannot become a *systematic feature* of such modes of production.
>
> To state the case schematically: 'production for profit via exchange' will have the systematic effect of accumulation and the development of the productive forces only when it expresses certain specific social relations of production, namely a system of free wage labour, where labour power is a commodity. (Brenner 1978, p.32)

Brenner's points can be analysed in the following way:

i) Capitalism involves the predominance of production for profit obtained in the process of exchange;

ii) But the converse does not hold true: widespread production 'for profit in the market' does not signal the existence of capitalism. Why not? Because, according to Brenner, capitalism involves the following essential features:

    a) A constant expansion of production;
    b) constant technological innovation;
    c) increased production of relative surplus-value;
    d) the existence of free wage-labour.

For Brenner, although capitalism is a system in which production for profit via exchange predominates this is not an *essential* feature of the system as pre-capitalist forms have also involved some types of production for profit through exchange. The essential features of capitalism that distinguish it from pre-capitalist economies are those listed above under points (a) to (d). Let us examine these points in more detail:

a) It is a gross exaggeration to suggest that pre-capitalist economies did not expand production. Expansion often occurred but was much slower than under capitalism; given the agricultural basis of the economy this involved either the cultivation of previously unused land or tribal, national and imperial expansion (see Chapter Seven above).

b) Technological innovation did take place under pre-capitalist conditions of production but the pace was much slower than under capitalism.

c) Production, given the narrow and relatively stagnant technological base, usually involved the production of absolute surplus-value (see Chapter Six above).

d) Wage-labour was used in pre-capitalist forms of production but not on an extensive basis.

As we have emphasized above in our discussion of the transition debate, the transition from feudalism to capitalism involved a major structural shift that increased the share of tradable goods relative to non-traded goods due to the rise of industry and manufacturing. But this transformation also involved increased commodification that could not be limited to internationally traded goods. By contrast, nearly all the essential characteristics of capitalism mentioned by Brenner can be deduced from the increased production of goods for sale in markets with the purpose of profit-making.

The rise of free wage-labour (as we have argued above) came about due to the break-up of the subsistence economy of agricultural workers. This change led to the separation of workers from their means of reproduction and the increased commodification of use-values. Under these conditions workers had no choice but to offer their labour-power for sale in order to buy commodities that were only available in the market. The constant expansion of production can also be explained in a similar way: the profit motive combined with the possibility of increased production (which depends on the greater availability of inputs as commodities and commodification in general) will lead to the expansion of production. Increased commodification implies the expansion of production. Technological innovation, which is closely related to the relative form of surplus-value can be explained on the basis of the logic of the development of capitalism. The development of capitalism, combined with natural and political constraints leads to an increased production of relative surplus-value and competitive pressures act as a motive force for innovation (both technical and managerial).

Thus all the essential features, all the so-called 'pre-conditions' of capitalism can be deduced from what Brenner considers to be a non-essential feature of capitalism. These features and pre-conditions are as much the *results* as premises of capitalist development.

The problem is that Brenner considers capitalism from the height of its most mature and developed forms. This would have been justified (as it is an attempt to define capitalism via an S.3 concept) except for the following considerations:

Brenner wishes to define capitalism as purely as possible, in fixed opposition to pre-capitalist forms of production. He uses concepts such as production, circulation and markets in a generic-analytical way. Thus for him circulation, trade and exchange have identical content and have identical relations with production in all modes of production. That is why he refuses to accept profit-oriented production for the market as a fundamental feature of capitalism, as for him markets have always existed. This rejection of exchange, based on his opposition to what he calls 'neo-Smithianism', ignores the fact that the most important social relation of production from his point of view, i.e. the sale of labour power, is itself based on exchange.

One may argue that Brenner's analysis is based on Marx's analysis of a pure capitalist mode of production in *Capital*. But Marx's analysis of capitalism cannot be so easily reconciled with analytical methodology. For instance we have shown (Chapter Six) that it is the absolute form of surplus-value (SV.3) that explains the increased use of the relative form. This analysis on the one hand shows the connection between pre-capitalist forms of exploitation and the capitalist form, and on the other hand points to the further development of surplus-labour in the form of relative surplus-value. Marx's analysis is conceptual but at the same time historical-developmental. The pure model of capitalism is deduced in *Capital* from the basic feature of capitalism, which is a system in which production takes place primarily in connection with circulation. To take this model as a ready-made construct and to attempt to detect the existence of capitalism in any given real economy is putting the cart before the horse.

The following quotation from Marx should clarify that for Marx capitalism was not a ready-made and already-complete blueprint but a system that develops in time and space; in particular the categories of *Capital* such as value, surplus-value, etc. which are used to define capitalism, are dialectical categories that unfold in time and in relation to the development of capitalism on world-scale:

> If surplus labour or surplus-value were represented only in the national surplus product, then the increase of value for the sake of value and therefore the exaction of surplus labour would be restricted by the limited, narrow circle of

271

use-values in which the value of the [national] labour would be represented. But it is foreign trade which develops its [the surplus product's] real nature as value by developing the labour embodied in it as social labour which manifests itself in an unlimited range of different use-values, and this in fact gives meaning to abstract wealth . . .

But it is only foreign trade, the development of the market to a world market, which causes money to develop into world money and *abstract labour* into social labour. Abstract wealth, value, money, hence *abstract labour*, develop in the measure that concrete labour becomes a totality of different modes of labour embracing the world market. Capitalist production rests on the *value* or the transformation of the labour embodied in the product into social labour. But this is only [possible] on the basis of foreign trade and of the world market. This is at once the pre-condition and the result of capitalist production. (TSV.III. p.253)

In this extraordinary passage we learn that all the fundamental categories of capitalism develop in historical time and in global space. We also learn that categories such as use-value and value which are often treated as analytical concepts are in fact two sides of a dialectical relationship to the extent that, for instance, it is only through the multiplication of the world of use values through foreign trade (and we might add internal trade as well) that abstract labour and abstract wealth develop.

It would be hard to reconcile these ideas with extreme forms of dependency theory and radical approaches to economic development that advocate virtually an autarchic regime and an inward-looking policy of industrialization for less-developed countries. It is equally hard to reconcile them with the 'productionism' of those like Dobb, Brenner and Laclau who attempt to degrade the role of foreign trade and to construct a model of capitalism purely on the basis of production relations. Such an approach implicitly proposes the possibility of *capitalism in one country*. Many Marxists have tried to come to terms with the dramatic trends in the world economy especially since World War II, such as the multinational explosion (initially American but increasingly European, Japanese and to a lesser degree even Third World), the rise of manufacturing industry in the Third World (on a grand scale in some countries like South Korea), the increase in global competition, the internationalization of production, regional economic integration such as the EC, the diffusion of technology (sometimes quite advanced) to less-developed countries, the rise of the modern 'service economy' and many other such phenomena. Clearly some of these trends have taken many by surprise, which may very well be due to a one-sided interpretation of the pure capitalist model — a model that we have been criticizing in this concluding chapter. But if Marx had been interpreted along the lines suggested

272

here then many of these modern trends should not have come as a surprise.

We find very similar ideas in the approaches to the transition from capitalism to socialism to which we now turn our attention.

The Transition from Capitalism to Socialism

There is a tradition of conceptualizing a socialist economy in complete opposition to a capitalist economy which can be traced to Marx's theory of commodity fetishism in *Capital I* but which was formulated in its dogmatic fashion by the economists of the Second International. While one can make a strong case for the influence of the nature of capitalist development in the late nineteenth and early twentieth centuries in the writings of these economists, an equally strong case may be made in the opposite direction: the very conception of the nature of the capitalist mode of production, especially compared with other modes of production, lay at the root of these economists' attitude towards the developmental tendencies of capitalism at this advanced stage of capitalist development. The foundation upon which this conception rested was the rigid conceptual opposition of the capitalist mode with pre- and post-capitalist modes of production. In this conception the capitalist economy is totally ruled by the 'anarchy' of markets, where human will, plan or desire plays no direct role, while the non-capitalist modes are ruled by some kind of central direction in which human will and purpose (individual or collective) plays a more direct part. In the work of these economists this fundamental 'dualism' often appeared in the form of the twin theses of: a) the 'opacity' of the capitalist economy compared to the 'transparency' of non-capitalist economies, b) The irrelevance of the 'science' of political economy for the pre-capitalist economies and its disappearance under socialism.

The following quotations represent a small sample.

In her pamphlet *What is Economics*, Rosa Luxemburg compares the capitalist economy first with a self-sufficient peasant economy and then with the household of Charlemagne. In both cases she reaches identical conclusions. In the first case production is directly oriented towards the needs of the community, work is organized consciously based on the available resources and the quantity of 'wealth' directly depends on the quantities of these resources.

> As a matter of fact, all the relations in such a peasant economy are so *open* and *transparent* that their dissection by the scalpel of Economics appear indeed idle

273

play. (Luxemburg, n.d. p.63, emphasis added)

In the case of the household of Charlemagne, furthermore, the purpose of production is the satisfaction of human needs; there is a division of labour, but no commodities are produced and the quantity of wealth depends on the quantity of factors of production.

> Thus in all probability, we should not be able to think up any kind of *mysterious* problems for the science of Economics to analyse and solve there, in as much as all relations, cause and effect, labour and instrument are *crystal-clear*. (Luxemburg. n.d. p.66, emphasis added)
>
> What is striking in both examples is the fact that the needs of human existence directly guide and determine the work, and that the results correspond exactly to the intentions and the needs, and that, regardless of the scale of production, economic relations manifest an astonishing *simplicity* and *transparency*. (Luxemburg. n.d. pp.67-8, emphasis added)

This simplicity and transparency makes pre-capitalist economies accessible to the knowing subject without a need for 'science'. The latter is required only when the nature of the economy envelops it with mysteries and riddles that need uncovering and solving. Such is the case with capitalism. The anarchy of markets transforms the results of human will, purpose and activity into riddles and mysteries:

> And it is precisely this anarchy which is responsible for the fact that the economy of human society produces results which are mysterious and unpredictable to the people involved . . . . Scientific analysis must discover *ex post facto* that purposefulness and those rules governing human economic life which conscious planfulness did not impose on it beforehand. (Luxemburg. n.d. p.80)

She then predicts that Economics will disappear with the demise of capitalism:

> If Economics is a science dealing with the particular laws of the capitalist mode of production, then its reason for existence and its function are bound to the life span of the latter and Economics will lose its base as soon as that mode of production will have ceased to exist. (Luxemburg. n.d. p.90)

We find the same trend of thought in Bukharin:

> Only unorganized social economy presents such specific phenomena in which the mutual adaptation of the various parts of the production organism proceeds independently of the human will consciously turned to that end. In a planful

274

guidance of the social economy, the distribution and redistribution of the social production forces constitutes a conscious process based on statistical data. In the present anarchy of production, this process takes place through a transfer mechanism of prices . . . . All these are characteristics of modern society and constitute the subject of political economy. In a socialist society, political economy will lose its *raison d'être*: there will remain only an "economic geography" — a science of the idiographic type; and an "economic politics" — a normative science; for the relations between men will be *simple* and *clear* . . . (Bukharin 1972, p.49, emphasis added)

Preobrazhensky argues along very similar lines. For him 'Political Economy is the science which reveals the law of development and equilibrium and (in part) the laws of decay of the commodity and commodity-capitalist mode of production, as a planless, unorganized mode of production'. As opposed to capitalism the socialist economy appears as planned economy in which

the commodity of the capitalist mode of production is replaced . . . by the product, value by the measurement of labour time, the market . . . by the book-keeping of planned economy, surplus value by surplus product, so in the sphere of science political economy gives place to social technology, that is, the science of socially organized production. (Preobrazhensky 1965, p.48)

The ideas of 'social technology', 'economic geography', etc. that presumably will replace the science of political economy under socialism, as fantastic as they may sound, were in fact based on a particular interpretation of Marx's theory of history. One of the most extreme versions can be found in Bukharin. For instance, this is how he tries to portray the nature of production relations in society in general. He uses the example of a factory where each worker is doing 'his own job' but that this job 'is only a part of the whole', i.e. the technical relations within a factory (Bukharin 1972, pp.90-1). He goes on to generalize this to society as a whole:

What we have just observed in the factory is also applicable on a more intricate and far greater scale in human society as a whole. For all of society constitutes a peculiar human working apparatus, in which the overwhelming majority of persons or groups of persons occupy a certain place in the working process . . . . And when masses of commodities pass from one country to another, from factory to market, from market through tradesman to consumer, all this constitutes a material bond between all these persons. They are a part of the material skeleton, the working apparatus of a single social life. (Bukharin 1972, p.91)

At this point he compares human society to a 'society of bees' and defines

275

production relations in the following terms:

> This 'body' is the labour skeleton, the system of material relations between persons in the process of labour, or, as Marx put it, the *production relations*. (Bukharin 1972, p.92)

Observe how Bukharin reduces social relations of production to mere technical and material relations and how he mixes up the social with the technical division of labour. This not only undermines Marx's theory of division of labour (representing a regression to the Smithian theory) but also his theory of history.

Adam Smith had advanced a single concept of the division of labour, embracing both the division of labour in the workshop and that in society at large (thus conceiving society as being similar to a 'giant factory'), with the difference between the two only a matter of degree and scale. For Marx, however, there was a qualitative distinction between the two concepts. His criterion for this distinction was the absence or presence of commodity exchange. Thus the difference between the two divisions is that under capitalism the social division of labour is mediated by commodities, while the technical division of labour within the factory is not so mediated (C.I. pp.474-5; see also Chapter Nine above).

This sharp distinction, however does not prevent Marx from recognizing a dynamic relationship between the two:

> Since the production and the circulation of commodities are the general prerequisites of the capitalist mode of production, division of labour in manufacture requires that a division of labour within society should have already attained a certain degree of development. Inversely, the division of labour in manufacture reacts back upon that in society, developing and multiplying it further. (C.I. p.473)

Marx, in fact, goes beyond this perspective and characterizes the division of labour within the workshop as 'an entirely specific creation of the capitalist mode of production' (C.I. p.480). Thus the factory, which is a sphere of 'direct' organization and allocation of labour as opposed to the market-place, far from being an 'island' in the great ocean of anarchy of market, is at the very centre of the social division of labour under capitalism. To present the capitalist mode of production as a system ruled completely by the anarchy of markets thus amounts to a misrepresentation of Marx's view of capitalism.

The later writers' rigid separation between the technical and social division of labour led to a strict dichotomy between the forces of production (the labour process, the 'factory') and the relations of production (the market). Associated with these ideas was the notion that the socialization of labour can somehow be identified with the enlargement of the scale of production (by 'bringing the workers together') and that this heralds the birth of socialism as a completely socialized system of production.

Indeed what was happening in the late nineteenth and early twentieth centuries involved an increase in the scale of production (e.g. via vertical integration). This development implied the triumph of planning over the anarchy of the market for these economists. But to identify the degree of the socialization of labour with the scale of production is justified only in a limited way. One may on the contrary conceive of the scale of production as a reaction to a low degree of the socialization of labour — the absence of developed markets. Let us be more specific. Marx analyses the early phases of capitalist development in Britain as an evolution from the 'putting-out' system through handicraftsmen brought under one roof, the manufactory, leading up to the large-scale machine industry. Surely the necessity of bringing the handicraftsmen 'under one roof', which according to Marx, achieved increased productivity without a change in technology was a result of the high costs of transportation and communication in general. Let us not forget that the premises of capitalist production are the scattered nature of labourers and their instruments of production. At this stage the socialization of labour assumes the form of aggregation precisely because the starting point is the fragmentation of labour and the means of production, which is costly due to the lack of the development of the infrastructure.

Today, developing countries also exhibit a large degree of concentration in industry, technologically as well as geographically — a fact much criticized by development economists as involving 'urban bias', capital-intensive technology, dualism and uneven income distribution. Thus in this case one can clearly see that large-scale production is not necessarily a sign of super-development but of under-development. In a similar way the early industrialization drive in both Germany and Russia in the nineteenth century assumed highly concentrated forms of production, i.e. through the role of the state and in the case of Germany large investment banks (the 'Trotsky-Gerschenkron effect').[13]

Marx does indeed characterize capitalist production as large-scale, as co-operative and as socialized. This has to do with the nature of capitalism as a system based on an unending search for surplus-value. But to base any conclusions about the precise nature of the technical

277

scale of capitalist units of production upon this observation is to confuse the social relations of a system with its technical basis. To identify any particular form that the capitalist socialization of labour assumes in different stages of capitalist development with the specific essence of socialization under capitalism is bound to lead to the wrong conclusions about the nature of capitalist development:

> Co-operation remains the fundamental form of capitalist mode of production, although in its simple shape it continues to appear as one particular form alongside the more developed ones. (C.I. p.454)

Here Marx is clearly distinguishing between co-operation as a fundamental basis of capitalism and the 'simple shape of co-operation' that may characterize an early phase of the capitalist development or function alongside more developed forms of co-operation.

One may claim, on the contrary, that the greater use of the market principle, an expansion in commodification and thus a deepening of the social division of labour as opposed to a mere expansion of the 'factory', achieves a greater degree of socialization of labour through greater competition among capitalists as well as workers. As a result, the labour of the individual worker acquires a greater social significance and determination. In other words the exchange process, compared with the enlargement of units of production, may prove to be a more efficient equalizer of the quantities of labour spent on producing various commodities, i.e. the amount of socially necessary labour.

If the exchange process is identified with anarchy and the 'factory' with planning then the definition of socialism as an economy without exchange-value, money and markets seems quite logical. But as we have just indicated, along the lines suggested by Marx's passage quoted at the end of the previous section, commodification and the expansion of the sphere of circulation is a potent force for socialization of labour. However, for the economists of the Second International (including Engels) this highly socializing factor under capitalism was treated as anarchic (anti-social) while the expansion of the factory seemed to embody the highest form of socialization. It was thus quite natural for them to banish value, markets and money from the realm of the socialist economy and identify the social relations of production with the technical forces of production in such an economy.

Bukharin's interpretation of Marx's theory of history involves a virtual identification of the social relations of production with technology, for which he was soon criticized by one of the best representatives of the 'Hegelian' opposition to the perspectives of the Second International, Georg Lukàcs.[14] Bukharin's position was indeed extreme but as we have seen above other economists of the time virtually endorsed this position by their twin theses of 'transparency' and the 'disappearance of political economy'. According to these economists the following correspondences are established:

DIAGRAM 6

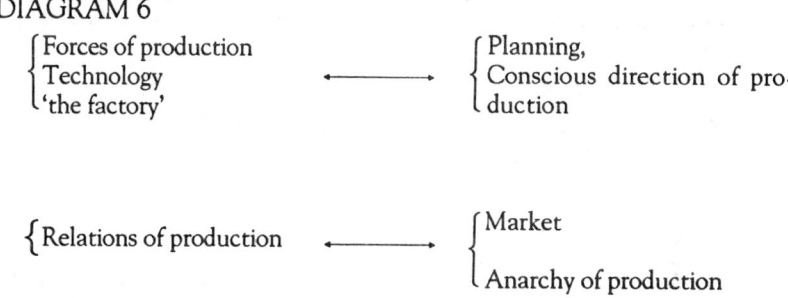

If we were to follow Bukharin, all societies are like 'giant factories', 'skeletons of labour' and thus the forces of production sum up the content and essence of every single society. But the capitalist market represents an exception to the rule, as it disrupts the regularity of production and its transparency. This discontinuity represents a 'dualism' in his train of thought as the social relations of production are identified with the market. Markets thus cannot exist under socialism since the latter consists of purely technical relations. This approach undermines Marx's theory of history which conceives of every mode of production as a combination of both the forces and relations of production.

The problem we again face is the attempt to define society, capitalism, socialism in generic terms, as pure and abstract concepts. This has been the underlying methodological point in all the debates we have reviewed so far. The history of centrally-planned economies (so-called 'actually existing socialism') clearly demonstrates that these ideas were taken very seriously indeed: the model of War Communism in Soviet Union (1918-21) (whose theoreticians included Bukharin and Preobrazhensky), the collectivization of agriculture and expansion of heavy industry under Stalin beginning with the First Five-Year Plan (1929-30); more recent experiments with 'socialization' such as Cuba's attempt in the earlier phase of its revolution (1960s) to construct a money-less

279

self-sufficient economy; China's Great Leap Forward; the Khmer Rouge attempt in Kampuchea in early 1970s to collectivize agriculture when a large proportion of the rural population had already settled in urban areas. We can see in these historical events the influence of ideas such as the primacy of production over exchange, the primacy of heavy industry over consumer industry and the disappearance of markets and money. The model of a pure socialist economy defined in fixed opposition to a capitalist economy lies at the root of all these attempts. Yet these experiments not only were carried out at a terrible cost in human life as well as in the physical 'forces of production' but also ended in failure. This was not because these countries were underdeveloped and thus not quite ready for socialism, as is often claimed.

Final Remarks

All these views on capitalism, socialism, underdevelopment, etc. merge to present a coherent problematic. For instance, we have seen how some economists and historians have tried to belittle the role of markets under capitalism (or indeed under feudalism) e.g. Dobb and Brenner. Such a position is quite consistent with the views of the economists of the Second International who similarly attempted to denigrate the place of markets under socialism. Similarly in the economic development literature we find strategies such as the 'big push', 'balanced growth', 'unbalanced growth', etc. which primarily emphasize technical complementarities in production without regard to the circulation process.[15] It is only recently that this literature has turned its attention to questions such as the role of money and finance in economic development.[16] Much of this failure is due to one-sided interpretations of the concepts of production, circulation, exchange, etc., and the assumption of linear causal relations between these categories — something that we have attempted to criticize throughout this book.

To return to our discussion of Japan, it is clear that what Japanese Marxists considered as the exceptional Japanese road to capitalist development was not exceptional at all but quite normal compared with other countries. The problem was as follows:

a) The pure model of capitalism in Marx was treated as an abstract model devoid of historic-developmental aspects, as a ready-made construct to be applied to a real economy.
b) In the application of this abstract model to the real economy those

aspects of the latter that were at variance with the former were treated as abnormalities, survivals, etc.

I find no better way of ending this concluding chapter than quoting Hegel again:

> In a more speculative sense, a concept's determinacy and its mode of existence are one and the same thing. But it is to be noticed that the moments, whose result is a further determined form of the concept, precede it in the philosophical development of the Idea as determinations of the concept, but *they do not go in advance of it in the temporal development as shapes of experience*. Thus, for instance, the idea determined as the family, presupposes the determinations of the concept from which the family will later on in this work be shown to result. But the explicit existence of these inner suppositions as shapes of existence also, e.g. as the right of property, contract, morality, and so forth, is the other aspect of development, and it is *only in a higher and more complete civilization* that the development has gone so far as to endow its moments with this appropriately shaped existence. (Ph.R. p.35, emphasis added)

Notes to Conclusion

1. See Hoston (1986) for an extensive discussion of these debates. Also see Itoh (1980), Chap. 1.

2. The following quotation from Marx's Preface to the first edition of *Capital I* supports the idea that he considered the British experience of capitalist development as the classic case: 'What I have to examine in this work is the capitalist mode of production, and the relations of production and the forms of intercourse that correspond to it. Until now, their *locus classicus* has been England. That is the reason why England is used as the main illustration of the theoretical developments I make' (C.I. p.90). He adds further: 'The country that is more developed industrially only shows, to the less developed, the image of its future' (C.I. p.91). It is this last statement that later proved to be very controversial (see below).

3. On these debates and Marx's involvement see Shanin (1983). This work also contains various drafts of Marx's reply to Vera Zasulich. See also Bideleux (1985), Chap.1.

4. See Lenin's *Two Tactics of Social-Democracy in the Democratic Revolution* (first published in Russian in 1905) in Lenin (1975), vol. 1. The following quotation is taken from this work: 'While recognizing the incontestably bourgeois nature of a revolution incapable of *directly* overstepping the bounds of a mere democratic revolution our slogan *advances* this particular revolution and strives to give it forms most advantageous to the proletariat; consequently, it strives to make the utmost of the democratic revolution in order to attain the greatest success in the proletariat's further struggle of socialism' (ibid. p.483). See also his *The Right of Nations to Self-Determination* (first published in Russian in 1914) in Lenin (1975), vol. 1.

5. On War Communism and NEP see Nove (1969), Chaps. 3-6. See also Szamuely (1974).

6. See Anderson (1987).

7. Dobb (1963).

8. Hilton (1976) contains the original contributions by Sweezy and Dobb as well as several papers by other contributors to the debate.

9. Institutional factors, in particular the development of secure property rights, in the rise of capitalism have been emphasized by North and Thomas (1973) and North (1981). For a detailed discussion of various approaches to the transition from feudalism to capitalism, including the property

rights approach, see Holton (1985).

10. Laclau (1971). For a detailed discussion of the history of dependency school see Bloomström & Hettne (1984). See also Brewer (1980), Chaps. 6 & 7.

11. For a review of modernization theories see Webster (1984), Chap. 3. For economists probably the most prominent work in this area is Rostow (1960).

12. See Chapter Four, section V above.

13. Trotsky in *Results and Prospects*, published in 1906 (see Trotsky, 1969, pp. 37-45) emphasized the role of the state in the industrialization of the less-developed Russia. Gerschenkron (1962) claimed that the role of state in economic development in a less developed economy was in direct proportion to the latter's degree of economic backwardness.

14. See his *N. Bukharin*: Historical Materialism. in Lukács (1972).

15. The theory of 'big push' was formulated by Paul N. Rosenstein-Rodan (1943) and later became known as the theory of balanced growth. Hirschman (1958) criticized this theory and, in turn, proposed his theory of 'unbalanced growth'. Both theories relied on technical complementarities in production.

16. See Note 1, Chapter Ten for references in this area.

BIBLIOGRAPHY

Albritton, R., 1986, A Japanese Reconstruction of Marxist Theory, Macmillan: London

Allan, D. J., 1952, The Philosophy of Aristotle, Oxford University Press: Oxford

Althusser, L., 1969, For Marx, Allen Lane: London

Althusser, L. & Balibar, E., 1970, Reading Capital, New Left Books: London

Althusser, L., 1971, Lenin and Philosophy and Other Essays, New Left Books: London

Anderson, P., 1987, The figures of descent, New Left Review, No.161, Jan-Feb

Auerbach, P., 1984, On the theory of social democracy, British Review of Economic Issues, 6/14, Spring

Auerbach, P., 1988, Competition, Basil Blackwell: Oxford

Auerbach, P. & Skott, P., 1988, Concentration, competition and distribution — a critique of theories of monopoly capital, International Review of Applied Economics, vol.2, No.1

Auerbach, P., Desai, M. & Shamsavari, A., 1988, The transition from actually existing capitalism, New Left Review, No.170, Jul-Aug

Banaji, J., 1980, From the commodity to capital: Hegel's dialectic in Marx's Capital, in D. Elson (ed.) 1980

Baran, P. & Sweezy, P. M., 1968, Monopoly Capital, Penguin Press: Harmondsworth

Baumol, W. J., 1974, The transformation of values: what Marx 'really' meant (an interpretation), Journal of Economic Literature, Vol. XII, No.1

Begg, D., Stanley, F. & Dornbusch, R., 1984, Economics, McGraw-Hill: London

Benton, T., 1984, The Rise and Fall of Structural Marxism, Macmillan: London

Bideleux, R., 1985, Communism and Development, Methuen & Co.: London

Blomström, M. & Hettne, B., 1984, Development Theory in Transition, Zed Books: London

Böhm-Bawerk, E. von, 1898, Karl Marx and the Close of his System, in P. Sweezy (ed. 1949)

Bortkiewicz, L. von, 1907, On the correction of Marx's fundamental theoretical construction in the third volume of *Capital*, in Sweezy (ed. 1949)

Brenner, R., 1977, The origins of capitalist development: a critique of the neo-Smithian Marxism, *New Left Review*, No.104, Jul-Aug

Brewer, A., 1980, *Marxist Theories of Imperialism: A Critical Survey*, Routledge & Kegan Paul: London

Bukharin, N., 1972(a), *Imperialism and World Economy*, Merlin Press: London

Bukharin, N., 1972(b), *Imperialism and the Accumulation of Capital*, Allen Lane: London

Bukharin, N., 1969, *Historical Materialism: A System of Sociology*, University of Michigan Press: Ann Arbor

Callinicos, A., 1976, *Althusser's Marxism*, Pluto Press: London

Carver, T., 1981, *Engels*, Oxford University Press: Oxford

Cassirer, E., 1923, *Substance and Function & Einstein's Theory of Relativity*, The Open Court Publishing Co.: Chicago

Cassirer, E., 1981, *Kant's Life and Thought*, Yale University Press: New Haven

Clark, N., 1985, *The Political Economy of Science and Technology*, Basil Blackwell: Oxford

Cleaver, H. M., 1972, The contradictions of the green revolution, *American Economic Review*, May, pp.177-88

Cohen, G. A. 1979, *Karl Marx's Theory of History: A Defence*, Oxford University Press: Oxford

Colletti, L., 1973, *Marxism and Hegel*, New Left Books: London

Cornforth, M., 1976, *Dialectical Materialism: An Introduction*, v.3, Lawrence and Wishart: London

Cutler, A., Hindess, B., Hirst, P. & Hussain, A., 1977, *Marx's Capital and Capitalism Today*, v.1, Routledge & Kegan Paul: London

Dalton, G., 1967, Primitive money, in G. Dalton (ed.) *Tribal and Peasant Economies: Readings in Economic Anthropology*, National History Press: New York

De Brunhoff, S., 1976, *Marx on Money*, Urizon Books: New York

Della Volpe, G., 1978, *Rousseau and Marx And Other Writings*, Lawrence & Wishart: London

Della Volpe, G., 1980, *Logic as a Positive Science*, New Left Books: London

Desai, M., 1974, *Marxian Economic Theory*, Gray-Mill Publishing: London

284

Dilworth, J. B., 1989, *Production and Operations Management*, Fourth Edn., Random House: New York

Dobb, M., 1963, *Studies in the Development of Capitalism*, Routledge & Kegan Paul: London

Drake, P. J., 1980, *Money, Finance and Development*, Martin Robertson: Oxford

Echeverria, R., 1978, Critique of Marx's *1857 Introduction, Economy and Society*, v.7, No.4, Nov

Eicher, C. K. & Staatz, J. M. (ed.), 1984, *Agricultural Development in the Third World*, Johns Hopkins University Press: Baltimore

Einzig, P., 1949, *Primitive Money*, Eyre & Spottiswoode: London

Elson, D. (ed.), 1980, *Value: The Representation of Labour in Capitalism*, Humanities Press: Atlantic Highlands, N.J.

Elster, J., 1985, *Making Sense of Marx*, Cambridge University Press: Cambridge

Engels, F., 1859, Karl Marx, "A Contribution to the Critique of Political Economy", in Marx (1970)

Fatami, A., 1972, The green revolution: an appraisal, *Monthly Review*, 2, June, pp.112-120

Fine, B. & Harris, L., 1979, *Rereading Capital*, Macmillan: London

Frankel, F. R., 1971, *India's Green Revolution: Economic Gains and Political Costs*, Princeton University Press: Princeton

Fransman, M., 1986, *Technology and Economic Development*, Wheatsheaf: Brighton

Frisch, R., 1965, *Theory of Production*, D. Reidel: Dordrecht

Fuchs, V., 1986, *The Service Economy*, National Bureau of Economic Research: New York

Gasché, R., 1986, *The Tain of the Mirror: Derrida and the Philosophy of Reflection*, Harvard University Press: Cambridge, Mass.

Gerestein, I., 1976, Production, circulation and value, *Economy and Society*, Vol.5, No.3

Gerschenkron, A., 1962, *Economic Backwardness in Historical Perspective*, Harvard University Press: Cambridge, Mass

Gershuny, J. & Miles, I., 1983, *The New Service Economy*, Frances Pinter: London

Gillis, M., Perkins, D. H., Roemer, M., & Snodgrass, D. S., 1987, *Economics of Development*, second edition, Norton: New York

Godelier, M., 1966, System, structure and contradiction in *Capital*, in Milliband, R. and Saville, J. (ed.), 1967, *Socialist Register*, Merlin Press: London

Godelier, M. 1972, *Rationality and Irrationality in Economics*, New Left Books: London

Griffin, K., 1974, *The Political Economy of Agrarian Change: An Essay on Green Revolution*, Harvard University Press: Cambridge, Mass

Griffith-Jones, S., 1981, *The Role of Finance in Transition to Socialism*, Frances Pinter: London

Gurley, J. G. & Shaw, E. S., 1967, Financial development and economic development, *Economic Development and Cultural Change*, vol.15, No.3, April

Harris, W. T., 1890, *Hegel's Logic*, Chicago, rep. 1984 by Garland Press: London

Hegel, G. W. F., 1873, *Logic*, tr. by W. Wallace, Clarendon Press: Oxford

Hegel, G. W. F., 1892, *Lectures on the History of Philosophy*, in 3 volumes, tr. by E. S. Haldane & F. H. Simon, rep. 1974 by The Humanities Press: Atlantic Highlands, New Jersey

Hegel, G. W. F., 1952, *Philosophy of Right*, tr. by T. M. Knox, Oxford University Press: Oxford

Hegel, G. W. F., 1967, *The Phenomenology of Mind*, tr. by L. B. Baillie, Harper & Row: New York

Hegel, G. W. F., 1969, *Science of Logic*, tr. by A. V. Miller, Allen & Unwin: London

Hegel, G. W. F., 1970(a), *Philosophy of Nature*, in 3 vols. tr. by M. J. Petry, Allen & Unwin: London

Hegel, G. W. F., 1970(b), *On Art, Religion, Philosophy*, (ed. by J. Glenn Gray) Harper & Row: New York

Hegel, G. W. F., 1971, *Philosophy of Mind*, tr. by W. Wallace and A. V. Miller, Oxford University Press: Oxford

Hegel, G. W. F., 1978, *Philosophy of Subjective Spirit*, v.1, tr. by M. J. Petry, D. Reidel Publishing Co.: Boston

Hibben, J., 1902, *Hegel's Logic*, New York, rep. 1984 by Garland Press: London

Hilferding, R., 1904, Böhm-Bawerk's criticism of Marx, in Sweezy (ed. 1949)

Hilferding, R., 1981, *Finance Capital*, Routledge & Kegan Paul: London

Hilton, R. (ed.), 1976, *The Transition from Feudalism to Capitalism*, New Left Books: London

Hirschman, A. O., 1958, *The Strategy of Economic Development*, Yale University Press: New Haven

Holton, R. J., 1985, *The Transition from Feudalism to Capitalism*, Macmillan: London

Hoston, G. A., 1986, *Marxism and the Crisis of Development in Prewar Japan*, Princeton University Press: Princeton, N.J.

Howard, M. C. & King, J. E. (ed.), 1976, *The Economics of Marx*, Penguin Books: Harmondsworth

Howard, M. C. & King, J. E., 1985, *The Political Economy of Marx*, 2nd edn., Longman: London

Hunt, E. K. & Schwartz, J. G. (ed.), 1972, *A Critique of Economic Theory*, Penguin Books: Harmondsworth

Ilyenkov, E., 1977, *Dialectical Logic*, Progress Publishers: Moscow

Ilyenkov, E., 1982, *The Dialectics of the Abstract and the Concrete in Marx's Capital*, Progress Publishers: Moscow

Inwood, M., 1985, *Hegel*, Oxford University Press: Oxford

Itoh, M., 1980, *Value and Crisis: Essays on Marxian Economics in Japan*, Pluto Press: London

Kant, I., 1929, *Critique of Pure Reason*, tr. by Norman K. Smith, Macmillan: London

Kant, I., 1952, *The Critique of Judgement*, tr. by James C. Meredith, Oxford University Press: Oxford

Kant, I., 1956, *Critique of Practical Reason*, tr. by Lewis W. Beck, Bobbs-Merrill: Indianapolis

Kolakowski, L., 1978, *Main Currents of Marxism*, vol.1, Oxford

Körner, S., 1955, *Kant*, Penguin Books: Hardmondsworth

Krause, U., 1982, *Money and Abstract Labour*, New Left Books: London

Lakatos, I., 1978, *The Methodology of Scientific Research Programmes*, Cambridge University Press: Cambridge

Laclau, E., 1971, Feudalism and Capitalism in Latin America, *New Left Review*, No.67, May-June

Leijonhufvud, A., 1977, Costs and consequences of inflation, in Harcourt, G. (ed.), 1977, *The Microeconomic Foundations of Macroeconomics*, Macmillan: London

Lenin, V.I., 1970, *Materialism and Empirio-criticism*, Progress Publishers: Moscow

Lenin, V.I., 1972, *Collected Works*, v.38, Progress Publishers: Moscow

Lenin, V.I., 1975, *Selected Works*, 3 vols., Progress Publishers: Moscow

Lippi, M., 1979, *Value and Naturalism in Marx*, New Left Books: London

Lukács, G., 1972, *Political Writings*, New Left Books: London

Luporini, C., 1975, Reality and historicity: economy and dialectics in Marxism, *Economy and Society*, v.4, Nos.2 & 3

Luxemburg, R., 1951, *The Accumulation of Capital*, Routledge & Kegan Paul: London

Luxemburg, R., n.d., *What is Economics?*, Merlin Press: London

MacGregor, D., 1984, *The Communist Ideal in Hegel and Marx*, Allen & Unwin: London

MacIntyre, A., (ed.), 1972, *Hegel: A Collection of Critical Essays*, Anchor Books: Garden City, N.Y.

Mandel, E., 1968, *Marxist Economic Theory*, Monthly Review Press: New York

Marx, K., 1963, *Theories of Surplus-Value*, Part I, Progress Publishers: Moscow

Marx, K., 1968, *Theories of Surplus-Value*, Part II, Progress Publishers: Moscow

Marx, K., 1970, *A Contribution to the Critique of Political Economy*, Progress Publishers: Moscow

Marx, K., 1971, *Theories of Surplus-Value*, Part III, Progress Publishers: Moscow

Marx, K., 1972, *Critique of the Gotha Programme*, Foreign Languages Press: Peking

Marx, K., 1973, *Grundrisse*, Penguin Books: Harmondsworth

Marx, K., 1975, *Texts on Method*, trans. & ed. by Carver, T., Basil Blackwell: Oxford

Marx, K., 1976(a), *Capital*, Vol.1, Penguin Books: Harmondsworth

Marx, K., 1976(b), *Value: Studies by Marx*, tr. & ed. by Dragstedt, A., New Park Publications: London

Marx, K., 1978(a), *Capital*, Vol.2, Penguin Books: Harmondsworth

Marx, K., 1978(b), The value-form, *Capital and Class*, No. 4

Marx, K., 1981, *Capital*, Vol.3, Penguin Books: Harmondsworth

Marx, K. & Engels, F., 1969, *Selected Works*, in 3 vols., Progress Publishers: Moscow

Marx, K. & Engels, F., 1975, *Selected Correspondence*, 3rd. Edn., Progress Publishers: Moscow

Marx, K. & Engels, F., 1983, *Letters on Capital*, New Park Publications: London

288

May, K. 1948, Value and price of production: a note on Winternitz's solution, *Economic Journal*, December

McKinnon, R. I. 1973, *Money and Capital in Economic Development*, Brookings Institution: Washington, D.C.

McLellan, D., 1979, *Engels*, Fontana/Collins: Glasgow

Medio, A., 1972, Profit and surplus-value: appearance and reality in capitalist production, in Hunt & Schwartz (ed. 1972)

Meek, R. L. 1973, *Studies in the Labour Theory of Value*, Lawrence & Wishart: London

Meek, R. L., 1976, Is there an 'historical transformation problem'? a comment, *Economic Journal*, June

Miller, R. W., 1984, *Analyzing Marx*, Princeton University Press: Princeton

Monden, Y., 1981(a), What makes Toyota production system really tick?, *Industrial Engineering*, January

Monden, Y., 1981(b), Adaptable kanban system helps Toyota maintain just-in-time production, *Industrial Engineering*, May

Monden, Y., 1981(c), Smoothed production lets Toyota adopt to demand changes and reduce inventory, *Industrial Engineering*, August

Morishima, M. & Catephores, G., 1975, Is there an 'historical transformation problem?', *Economic Journal*, June

Morishima, M. & Catephores, G., 1976, The 'historical transformation problem' a reply, *Economic Journal*, June

Morishima, M. & Catephores, G., 1978, *Value, Exploitation and Growth*, McGraw-Hill: London

Mure, G. R. G., 1940, *An Introduction to Hegel*, rep. 1970, Oxford University Press: Oxford

Mure, G. R. G., 1965, *The Philosophy of Hegel*, Oxford University Press: Oxford

Mure, G. R. G., 1950, *A Study of Hegel's Logic*, rep. 1984, Oxford University Press: Oxford

Nicolaus, M., 1973, Foreword to *Grundrisse*, in Marx (1973), pp.7-63

Norris, C., 1982, *Deconstruction: Theory & Practice*, Methuen: London

North, D., 1981, *Structure and Change in Economic History*, Norton: New York

North, D. & Thomas, R., 1973, *The Rise of the Western World*, Cambridge University Press: Cambridge

Nove, A., 1969, *An Economic History of the USSR*, Allan Lane The Penguin Press: Harmondsworth

Oakley, A., 1983, *The Making of Marx's Critical Theory*, Routledge & Kegan Paul: London

Pilling, G., 1980, *Marx's Capital: Philosophy and Political Economy*, Routledge & Kegan Paul: London
Plekhanov, G., 1956, *The Development of the Monist View of History*, Moscow
Polanyi, K., 1968, The semantics of money-uses, in Dalton, G. (ed.) *Essays of Karl Polanyi*, Doubleday: New York
Preobrazhensky, E., 1965, *The New Economics*, Oxford University Press: London

Ricardo, D., 1951, *On the Principles of Political Economy and Taxation*, Edited by P. Sraffa, Cambridge University Press: Cambridge
Roemer, J., (ed.), 1986, *Analytical Marxism*, Cambridge University Press: Cambridge
Rosdolski, R., 1977, *The Making of Marx's Capital*, Pluto Press: London
Rosenstein-Rodan, P. M., 1943, Problems of industrialization of Eastern and South-Eastern Europe, *Economic Journal*, Jun-Sept
Rostow, W. W., 1960, *The Stages of Economic Growth*, Cambridge University Press: London
Rubel, M. 1981, *Rubel on Karl Marx: Five Essays*, ed. & tr. by J. O'Malley and K. Algozin, Cambridge University Press: Cambridge
Rubin, I. I., 1972, *Essays on Marx's Theory of Value*, Black & Red: Detroit
Rubin, I. I. 1978, Abstract labour and value in Marx's system, *Capital and Class*, No.5
Rubin, I. I., 1979, *A History of Economic Thought*, Ink Links: London

Saussure, F. de., 1974, *Course in General Linguistics*, Peter Owen: London
Sayer, D., 1979(a), *Marx's Method*, Harvester: Sussex
Sayer, D., 1979(b), Science as critique: Marx vs. Althusser, in Mepham, J. & Ruben, D-H., (ed.), *Issues in Marxist Philosophy*, v.3, Harvester: Sussex
Schonberger, R. J., 1982, *Japanese Manufacturing Techniques*, Free Press: London
Schumacher, E. F., 1973, *Small is Beautiful*, Blond & Briggs: London
Schwartz, J. G., 1977, *The Subtle Anatomy of Capitalism*, Santa Monica
Sekine, T., 1975, Uno-Riron: a Japanese contribution to Marxian political economy, *Journal of Economic Literature*, vol. xiii
Sekine, T., 1980, The necessity of the law of value, *Science and Society*, Fall

Sekine, T., 1981, The circular motion of capital, *Science and Society*, Fall

Sekine, T., 1984, *The Dialectics of Capital*, v.1, Yushindo Press: Tokyo

Seton, F., 1957, The 'transformation problem', *Review of Economic Studies*, Vol.24, pp.149-60, reprinted in Howard & King (ed. 1976), 162-76

Shaikh, A., 1977, Marx's theory of value and the 'transformation problem', in Schwartz (ed. 1977)

Shamsavari, A., 1983, *Marx's Concepts in Capital in the Light of Hegel's Logic*, Unpublished Typescript, Kingston Polytechnic: Kingston upon Thames

Shamsavari, A., 1986, On the foundations of Marx's theory of money, *British Review of Economic Issues*, May

Shamsavari, A., 1987, A Critique of the Transformation Problem, *Kingston Discussion Papers in Political Economy*, No.58, Kingston Polytechnic: Kingston upon Thames

Shanin, T., 1983, (ed.), *Late Marx and the Russian Road*, Routledge & Kegan Paul: London

Shaw, E. S., 1973, *Financial Deepening in Economic Development*, Oxford University Press: Oxford

Smith, A., 1970, *The Wealth of Nations*, Books I-III, Penguin Books: Harmondsworth

Sraffa, P., 1960, *The Production of Commodities by Means of Commodities*, Cambridge University Press: Cambridge

Steedman, I., 1977, *Marx after Sraffa*, New Left Books: London

Steedman, I, 1981, (ed.), *The Value Controversy*. Verso: London

Stenback, T., 1979, *Understanding the Service Economy*, Johns-Hopkins University Press: London

Stewart, F., 1978, *Technology and Underdevelopment*, 2nd edn., Macmillan: London

Sturrock, J., 1986, *Structuralism*, Paladin: London

Sweezy, P. M., 1942, *The Theory of Capitalist Development*, rep. 1968, Monthly Review Press: New York

Sweezy, P. M., (ed.), 1949, *Karl Marx and the Close of his System*, Augustus Kelly: New York (Reprinted by Orion Editions: Philadelphia, 1984)

Szamuely, L., 1974, *First Models of the Socialist Economic Systems*, Akadëmiai Kiadö: Budapest

Trotsky, L., 1969, *The Permanent Revolution*, Merit Publishers: New York

Uno, K., 1980, *Principles of Political Economy: Theory of a Purely Capitalist*

Society, Harvester Press: Sussex

Wallerstein, I., 1979, *The Capitalist World Economy*, Cambridge University Press: Cambridge

Webster, A., 1984, *Introduction to the Sociology of Development*, Macmillan: London

Weiss, F. G., 1974, *Beyond Epistemology: New Studies in the Philosophy of Hegel*, Martinus Nijhoff: the Hague

Winternitz, J., 1948, Values and prices: a solution of the so-called transformation problem, *Economic Journal*, June

World Bank, 1987, *World Development Report*, Oxford University Press: Oxford

Zelený, J., 1980, *The Logic of Marx*, Basil Blackwell: Oxford

INDEX

300

302